PRESENT HOPE

Philosophy, Architecture, Judaism

Andrew Benjamin

London and New York

First published 1997
by Routledge
11 New Fetter Lane, London EC4P 4EE

Simultaneously published in the USA and Canada
by Routledge
29 West 35th Street, New York, NY 10001

Typeset in Perpetua by Routledge
Printed and bound in Great Britain by Redwood, Trowbridge, Wiltshire

British Library Cataloguing in Publication Data
A catalogue record for this book is available from the British Library

Library of Congress Cataloguing in Publication Data
A catalogue record for this book has been requested

ISBN 0–415–13385–8 (hbk)
ISBN 0–415–13386–6 (pbk)

For Sam and Lucy
with love

CONTENTS

PREFACE

This book could have been called *Contra Melancholia*. On one level its concerns are reasonably straightforward. Absence and loss insist at the present. And yet given their insistence, how are they to be understood, once it is recognised that the envisaged counters of either full presence or real presence are themselves no more than founding myths? Neither lament nor remorse will be able to serve as adequate responses to the set up established by the interplay of loss and myth. There are two reasons why this is the case. In the first place, it is because, as responses, they normalise and naturalise the opposition between loss or absence, as well as the suggested possibilities opened up by differing forms of presence. In the second, it is because lament and remorse entail, and thus demand, a thinking conditioned by a fall; both envisage, therefore, either a return or a continual preoccupation with the impossibility of return. Rather than the fallen, and in the place either of return and recovery, or of a resigned embracing of the aporetic as 'our' only condition, there exists the fragmentary, the incomplete and the partial. As will be shown in what follows, the temporal correlates of these terms will be repetition and renewal.

The presence of these latter possibilities – the fragmentary and the incomplete on one side and repetition and renewal on the other – will continue to have a significant force. That they came to be incorporated into the project of totality, unity and completion signals no more – though equally no less – than the presence of a dominant intellectual, philosophical and theological tradition. Tradition's elimination of both materialism and the place of the world in favour of differing forms of transcendence does not yield the locus of value, as though value existed in itself. Rather, what comes to be established are sites of contestation and, therefore, places where the exhibition and exercise of power occurs. What will allow both for the exposure of tradition's work as well as for the failure of the permanence of transcendence, is the interruptive possibilities held by repetition and renewal which are occasioned by the effective presence of the incomplete. The presence of the potential for repetition, and thus for renewal within the present, reinforces the incomplete nature of the present by refusing it the possibility of its ever being – or ever having been – self-identical. It should be added that repetition will have different and incompatible forms. It will always be necessary to distinguish between a repetition of the Same – i.e. the reiteration of tradition's work – and a repetition in which something occurs again for the first time. This latter form of repetition is a possibility that can never be excluded absolutely. The continuity of its presence becomes that which holds the continuity of the incomplete in place.

Allowing for the inherently incomplete nature of the present, maintaining, thereby, a productive and ineliminable caesura as the present's own condition, disrupts that flow of time which moves from past to the present and then to the future. Breaking this flow is to reposition the future. Rather than positing it as the yet to come – a positioning that robs the present of any specificity it may have had – the future will become a condition of the present. What this means is that the future is generated by the differing ways in which the present may come to be repeated. The present's repetition is only possible because it remains incomplete. By refusing the possibility of a completing self-identity, the principle of change will always remain internal to the present. Once enacted, that principle takes on the differing permutations of repetition. This reinforces the sense in which the future is a condition of the present. As such the future's own inscription within – as part of – the present, allows the present to guard the future and thus to be the guardian of hope.

Allowing for the partial and the incomplete on the one hand, and the complex interplay of repetition, renewal and hope on the other, is to open up the possibility that the response to real presence, as with the response to an enforcing structure of melancholia – two positions which function as differing sides of the same coin – need not be mythic. Here, therefore, the process of demythologisation will not have to depend upon a counter-myth. Specifically, the response to the oscillation between loss and presence need not be based on an inexorable teleology, the presence of theology within philosophical thinking, nor on the utopian, the mythic response par excellence both to loss as well as to that conception of the partial that is generated by the retention of either destiny or an envisaged plenitude that is yet to be fulfilled or which has come undone. There is another possibility. This possibility will arise with the recognition that once the interdependence between loss and completion is put into abeyance, then what will have to emerge is another thinking of the incomplete. No longer will it be that conception of the incomplete that is held by its opposition to differing forms of plenitude. Rather than being simply other, or merely different, its difference will raise the philosophical problem of how that alterity is to be thought. There will be an-other conception, one which thereby gives an-other possibility to the incomplete. Again, the philo-sophical challenge involves responding to the questions: In terms of what is such a possibility to be thought? Is it possible to hold to an ontology and thus to a temporality of the incomplete? Part of the answer to these questions will depend upon having shown that repetition and renewal are fundamental to the development of an ontology and temporality of the incomplete.

What this means is that once relativism is put to one side, and once differ-ence can be assumed to involve more than variety or diversity, then the philosophical problem concerns how that which is different is to be under-stood. Thinking the incomplete outside the oscillation between the complete and its opposite, and thus outside the oscillation between plenitude and loss, demands the introduction of another conceptual apparatus. While terms will be similar, their practice and thus their work will be importantly different. Tracing that difference, allowing these concepts to work, is what is being staged within the realisation of this project.

Rather than defining what is contra melancholia in a purely negative manner, it will emerge as a strategy that takes different forms. It is there in holding to the presence of contestation as primary, there in allowing the presence of antinomies to be real rather than mere surface effects (thereby enjoining the necessity for judgement), there in an openness risking closure, there in having to work with the inevitability of repetition, there in the affirmation of anoriginal difference. These differing conceptual moments can only be clarified by allowing them to be effectively present. Thus, what becomes essential is tracing the effect of their work. All of these possibilities – and it is a list to which other instances could be added – involve differing permutations of affirmation. However, affirmation is not joy. Thinking or acting contra melancholia yields neither a site of celebration nor a place of dance. The naive celebration of the carnival would always have to have forgotten carnival's original inscription of the violence of exploitation as well as its own manipulation of power.

Finally, rather than marking the presence of philosophy's constant applica-tion to areas outside of itself, moving backwards and forwards between poetry, architecture, Judaism and the nature of historical time, is meant to indicate that another possibility exists within philosophy, a possibility other than the one given by the posited opposition between the pure and the applied. What is involved here stems from the attempt to think philosophically about such topics. Rather than allowing philosophy to dominate their pres-ence, they will be positioned within the philosophical, once philosophy comes to be seen as concerned with the present. In other words, their inscription into the philosophical emerges within that project whose orientation is to think philosophically about the present.

ACKNOWLEDGEMENTS

I have benefited greatly from being able to give early versions of some of these chapters as lectures in different institutions. I would like to thank Monica Bohm-Duchen for inviting me to present elements of Chapter 1 at the *Art after Auschwitz* conference which was held at the Courtauld Institute in London in 1995; Bernard Tschumi for inviting me to give a version of Chapter 5 to The Graduate School of Architecture, Planning and Preservation at Columbia University; Charles Bernstein for the opportunity to present a version of Chapter 6 to his Graduate Poetry Seminar at the State University of New York at Buffalo. The work on Walter Benjamin in Chapters 2, 3 and 4 arose out of my graduate seminars on Benjamin which took place in the Department of Philosophy at the University of Warwick. Earlier versions of Chapters 2 and 3 appeared respectively in A. Benjamin and P. Osbourne (eds) *Walter Benjamin's Philosophy*, London: Routledge, 1994 and *New Formations*, vol. 10, 1, 95–111. I would like to acknowledge the enthusiasm and dedication of the participants of that seminar over the last four years. I would also like to thank Simon Sparks for his invaluable help in the preparation of the manuscript.

1

HOPE AT THE PRESENT

OPENING

Opening this project – *Present Hope* – involves establishing the positions that will continue to be developed and related in the writing to come. That they form a relation without end needs to be interpreted as symptomatic of the type of questioning they stage. Moreover, the force of this project will hold to hope as a structural condition of the present rather than as the promise of a future, the continual promise of a future that will always have to have been better.

The first of these positions concerns the way in which the present comes to be thought philosophically. As a point of departure it will have to be recognised that the present is already thought within differing philosophical positions. Instances of the differing ways in which the present works within philosophy will, in this instance, centre around the writings of Martin Heidegger and Walter Benjamin. In addition to philosophy, poetry, architecture and Judaism will also figure as an integral part of the argument to come. In more general terms, however, the presence of conflict at the present, conflict concerning the nature of the present, entails that, in the end, philosophy will have to allow for the possibility of antinomies that are not purely phenomenal. Allowing for this possibility will entail a reconsideration of the philosophical. What comes to be reworked is the relationship between the phenomenal and the essential and, therefore, the particular and the universal. Reworking is not destruction. Philosophy is constituted by an act of engagement with its own history. Engagement can take many forms. Here, and in contrast to a simple repetition of the Same, it is present as the process of reworking.

Philosophy has always attempted to justify itself in terms of universality. Even though, for example, the Cartesian project of absolute knowledge differs fundamentally from the Hegelian, their insistence on absolute inclusivity provides a fundamental point of contact.[1] Within Descartes and Hegel's own terms the limit of philosophy becomes the limit of the possible or the limit of the real. Philosophy will have always been linked to the project of completion and thus to the necessity for a temporal as well as an' ontological finality. This set up gives rise to questions which, despite their simplicity, harbour a necessary and insistent complexity. Is it possible to continue with philosophy if the projects of completion and finality have been rendered redundant for reasons as much philosophical as political? If philosophy is linked to the necessary identification of thought and being, and of the real and the ideal, can philosophy continue if what is taken as central, with the abeyance of these forms of finality, is the incomplete?

Responding to these questions can take at least two specific forms. The first laments the impossibility of philosophy's project, and thus condemns itself to a ceaseless preoccupation with impossibility, the aporetic and a thoughtful melancholia. The second involves a complex re-reading of philosophy's history in which what comes to be affirmed is the identification of the productive presence of the incomplete as always having formed part of the philosophical project. Part of that undertaking will have to involve a sustained engagement with the ontology and the temporality of the incomplete.[2] Assuming the effective presence of ontology and time will allow the work of the incomplete to be traced in different sites which thereby lend themselves to a philosophical engagement. Philosophy is able to continue once continuity is understood as involving a series of complex repetitions in which repeating needs to be understood as a continual reworking. It is the second of these options that provides the basis of the chapters to come.

At work within this set up, therefore, is the necessity to rethink and thus to rework the philosophical project in terms of an affirmation of the incomplete and thus to develop further an ontology and temporality of the incomplete. Rather than writing an abstract philosophical treatise – a project that has already been rendered otiose by the nature of the philosophy in question – the insistence of the present and its possible interarticulation with hope will be taken as providing the continual point of departure. (As will emerge, this defers the possibility of abstraction because the present will always be a particular that is no longer held within the relation of dependency demanded by the interconnection of universal and particular. Abstraction will be limited to that relation.) What is at stake, therefore, is the possibility of thinking philosophically about the present. Once again, this is not intended to be a question devoid of specificity, but one in which the problem of what type of thinking and what particular formulation of the present is involved will already be implicated in the specific form of philosophical activity undertaken. Furthermore, rather than being a spurious attempt to apply philosophy, an integral part of the project here will involve questioning philosophy's relation to architecture and to poetry once the site of engagement is taken to be the present – or, more precisely, the interrelationship between modernity and the present.

The position at work within this project therefore involves the complex set up that emerges when it becomes essential to address that which marks out modernity: i.e. modernity's own specificity. (The problem of the relationship between the present and modernity can be put to one side at this stage.) Here, there is a three-part formulation. The first part is that modernity is delimited by a founding dislocation.[3] An instance of this fundamental moment is the impossibility of identifying either a possible coextensivity or continuity between sign and thing or between signifier and signified. (There are many moments that mark out this divide. Perhaps one of the most emphatic is the Freudian formulation of the unconscious.[4]) Second, there is the continual attempt to efface the presence of this founding moment by the formulation of differing conceptions of continuity and totality: e.g. human nature, eternal values, myths of origin, the naturalisation of chronological time. Third, these attempts to establish or re-establish continuity generate their own version of particularity, or perhaps in a more limited sense, of the fragmentary. What makes this more difficult is that such a set up generates a conception of the particular that has three defining characteristics. Their potentially exclusive characteristics delimit how particularity is to be understood once it is viewed as having been generated by an enforcing continuity, and thus when it only exists in relation to that continuity. Particularity, now robbed of either generality or the simple assumption of existence, is here defined in relation to continuity, the continuity generating these differing conceptions of the particular. What this leaves open, of course, is the possibility of another sense of particularity.

The first characteristic is that, as particulars, they will be able to be absorbed into the whole, perhaps, for some positions, re-absorbed into the whole. The second is that a consequence of being absorbed is that, despite the presence of particulars, particularity, taken as that which may exist in itself, cannot be thought. Particulars will have been no more than mere predicates of a universal. The third characteristic is the melancholic. It is marked by a preoccupation with particularity in which the particular is haunted by either the loss of an unspecifiable whole or the fall from totality. Here particularity presupposes a founding plenitude and envisages either redemption or, more straightforwardly, the future, thought in terms of completion and thus of recovery.

3

What this means is that since modernity is to be understood as a dislocation that comes to be effaced, thinking that dislocation cannot involve mere
attention to particulars or fragments, as though they existed in themselves.
Here, in contrast, there has to be that act, that moment of work, which
allows for the presence of dislocation. It should also be clear that there are
different thinkers, and thus thinkings, of modernity, different ways of
arguing for the founding presence of dislocation. The reality that some of
these positions are, in the end, irreducible will only reinforce the fact that
what marks out the present site of philosophical activity is the presence of a
founding conflict concerning the nature of modernity. (Indeed it will be in
precisely these terms that it will become possible to stage the encounter
between Heidegger and Benjamin.) Finally, it must be noted that the
differing arguments denying the particularity of modernity only become
further symptoms of its ineliminable presence.

The third and final position marking out this project arises once it becomes
essential to link modernity to the present. Here, it will be assumed that what
yields this link is the Shoah.[5] In sum, what marks this founding moment – the
Holocaust within thinking – is the impossibility of maintaining simple continuity.[6] However, rather than abandoning the All in the face of the Shoah, the
emergent question must concern how to continue. That the tradition of
European culture could not have prevented what occurred means that instead
of either allowing that tradition to be repeated unchecked on the one hand, or
of abandoning key elements within it and thereby employing a dangerously
destructive logic on the other, the central question, one which will figure as
much in the visual arts as it will in philosophy and literature, will concern
how it is that what is given is able to be repeated. In what way can repetition
work without the hold of either complicity or nihilism? While demanding a
more precise description, complicity can initially be understood as allowing
for the unchecked repetition of tradition; nihilism is the name given to the
varying forms taken by what in more general terms could be described as a
metaphysics of destruction.

And yet, because the Shoah can always be incorporated within the gestures
of universal history or redescribed such that it forms part of a general history
of racism or, even more specifically, a general history of anti-semitism, what
allows it to be granted this status within this particular project? (The fact that
this question still needs to be acknowledged is itself one of the motifs that
marks out the current state of thinking.) There are at least two ways of
addressing this question. The first would be to invoke a form of precedent. It
would involve recognising that thinkers, writers and artists – including
Adorno, Lyotard, Celan, Beuys and Kiefer – have not just noted the presence

of a problem, but that the question of how to continue after the Shoah dominates their specific undertakings.[7] This is not to argue that their projects are
reducible to dwelling, straightforwardly, on questions arising from the Shoah.
Rather, their projects can be situated within the more nuanced position in
which there is the recognition that any work seeking to confront and thus
engage with the present cannot avoid the Shoah's insistence. The second
response to this question almost defeats the description of its being an argument. It is tempting to resort to the claim that the Shoah is an occurrence for
which there could be no universal, as though that were an argument complete
in itself. This would have the consequence that any attempt to establish such a
universal/particular relation would only trivialise the enormity of what took
place. While this position has a great deal of cogency – indeed it will be necessary to deploy elements of it at a later stage – the problem of privilege
remains *precisely* because it is a position which needs to be contested. Allowing
for the ineliminable presence of such a contest means that questions of proof
and certainty are no longer apposite. (Again, it may be that this is the consequence of the position being described.) At this stage, therefore, all that can
be done is to acknowledge a certain privileging of the Shoah as the occurrence
that, within the visual arts, literature and philosophy, brings modernity and
the present into conjunction. What this involves is, of course, a move that
cannot be justified if justification becomes a prescription for all. In what
follows this privileging is assumed. The viability of that assumption will be
shown in the work that it sustains. The problem of the lack of explicit justification should be taken as one of the enduring problems governing
contemporary thought.

The major difficulty to be addressed in this opening concerns the relationship between, in the first place, a general philosophical thinking of the present
– a generality that will have many specific forms; in the second, modernity
understood as dislocation; and finally, the present as given by the Shoah. There
is a generalised thinking of the present within philosophy. It occurs as much in
Kant and Hegel as it does in Benjamin and Heidegger.[8] This thinking of the
present has a generality which will be addressed in terms of the reciprocity
between time and task. Time, and that means the way in which the present is
understood, will determine the nature and with it the direction of philosophical activity. The latter is the task. The formulation of the present arising out of
a thinking of the reciprocity between time and task will be identified henceforth as the *epochal present*; as such, it can be held apart from the chronological
present. (It will be necessary to return to the details of this conception of the
present.) Nonetheless, it remains the case that once the Shoah is introduced,
another element enters into consideration.

It has already been suggested that not only is modernity given by founding dislocations, but that these dislocations are able to be effaced by the reintroduction of forms of totality. Particularity will always be able to be incorporated. Part of the challenge, therefore, will be to maintain the particularity of modernity. Related to this are the differing ways in which philosophy conceives of the present. Some will be connected to modernity, others will not. However, once the Shoah is attributed the status of allowing for an interconnection between modernity and the present, then that has to be understood as claiming that modernity as dislocation will have a specific engagement with the Shoah, given that the Shoah is taken within that formulation of philosophical activity which allows it to have a determining effect on thinking. This will be the site in which the effective interconnection of time and task is to be situated. And yet despite that, there is here the absence of a generalised, and indeed generalisable, necessity. What this means is that not only is there the inescapable possibility of the Shoah's absorption, but that this possibility defines the particularity of this project. In other words, resisting assimilation means having to grant that what is being staged here is a particular enactment of the relationship between time and task. There is no way of justifying this as a general or universal claim. As such what it provides is the point of dispute between this project and that thinking of modernity which presumes itself to be addressing the present even though the Shoah is completely absent as a determining occurrence. Moreover, in providing the site of conflict, it reinforces the necessity for judgement. It is only the presence of conflict that demands judgement. Once antinomies are taken to be anoriginally present – and here they must be, insofar as what is at stake are ways of thinking the present that cannot be reduced to each other – judgement becomes the only apposite response. What this means is that if the antinomic or the conflictual cannot be eliminated by recourse to another level of analysis, then their copresence will demand a decision. As the decision cannot have recourse to the structure of universality – if it could then the antinomies or the conflicts would have been eliminated from the outset – the decision will necessitate another response. A way of identifying the ineliminable necessity of this form of decision making is in terms of judgement. Judgement will only arise once a particular set up, while unmasterable, still necessitates a decision.

Before taking up the concerns of this text, a warning needs to be introduced. It concerns the name Auschwitz. Indeed, it will have to touch on any use of this name after Auschwitz. Perhaps one of the most acute versions of this warning has been advanced by Jacques Derrida in 'Canons and Metonymies'. Derrida's contextual concern is the role this name has played in a number of contemporary philosophical studies. His questions are both explicit and uncompromising.

> What is the referent of this proper name Auschwitz? If, as I suspect, one uses the name metonymically, what is the justification for doing so? And what governs this terrible rhetoric? Within such a metonymy, why this name rather than those of all the other camps and mass exterminations? Why this heedless and also troublesome restriction? As paradoxical as it may seem, respect is due *equally* to *all* singularities.[9]

Central to what is being suggested in this passage is the possibility that Auschwitz may have moved from being a simple proper name and thereby designating a specific geographical site, to its having become the name for all such sites. Why is Auschwitz evoked in this way and not Treblinka? On one level there is a pointlessness attached to this question. And yet echoing within it is the problem of how it is possible to 'respect' – to use Derrida's term – those who suffered elsewhere by only having used the name Auschwitz. How are they named by the name Auschwitz? Part of what is being demanded by Derrida is a grammar. It will be essential to return to the possibility of a justification for this use of language, here and initially, the justification for the use of metonymy. Derrida's relentless questioning introduces the need for caution and thus of holding back from an immediate oscillation between pathos and polemic. In the first place, respect will be linked here to this caution. Second, however, respect will be linked to memory. Both respect and memory demand continuity. Forgetting would be the failure to respect. The problem, therefore, is beginning to understand the possibility of a conception of memory that maintains respect. What would disturb this set up is the possibility that mourning may fail to maintain a relation of distance to the object. It would have failed precisely because it would have to have been overcome. Once this occurred, what it would entail is not just the incorporation of the object, but the elimination of a certain spacing that held the object in place. Place would have demanded distance. Incorporation and the denial of distance would, as a consequence, also fail in every respect to continue. Respect may, therefore, be necessarily linked to holding to a relation of distance.

In sum, modernity and the present are interconnected here precisely because this project – *Present Hope* – is an attempt to think the present from within that conception of the philosophical that takes the dislocation which yields modernity as the necessary point of departure. An inherent part of that thinking takes the presence of the Shoah to be the occurrence that brings the present and modernity into connection. What is being staged here, therefore, is a particular thinking of the present. Rather than offering an account demanding what would, in the end, be no more than putative universality, insisting on this connection has the twofold consequence of yielding a thinking of the present which projects a contemporary site of philosophical activity precisely because generality – both with regard to the present and modernity taken as existing *tout court* – is resisted. And yet, this resistance opens a conception of particularity that cannot be readily reinserted into the universal/particular relation. This is a fundamental part of Walter Benjamin's philosophical undertaking. The further consequences of this possibility will be developed in the following engagements.

As a final opening point, an additional consideration needs to be noted. Here it concerns the relationship between the incomplete, the differing particularities within which the present can be said to be thought, and an ontology of the present. A problem would seem to arise with the suggestion that the very necessity of having to think particularity within the abeyance of the universal/particular relation is incompatible with the project of ontology. The assumption in the above is, of course, that ontology will have to demand that particular form of inclusivity that would, in the end, render all particulars the Same. Responding to this position does not demand the introduction of relativism. It is not as though all that is at work here are different explanatory narratives. There is a more fundamental project which involves having to think the presence of different formulations of philosophical activity; again, this will be an activity defined in terms of the relationship between time and task. The presence of these differences is another way of understanding the presence of the incomplete. The challenge involves the further recognition that the only adequate philosophical account of this set up involves a reformulation of the project of ontology in terms of an ontology of the incomplete. Once this is taken up as a real possibility then it would, in its very realisation, provide an ontology of the present. Part of this project therefore involves precisely that undertaking. What will emerge is that the interrelationship between the incomplete and the present allows a similarity of thinking. What this means is that both articulate the same ontologico-temporal set up. Here, the ontological will have a productive or generative quality. Moving to the effective or the actative is the mark of already having moved from considering the ontological in terms of stasis, namely the fixed and the permanent, to allowing for the ontological to be explicated as becoming or force, and thus in terms of presencing rather than the already present.[10]

While it remains the case that these opening formulations of the interconnections between modernity, the present and the incomplete, and the differing demands they make on thinking, stand in need of further clarification, such an undertaking cannot be done in the absence of particulars. Particularity has become essential. Nonetheless, it will be in terms of these initial positions that it will have become possible to turn with greater precision to the question of the present. With this turn, both the difficulty of the present – a difficulty that is in part generated by the present's insistent quality – and the possibility of its interconnection with what will be developed here in terms of the structure of hope, will themselves have to return.

AT PRESENT

Part of what marks out one of the dominant trends within philosophy is the recognition that its own concerns are staged in time.[11] What comes to be introduced with this recognition is the possibility that time will have a determining effect on the specific forms taken by philosophical activity. These forms will be differing permutations of the philosophical task. As formulations, they do not occur within the simple present; that would be to reduce the present to a mere moment of chronological time. More exactly: they define the present by invoking and holding to different formulations of the time of writing. What this entails is that the complex relationship between time, task and the present – recognising that the relationship has no one unique form – will work to define differing philosophical possibilities by generating different conceptions of the epochal present. (These differing conceptions can, of course, all bear the same date.) Consequently, and as a way of taking up the question of thinking philosophically about the present, rather than giving time a tangential position, it will be taken as playing a determining role. Time, understood as involving differing formulations of historical time, will have already been at work, therefore, within what has already been identified as the complex relation of time and task. This latter relation will be marked by an inherent reciprocity, perhaps even a symbiosis, between its constituent elements. Furthermore, time will also figure in the other central component of this project, namely hope. Once there is the possibility of connecting hope and the present then time will be even more central. Hope necessarily brings time into consideration.

Prior to pursuing the detail of these founding relations, there is a preliminary problem which demands discussion. It occurs because of the introduction of hope, and precisely because hope seems to be linked inextricably to time. However, the nature of that temporality seems to check the project in question. After all, is there not an inherently paradoxical element in any attempt to insist upon a relationship between hope and the present? Is it not the case that hope is already implicated in a future which it intends? The project of hope, and with it the possibility of hope's realisation, would seem to be necessarily futural and therefore to cast doubt on the viability of any attempt to bring hope into conjunction with the present. How could there be any real connection between the present and hope? It is the self-evident force of this question that reveals the problem. If, as a question, it harboured an inner truth, the consequences stemming from it would efface the present. In other words, if it were accepted that hope is opened up by gesturing towards a future, then the question that immediately arises concerns the present. What happens to the present – the site in which hoping takes place – if hope is unequivocally futural? Not only would the present remain unthought, but its considerations and its concerns would be effaced in relation to the future. In this instance, rather than allowing the present to remain unthought, there is the possibility of another form of questioning. It arises precisely because of the failure to address the present which occurs when hope is taken as only ever futural. The question is: What happens to hope once the present rather than the future is taken as central? In sum, if it can exist, then what is hope at the present?

Part of this project involves responding to these questions by repositioning hope, stripping it of its utopian garb by locating it in the present. What this will mean is that hope would be positioned as part of an ontology of the present. Hope would become one way of naming the present's inherently incomplete nature. As such, rather than a futural projection bringing with it the appearance of the ethical, hope will have a structural force, insofar as it will hold the present open and thus as being unfinished. Rather than allowing for the present to be effaced, the possibility of an inherent interconnection between the present and hope will entail that both terms come to be rethought in the attempt to explicate that relation. Part of this particular project will necessitate working with the consequences of the understanding that the present admits of an already present complexity. Tracing the work of this complex state of affairs will mean pursuing the interplay of time and task. The copresence of time and task not only indicates the possibility of work in the present; it has a further effect. Noting their presence means noting work that is already taking place at the present. The epochal present which arises from the reciprocal relation of time and task is, as a consequence, the work of the present. Even though such work need not eschew universality or continuity, it is already an engagement with the particularity of the here and now.

At this stage, however, rather than developing the differing nuances of this complex set up, it will be necessary to stay with the reciprocity between time and task as that which is given once a generalised present is allowed to bear upon philosophy. Here, two positions will be sketched to indicate how this process works and thus how two differing conceptions of the epochal present may come to hold sway. (They will be developed in more detail at a later stage).

In 'On the Concept of History', Benjamin underlines the importance and the urgency of his project of 'rescue' (*Rettung*) by claiming that

> every image of the past that is not recognised by the present as one of its own concerns threatens to disappear irretrievably.[12]

There are two questions here. The first concerns what is meant by 'the present'. The second question concerns how the explicit sense of project – the task – that is announced in these lines is to be understood. Before responding to these questions, the way in which the present is announced in Heidegger's own work needs to be noted.

In *An Introduction to Metaphysics*, Heidegger formulates the concerns orienting his philosophical project in light of his detailed treatment of the distinctions between Being and Becoming, Being and Appearing, Being and Thinking and finally Being and Ought. What is important about this formulation is the interconnection of what has already been identified as time and task.

> If one asks the question of Being radically, one must understand the task [*die Aufgabe*] of unfolding the truth of the essence of Being; one must come to a decision regarding the powers hidden in these distinctions in order to restore [*zurückbringen*] them to their truth.[13]

This passage needs to be set against another slightly different yet nonetheless programmatic expression of what determines the philosophical task. In the second of the *Nietzsche* volumes, Heidegger takes up the time of writing in the following way:

> Our epoch reveals a particularly casual matter-of-factness with the respect to the truth of beings as a whole.[14]

While the detail of this second quote will also be taken up at a later stage, what is clear is that the project of restoration is intended to overcome the identified 'matter-of-factness'. Not only is this the intention; it is, to use Heidegger's own term, 'the task'. The 'task' is determined by the nature of the 'epoch'. Here, it would have to be argued that the relation between the two is not only necessary, but that there is a reinforcing reciprocity. As is clear, in each case the structure and the specific determination of one is given by the other. This complex giving is inescapable. It marks the reciprocity of time and task. Responding within this set up will be intentional. It will be the result of a 'decision'. Moreover, it will be in terms of the necessary force of this decision – necessity here is both the decision's ground and as well as its projection – that a form of philosophical authenticity will become inescapable.

Benjamin's concern with the present is not with a present explicable in terms of a simple reference to chronology. While able to be dated, the present in question is not reducible to mere chronology. Rather what is given with the present is that which determines the nature of the philosophical task. (It goes without saying that in Benjamin's case, as with Heidegger's, there will also be a linked political task in the exact sense that the formulation of the present determines the nature as well as the form of such activity.) Thus, the significant point here is that making something a concern for the present determines what it is that defines the nature of philosophical activity. The present is such that it demands that certain things be made a concern for it. Benjamin's own concern, that were this not to happen then things could be lost forever, is neither nostalgic nor driven by a desire to maintain the present's heritage. Indeed, his concern is only explicable in terms of a conception of the present – here modernity – that is constructed by a dislocation that is not at hand. The importance of rescue is that what comes to be disrupted in the action – in the process of dislocation itself – is the time of historicism or the time that effaces the actual dislocation that determines the nature of the modernity. Dislocation reveals the nature of modernity as dislocated. For Benjamin, the present is the thinking of this set up.

It is, of course, the time of continuity that accounts for the dominant conceptions of temporality that are taken to work the present. (While this appears to equate the chronological present with the epochal present, the contrary is the case insofar as it reinforces the point that the positing of chronology will already be a specific thinking of the present.) Accounting for this process involves working with the fact that the interarticulation of chronology and continuity comes to be naturalised and, as such, is taken to be the expression of time itself. Part of the acuity of Benjamin's own analysis of modernity is that it shows how this set up brings a certain politics with it. The relationship between time and politics is such that one cannot be thought without there being, either implicitly or explicitly, a thinking of the other. With the naturalisation of time there is a related effacing of the specificity of modernity; to the extent that continuity is maintained, one move will have been given by the next. Consequently, there could be nothing that will have already been exclusively modern. The one exception would be that conception of modernity in which the contemporary would be the current form taken by that which endured either perennially or eternally. Detailing

12

Benjamin's own position will form a fundamental part of this project. And yet there will be a further opening, since this reciprocity will have far greater extension than that which bounds his writings.

In broader terms, therefore, indicating the essential reciprocity between time and task returns to philosophy not just the possibility of its own engagement with modernity, but the recognition that such an engagement is taking place. Here, the interconnection between modernity and the present brings with it three interrelated areas of concern; namely loss, memory and experience. While these terms have an important generality, they will have already been mediated by that occurrence that will have already determined *our* modernity, namely the Shoah. With regard to the Shoah, thinking its emphatic presence will, in the first instance, be staged, via a long and detailed engagement with Freud's most sustained attempt to think loss, namely 'Mourning and Melancholia'.

Questions concerning the singularity of the Shoah are, in this instance, not the issue. What is of importance are the problems posed for philosophy by having to think what took place. Again, it is not just a question of historical specificity, but of the way in which the Shoah has affected the project of memory, the status of knowledge and the problem of experience. It is this set up that will check the work of representation since memory and knowledge are traditionally understood as given within the general problematic of representation. Some of the direct consequences of the Shoah for the task of thinking can be located here. Once this occurrence is allowed to register within philosophy, then philosophy is constrained to think its own engagement with the Shoah's insistence. The contention will be that an integral part of this formulation of the interconnection of modernity and the present – amounting thereby to a thinking of the present will have to be both the awareness of this insistence and the sustained attempt to engage with its presence. It will be in terms of what is opened by this insistent engagement that the interplay of value and judgement can be situated.

However, the counter-move to this must not be overlooked. As has already been suggested, modernity also brings with it attempts to force and thus to reinforce generality and continuity. Whether it is in terms of the project of a universalising history – and this need not be on the grand scale of Hegel but could be on the particular scale of the generalised history of certain topics – or in terms of a general thematics of perfectibility, one of modernity's defining tropes will be the attempt to efface insistent particularity. Once this occurs with the Shoah, then a further part of the contention being advanced here is that such work either fails to think the conjunction between modernity and the present, or would fail to allow that conjunction to be thought.

MOURNING AND MELANCHOLIA: FREUD'S LOSS

Taking up the problems posed for philosophy – though this will also be true for literature and the visual arts – by its having to think its own response to the Shoah, means encountering the problematic of representation. As has already been suggested, with the Shoah the project of representation, the conception of the object and thus the conception of the project of episte-mology proper to representation, encounter a limit. While there will always be the need to know, while the detail of knowledge remains indispensable, the project of representation and the way it structures both memory and knowledge will no longer pertain in an unproblematic sense. Avoiding this consequence of the Shoah's insistence is to move to a form of forgetful nihilism. Resisting, if not overcoming, the force of nihilism, means that presentation after the Shoah will have to involve reconsidering the nature of re-presentation itself.[15] Representation raises the problem of iconoclasm and thus the control not just of images but of what can be represented. With the Shoah what is of central concern is the possibility of representation. Identifying this concern in this particular way is not intended to address the question of physical possibility; it is, after all, always possible to represent. Rather, what is at stake in this instance is the activity of representation once it has been linked to a form of interdiction concerning the nature of repre-sentation itself.

There is a general problem of iconoclasm. Within Judaism it will have specific though different forms, in the same way as Judaism itself will have different and, at times, almost incommensurable forms. Even in recognising the importance of this limit, the question of representation and thus of the process of instantiation must have greater extension. Part of its range is found in time since it is time that figures with representation. The movement of representing takes place across time. Representation is inextricably bound up with time and memory. At its most minimal, memory is, after all, the name for a relation across time. At work within this set up, therefore, is an abstract formulation of the site of representation. It is an abstraction that will come to be mediated by the present, demanding thereby that the present be thought.

Laws restricting the process of representation are positioned in relation to the present thus construed. Law here must have an ambiguous status. It will refer to the commandment within the Hebrew Bible that seeks to delimit the representation of God, thus giving rise to the general problem of iconoclasm. This continuity is, of course, shattered by the problem of representation, of imagining and of remembering after the Shoah. There is another law which will have become linked to this occurrence. Equally, the centrality of repre-sentation and thus the linking of interdiction and representation will emerge not as a direct result of but in relation to Adorno's claim that 'after Auschwitz writing poetry is barbaric'.[16] Here the restriction lies not in a simple interdiction but the identification of an impossibility. Adorno continues: 'And this corrodes even the knowledge of why it has become impossible to write poetry today [*heute Gedichte zu schreiben*]'. What will have to be recognised is the extent to which this is a formal claim; i.e. given the historical context – a context marked in the passage by the word 'today' – it is a claim about the form of a certain poetic practice within the determinations of the present. With the use of term 'today', the present will have already been thought. Furthermore, the claim about possibility needs to be understood in relation to what is still able to be done. In other words, it needs to be interpreted as a claim about repetition, though equally as a claim about the complexity of repetition's inherent presence. Part of that complexity lies in repetition's own continuity despite its having been sundered by Auschwitz. Acting while ignoring Auschwitz will be a type of barbarism. Loss will have to be both acknowledged and thought. The question, however, is the following: How is an acting possible that acknowledges the specificity of Auschwitz and which allows for loss? In sum, there are two central questions. The first concerns how the response to loss is to be understood, how it is to be understood in being represented. The second is related because it pertains with equal force to the concerns of representability. How is another form of remembering possible? Such questions are neither abstract nor prevaricatory. They are concerned as much with the conditions of judgement as they are with possibility.

Answering such questions will necessitate holding to the effective centrality of repetition. More specifically, approaching loss will need to be undertaken via a consideration of Freud's own attempt to generalise the process of loss – the project of 'Mourning and Melancholia'. It is not just that this text plays an important role in more general examinations of loss; it is the one place in which Freud's ostensible concern is thinking through the site of loss as it is constructed by the temporal and experiential structures of mourning and melancholia. Both will figure in thinking as responding to the presence of the Shoah.

Freud's 'Mourning and Melancholia' occasions the possibility for a certain type of thinking.[17] What will it mean to have to think this loss? This question is asked rather than the more straightforward one of what is it to think this loss. To have to think it will mean coming to the recognition of the insistence of thinking, of having to think it. Thinking will involve and demand a decision. Not thinking it, therefore, will be linked to the resistance to this form of recognition. It would not have emerged as something that one had to think. In addition, the expression 'to have to think' brings with it the form of an obligation. There is something that one has to do. This is the case even though the text's ostensible concern is loss for an individual. The question that will endure, however, concerns the extent to which it allows for this other loss to be thought – the loss that comes to be connected with the name Auschwitz. Part of what is at issue, therefore, is having to take up of the complexity of loss. It is not enough to ask: How, with the Shoah, is loss to be understood? There is a more emphatic question: In terms of what is that which insists to be thought? This question marks the limits of the possibility of thought by allowing thinking to emerge as given in response to a need. It also allows for the Shoah to endure as a challenge to thinking and thus as not automatically assimilable to already present conceptual and categorial frameworks. Part of the singularity of this occurrence emerges at this point. The difficulty is that almost by definition there cannot be a general, or even a generalisable, argument that would establish this claim. This is part of the difficulty. Indeed, it can also be taken as attesting to the viability of the initial proposition. In fact, it is the problem of singularity – its impossible possibility if what is at stake is justification – that will be the continual site of engagement in a number of the arguments which follow. The problem of proof will always remain a burden.

In both mourning and melancholia there is an impoverishment of the world. Nonetheless, the worlds proper to each one, are importantly different. The way that difference comes to be formulated by Freud is that in 'mourning it is the world which has become poor and empty; in melancholia it is the ego itself' (246). What is of significance here is that, despite the distinction, there is a reciprocity of structure. One position mirrors the other. It is thus that both come to be worked out in similar ways. Freud describes their relation in terms of an 'essential analogy'. With the existence of this analogy it becomes possible to indicate what a resolution in each case will be like. After having described 'normal mourning' in terms of an emerging capacity to 'overcome the loss of the object', the point of real connection is established in the following terms.

> Just as mourning impels the ego to give up the object by declaring the object to be dead and offering the ego the inducement to continue to live, so does each single struggle of ambivalence [in melancholia] loosen the fixation of the libido to the object by disparaging it, denigrating and even as it were killing it. It is possible for the process in the Ucs to come to an end, either after the fury has spent itself or after the object has been abandoned as valueless.
>
> (257)

What is immediately apparent with both mourning and melancholia is the extent to which there is the possibility of an overcoming. Part of that particular process must be the movement from mourning to remembering. Overcoming loss will not involve a denial of the loss. Rather, loss is registered with the result that the ego releases its hold by 'declaring the object to be dead'. Even though melancholia repeats the structure, except this time as internal to the self and then where this internality in fact involves an exteriority, it remains the case that melancholia will allow for its own specific cessation. Furthermore, despite there being a pathological stage or possibility within both mourning and melancholia, their specific temporal form involves a completion. Freud will speak of the possibility of 'bringing melancholia to an end'. It is worth noting the detail of Freud's own 'conjecture' concerning how, economically, the process of 'normal' mourning works.

> Each single one of the memories and situations of expectancy which demonstrate the libido's attachment to the lost object is met by the verdict of reality that the object no longer exists; and the ego, confronted as it were with the question whether it shall share this fate, is persuaded by the sum of the narcissistic satisfactions it derives from being alive to sever its attachment to the object that has been abolished. We may perhaps suppose that this work of severance is so slow and gradual that by the time it has been finished the expenditure of energy necessary for it is also dissipated.
>
> (255)

With this description it becomes possible to see what is involved in mourning for a lost individual. The ego is driven back into itself by its own awareness that it does not share the fate of oblivion. It gives up the lost object for precisely that reason. Part of this movement will allow for memory in the sense that memory must emerge at that point at which the hold of mourning is broken.

As something other than the form of recollection given within mourning, memory will necessitate a gradual release of the hold on the lost object. The release is not simply ideational; it pertains to the expenditure of energy that is necessary to keep it in the ego's grip. As it slips free – a state of affairs arising out of 'reality testing' – it is released into death. Its being released is thus the *sine qua non* for its being able to be remembered. A question arises at precisely this point. Will this same structure pertain when what is involved is mass death and where the individuals are not known and therefore even the horrific accumulation of names will not make them any more known?[18] Absence and loss here take on a different form. Indeed it may be the case that what mass death introduces is the necessity and the limit of epistemology; in other words the impossible possibility of knowledge. What is being questioned here is not mourning itself but its dependency upon knowledge. Mourning needs to be connected either to the known or to the knowable. What this entails is that part of what has to be pursued is the interconnection between mourning, memory and knowledge. However, the problem posed by the presence of the Shoah concerns the relationship between memory and that which is no longer delimited epistemologically, where epistemology is understood as necessarily interarticulated with the problematic of representation. Prior to addressing these questions and problems it is necessary to allow for the possibility of being able to pursue the presence of mass death through the structure of melancholia.

While melancholia and mourning maintain important points of contact, they are held apart at a certain crucial moment. Part of the reason lies in the enigmatic quality that is present within melancholia. The melancholic 'knows whom he has lost but not what he has lost in him' (245). Loss, specifically the object of loss, has an unknown quality. It is caught with a space opened up by disavowal and misidentification. Part of the work that allows for an account of the 'liberation' from the hold of melancholia involves understanding that it is characterised by what Freud describes as a formative 'ambivalence'. What this means is that melancholia is marked by a more complex structure. Operative here are different activities.

> In melancholia, accordingly, countless separate struggles are carried on over the object, in which hate and love contend with each other; the one seeks to detach the libido from the object, the other to maintain this position of the libido against the assault. The location of these separate struggles cannot be assigned to any system but the Ucs.
>
> (256)

Departing from this set up involves a victory for that aspect of the libido which seeks supremacy over the object. What accounts for the difficulty here is the movement between that which pertains to the unconscious and what it is that is possible for consciousness. Again it is essential to pursue the detail of Freud's own formulation.

Initially melancholia arises out of the destruction of the relation between the libido and its chosen object. However, rather than this meaning that there was a movement from one object to another, it means that the libido was 'withdrawn into the ego'. Consequently, part of the ego came to be equated with the object that had been discarded. The division within the ego amounted to what has already been identified as a state of conflict. This arises because the shadow of the object fell upon the ego, and the latter could henceforth be judged by a special agency, as though it were an object, the forsaken object. In this way an object-loss was transformed into an ego-loss and the conflict between the ego and the loved person into a cleavage between the critical activity of the ego and the ego as altered by identification.

(249)

It is this particular process which is located in the system Ucs and which can be terminated only by the complete vanquishing of the other part of the ego or, more importantly, by denying any value to the object whatsoever. In other words, what is fundamental to the extraction of the ego from the situation of melancholia is the removal of the object from the position of psychic or libidinal worth. It is almost the case that, in being stripped of value, the object would have been reified and thus would lack any determining particularity. It would be without an identity that held it apart from other things. The ego's survival would lie in the necessary denegation of the object. In the case of the Shoah, not only would this be an unacceptable way of overcoming its presence, but the denegation of the object would inevitably fail to allow for that conception of remembrance linked to loss, once loss needed to be thought beyond the hold of a question pertaining to worth. The presence of worth – be it in either a positive or negative sense – cannot delimit the presence of loss and thus the question of remembrance. These problems and difficulties arise with mourning and melancholia. In sum, what emerges with them is that they unite in their both having to demand the object's release. Whether release takes the form of incorporation or denegation, what cannot be avoided is the effacing of the relation of distance that is given by the object's being released.

Two interrelated components arise as central to the structure of both mourning and melancholia. Both components will need to be linked to whatever it is that conditions a response to loss in what has been described as the age of 'mass death'.[19] The first is the emergence of memory arising with the cessation of their hold; the second is that what comes to be established, though perhaps more accurately, re-established, is the continuity of the world. Clearly, what is involved here is the normalising of mourning and the presentation of melancholia as allowing for a satisfactory resolution. Even though it remains the case that both allow for an exacerbating pathology, both economically and topographically it is clear that the re-emergence of the ego reunites the ego with its life. Memory, therefore, as it is present here, is part of this process. In more general terms this indicates that it cannot be an essential question about memory. Memory is already tied up with and thus comes to

19

articulate specific and hence differing conceptions of historical time. These conceptions bring with them their own formulations of loss and thus their own different projects of remembrance. Neither memory nor the monument admit of essential thinking.

In the case of mourning and melancholia, what can be said to have taken place is an occurrence that gives rise to a certain response. (Either the death of a loved one or the dissatisfaction with a particular object choice which then becomes incorporated. As regards the former, this results in mourning, and with the latter, in melancholia.) Part of the nature of the response to particular loss is that the individual ego, either in itself or in its own internal conflictual division, severs a relation to the world. The individual has become discontinuous with the continuity of the world. Successful mourning or the overcoming of melancholia is the sustained elimination of this discontinuity. Memory is the process in which the lost object can be retained within the world's continuity. With the Shoah, however, there is the possibility that instead of an individual's discontinuity with the world, the world may have become discontinuous with itself. As is true of mourning and melancholia, it is a discontinuity that will allow for its own disavowal. If this is the case, what will be entailed is the necessity of thinking through a conception of memory as linked to a world that has been sundered, but which continues with, and thus within, its having been sundered.[20] Taking this a step further will mean having to insist on the centrality of repetition. However, it will be a conception of repetition that will need to be thought outside the continuity of the Same. After all, the latter is that temporal sequence to which a return is to be made with the completion of mourning.

What is being addressed is the applicability of mourning and melancholia to that state of affairs generated by the Shoah. The forced neutrality of this position indicates that a stand will have to be made that is neither moral nor straightforwardly political. Such a stand will be linked to what has already been identified in Adorno's use of the word 'today' (*heute*). At work within this term is the present, namely a thinking of today that is not reducible to the unproblematic play of chronology and thus the time of dates. Consequently, if there is a politics in this set up it arises out of that which is already implicated in thinking the ontology of the present. Another way of addressing what is at stake here would be by taking up the applicability of mourning and melancholia to the question of remembrance once it is posed as a question at the present. Taking this a step further necessitates resuscitating the link between mourning, knowledge and memory to which allusion was made earlier.

The importance of this link is that a fundamental part of mourning is the proximity of the loved object. It must be familiar, almost in every detail. It must be known, almost absolutely. What is known has to do with a body, one that touches, was touched, but now no longer reaches out; a mouth that opened, but now is silent; a body that was animated and is animated no longer. It is almost as though knowing both states of animation – from the quick to the dead – is essential for mourning. While the life in question may have been fantasmatic it could always be contrasted to death, to its own death, to its own having died. Here, knowledge is essential. Its link to mourning is inescapable, as is mourning's dependence on the structure of knowledge. With melancholia there will be a different state of affairs, or at least initially, since melancholia misconstrues the object. It misidentifies it and for that reason is marked by a type of epistemological failure. It is, however, a failure that can be overcome. It is neither the failure nor the limit of epistemology. The absence of knowledge is an absence given within the structure of epistemology insofar as it is an absence that can be replaced. Absence will yield to presence through a form of knowledge. Overcoming melancholia will mean that the correct identification of the object has taken place. It will arise because of having moved from a misidentification to the correct identification.

It is the nature of the interrelationship between mourning, knowledge and memory – here only tersely sketched – that may limit the possibility of knowledge in relation to the Shoah. Plotting the limits of knowledge is not intended to deny either the importance of knowledge or the necessity of history. The limit pertains to how what occurred is to be understood; it brings with it a structure of completion that will have come undone. It goes without saying that the limit of knowledge is equally the limit of mourning and melancholia. Furthermore, their limit also works on that conception of memory that seeks continuity with the world.

In *L'Écriture du désastre*, Maurice Blanchot asks how one could accept not knowing. How, in other words, could the project of knowledge ever be repudiated: 'how, indeed, to accept not to know [*comment, en effet, accepter de ne pas connaître*]?' However, immediately after identifying this necessity he goes on to draw an important limit.

> One reads books on Auschwitz. The wish of everyone there, the last wish: know what has happened, do not forget, and at the same time know that you will never know [*sachez ce qui s'est passé, n'oubliez pas, et en même temps jamais vous ne saurez*].[21]

On one level there is the imperative to know and thus not to forget; but equally there is the possible experience of a limit, of never knowing and of never being able to know. The complexity of this almost paradoxical situation is given by Blanchot not in the words marking the apparent paradox *sachez . . . jamais vous ne saurez*, but in their location. They occur within and thus designate a location that is one and the same. Here, it is identified temporally: 'at the same time'. What is the time of this 'at the same time'? What location has been thus timed? What time has been thus located? Here, this time, this interplay of time and place, is neither the *punctum* nor the *nunc stans*. What has been identified is the present. The location of this impossible possibility – and indeed a possibility that is equally marked by an ineliminable impossibility – is the here and now of writing and thus the site of philosophical activity. Equally, it can be taken as the here and now of a more generalised form of artistic activity. The present is thought within, and as, the affirmed reciprocity of time and task.

Where does this leave mourning and melancholia? And if they were to be left, what then comes to be opened up beyond the hold of pathos? Though it means cutting a path through a more complex argument, the answer to these questions lies in the difference between representation and repetition. Freud's sense of mourning and melancholia comes to be inappropriate because it depends upon a structure of knowledge that has been rendered redundant by the nature of the present. The precise nature of the present is, in a real sense, always to be determined. The reason why this is the case is that if the opening up of melancholia and mourning – an opening in which their acuity begins to fade as that within which loss is to be thought – reveals that it is the world that has become discontinuous with itself, then what this means is that living with the Shoah, living in the era of mass death, entails taking over an impossible heritage. Recalling Adorno's interdiction, what is at issue here is having to work with the incorporation of a range of artistic, literary and philosophical forms within a tradition whose continuity has been sundered and thus which cannot be continued without some type of acknowledgement of what it was that caused it to fall apart. Part of any such acknowledgement would be the refusal to repeat – simply to repeat – the artistic forms that sustained that tradition. In sum, it is a question of linking memory to a particular type of intellectual and political activity. Taking the presence of tradition seriously and therefore having to allow the presence of the Shoah a determining effect within both philosophical, literary and artistic production and the interpretation of such activities, means recognising that the real site of engagement is repetition.

What is at issue here is the suggested impossibility, for political and ethical reasons pertaining to the present rather than existing in themselves, of allowing one position or form to be repeated. And yet, to retain the link to poetry, it is not as though poeticising founders absolutely. There will be a type of continuity. Expanding this point will mean that these activities will have to involve the possibility of the thinking and thus the acting out of another conception of repetition. (It is precisely this point that will provide the basis of the analysis of Jabès and Celan in Chapter 6.) It is in terms of the distinction between an interdiction and this other repetition that it becomes possible to draw a connection between a number of the threads introduced thus far.

INCOMPLETE PRESENT

The force of the complex juxtaposition *sachez . . . jamais vous ne saurez* entails proceeding with an impossible possibility. What dominates is the hold of the negative held outside of the logic of negation (and by extension, the logic of identity). Not knowing is mediated by the status of what is known, known as a consequence of the necessity to know, perhaps even the obligation to know, captured by the use of the imperative form *sachez*. And yet this is not a site of lament in the precise sense that what would be lamented would be the lack of knowledge. Mourning the dead, mourning the loss occasioned by the Shoah, demands a conception of memory that is linked to the impossibility of mastering what took place. Not a memory admitting of failure, but a memory that, in responding to the threat of forgetting, comes to be repositioned in terms of vigilance. Part of what will structure this site is the presence of an insistent spacing. The impossibility of closure endures because of a present spacing that holds the object *apart* because it holds to it as *a part* of the work of memory. Figuring within the interplay of the logic of the apart/a part, memory will come to be reactivated in terms of present remembrance.[22] The force of this latter designation is that it holds to what will be developed as an insistent relation of distance. It is thus that it is the question of memory – both in itself and in terms of present remembrance – that will open up further ways of interconnecting modernity and the present.

As a defining problem, memory registers loss. What is to be remembered is no longer at hand. Understanding this set up means working with the recognition that rather than there being an explicit epistemological problem, the interplay of loss and memory has to be understood as pertaining to experience. Experience, rather than the hollow tone of knowledge, will have become central. Its centrality works to define the contours of modernity. (This will also be the case even with those conceptions of the present that do not envisage a founding link between modernity and the Shoah.) The trap of defining loss in terms of either melancholia or mourning is that what is projected is an object over which control and thus mastery can come to be exercised. As the object is recovered – and in being recovered is known – it comes to be absorbed. Against absorption there needs to be set a conception of monumentality. However, the monumental cannot refer to scale. It must refer to that which maintains a spacing, a relation of distance and thus a locus of tension. The monument will need to be linked to experience. In order that experience not be generalised to the point of becoming banal, it will always have to demand specificity. Indeed, not only will it be the term proper to any understanding of the work of tension, distancing and spacing, it will also be in terms of specific expectations and determinations – sites of repetition – that the locus of transformative experiences can be located. Transformation involves an interrelated twofold possibility. In the first place, it relates to repetition understood as transformative and therefore transformation as a form of reworking. In the second place, dislocations revealing the founding dislocations marking modernity's inception become other ways of describing this transformative experience.

There is an initial problem attached to this second form of transformation since linking the Shoah to such a conception of experience may appear to aestheticise it, turning it into an occurrence whose register has marked similarities to the avant-garde art object or even the experience of the sublime. What would give such a charge its force is that both resist incorporation and thus have a potentially transformative effect. (Equally, of course, both are subject to an enforcing incorporation presented in terms of differing temporalities of continuity.) Two arguments need to be adduced here. The first, which will be taken up at a later stage, involves showing how concepts of sublimity are necessarily linked to the problematic of representation and thus do no more than indicate its limit. The second, which will be pursued here, involves discriminating with regard to the site of transformation. In relation to the second of these arguments, it is the site of transformation that establishes how the difference – thus the quality of that difference – is to be thought while the centrality of experience is still maintained. Establishing this difference means restating and developing some of the points already noted.

The distinct nature of the Shoah is the emergent discontinuity of the world with itself. It is not, therefore, a question of whether to go on, but of how going on has to incorporate that discontinuity. As has already been indicated, one way to assimilate the Shoah would be to identify it as a particular instance of racism or oppression. Once this were done then the singularity of its occurrence could no longer be maintained. The problem of its possible, albeit impossible, incorporation defines both the site of complacency as well as the site of vigilance. (Mastery of this site will never have been possible. It is thus that it locates the inevitability of decision and thus the potential necessity for judgement. Acts within this site are already decisions. Explicit acts are necessarily judgements.) In the case of the avant-garde art object, the experience of dislocation – of the object's having a dislocating effect – will always be generic. The site of dislocation and thus of a subsequent relocation will be the genre. Genre provides the site of repetition. Continuing with the genre will always be a question of the nature of the repetition. The point of connection but equally of disassociation with the Shoah is that all domains of experience are subject to the anaesthetising effect introduced by the thinking, the architecture or the artistic forms of historicism and therefore of enforcing continuities. From within a certain conception of the interrelationship between modernity and the present, the disruption of those continuities may be taken to be the task at the present.

What follows, therefore, are different attempts to investigate both the complex ways in which the interrelationship between time and task comes to be formulated, and, with it, the development of a particular formulation of the present which locates that structure within it as an integral part of its make up. As has already been made clear, central to this project will be the necessity of responding to the presence of the Shoah. This should not be interpreted as applying philosophy to this 'topic'. Rather, it needs to be understood as a consequence of having already taken the Shoah as that occurrence which brings modernity and the present into a determining relationship. Thus it is their conjunction – the productive interconnection of modernity and the present – that works to define not just the contemporary, but the locus of present hope.

2

TIME AND TASK
Benjamin and Heidegger showing the present

OPENING THE PRESENT

Writing takes place in time. There is, in addition, the time of writing. This twofold positioning of time – an ineliminable doubling of time, the recognition of which becomes the affirmation of anoriginal difference, the truth of ontology – is, from the start, in this particular presentation, mediated by another presence. In this instance the mediation is given by the effective presence of an announced task. The task's enactment, an enactment which must maintain a link to its founding articulation within intentionality – e.g. its being the result of a decision – reiterates the twofold temporality already located in the connection between writing and time. What emerges from this given relation is the interplay of writing, time and task. What is involved in this relation is the possibility of thinking the relation between politics and time. This possibility arises because such a thinking must occur in a 'now' that, in eschewing its reduction to the *nunc stans* while nonetheless maintaining a relation to it, a relation that marks a presence that takes place at the same time, demands to be thought at the present as the present. In opening this 'now', what is opened up is the ontology of the present. What is proposed therefore, with Benjamin, is furthering the possibility for a philosophical thinking of the present.

In broad terms what is involved here is a specific opening of the present. This is a task made all the more difficult by the demand that it also involve an already existent consideration, at the present, as the present, of the possibility of thinking philosophically about philosophy's history. (The problem of the relationship between history and philosophy's history is raised by having to pursue this particular path.) As the present is itself already thought within the work of Benjamin and Heidegger, to engage with their thinking is itself to take up the present and therefore to move towards a consideration of the ontology of the present by maintaining it as the site in which such movements are sustained. The identification of the present determines the nature of the philosophical task. Reciprocally, of course, the nature of the philosophical task will

26

have a determining effect on the construal on the present. One cannot be thought without the other.

As yet, however, the need for taking up this particular emergent connection between time, task and writing is yet to be announced. It is not as though need is yet to be given a specific determination within philosophy. Amongst other possibilities, need can be taken as opening both the Cartesian and the Hegelian philosophical projects. (Its presence in Heidegger and Benjamin will be just as insistent.) In both instances, need is present as what advances a necessity that orients the project and which in its projections continually comes to be addressed by them. As such, it is maintained within, while maintaining, an ineliminable reciprocity. In both instances, need is a demand given by the present – the present being the construal of the contemporary at (and as) the time of writing, again need's time. As such, the response to need is itself contemporary.[1] With need, with its instantiation, its having a time at a given instant, a relation to the given is established. In other words, if need is a response to what is given – the gift of tradition creating the specificity of the moment – then the response occurs at a particular instant. While bearing a date, the instant is not the present as such. The reason for this being the case is that thinking the present will necessitate taking up the construal of the given and its (the given as construed) enjoined response. Articulated as need, the response can be formulated as a specific stand in relation to a particular repetition. Repetition here is the reiteration of the already given. Need exists in relation to the gift and yet the gift, that which is taken to have been given, is itself determined by need: again, the presence of a founding and original reciprocity. Accepting the generality of this description cannot obviate the necessity of giving it specificity and thereby opening up the multiplicity inherent in the stance. Indeed what must be maintained is the suggestion that it is only in terms of its actual specificity – the effective interplay of dating, present and need – that any philosophical thinking of the political will come to be acted out, since it is the differences given at the level of this interplay that mark the primordiality of conflict. (It is this possibility that will be addressed in detail in the final chapter.) Regarding their actual projects, the point of connection and divide between Benjamin and Heidegger can be located at this point. Multiplicity therefore becomes the site of conflict. Once given a precise designation, it becomes a site that resists the possibility of any automatic synthesis.

In sum, and if only to provide a name with which to work, the present as giving rise to a specific task – where that specificity is itself moulded and determined by the construal of the present – will be termed, as has already been suggested, the epochal present. Such a present gives itself. It is given within its own self-conception. It is *not* the giving of that which is distanced because of its being either originating or primordial, and whose presence and hence its being present (were it ever to be present) would then become the epochality of its founding and maintaining origin. In working with the abeyance of such a conception of epochality, and, moreover, in allowing for the determining interplay of the epochal present and the *nunc stans* (the latter being the time of dating, the temporality of the instant), this will serve to maintain the ineliminable presence of a different politics insofar as this other possibility (a politics thought within a different philosophical frame) can be reworked as the primordial conflict over the nature of the present. Such a reworking sustains the present as that site, while at the same time providing a different instantiation of the primordial. What is proposed is a conflict that cannot be resolved by a simple deferral to the instant. The conflict staged between Benjamin and Heidegger is political for precisely this reason. The inability of the instant to resolve conflict opens up the necessity not just to rethink its presence, but to take its presence as determining and thus as real. However, the reality in question is not coextensive with the instant (which marks both the ontological as well as the temporal location proper to the time and the place of dating). As a name, the epochal present names another, yet related, reality.

The ineliminable reciprocity between action and the ontology of the present, where the former is a constitutive part of an inherent actative dimension forming an integral part of the present, is of an order such that it will sanction the possibility that this engendered construal may become the present within philosophy's history. The actative is simply the constitutive part of the present that will demand action and thus be what gives rise to a task while at the same time sanctioning its reality. As a consequence, the epochal present will always attempt to legitimatise actions done in its own name. An additional point must be made, namely that it will always be possible for the epochal present to be declared to be, in all senses, commensurate with the time marked by 'calendars' and 'historical occurrences'. However, such a conception becomes no more than the intended, unmediated positing of objectivity which, in the attempt to rid the present of its construction and thus of its proper reality, in the end only maintains that relation and with it the distance between the present and the instant by representing it in the guise of objectivity (reality here marking out the space of conflict). The doubling of objectivity resists exclusion. Thus, the positing of objectivity will always occupy the space of construction. Objectivity, in other words, becomes a part of an interpretative structure given by construction.

What is central within this opening, in its having opened an approach to the present as it figures in Benjamin and Heidegger, is that it entails working through the site of the task's founding formulation; in other words, the task and its interpretation demand working through the foreword.[2] Even in allowing for a certain plurality, namely an oscillation between the formal (an actual foreword) and projection (an intended project), the foreword always has an attendant risk. This risk lies in that the foreword may always be viewed as being either provisional or redundant and hence as no more than an addition that can be either subtracted or added; it could even become a gratuitous afterword. Nonetheless, it is by beginning with a foreword that Benjamin will set the scene for his writings on *Trauerspiel*, Baudelaire, Paris and the nineteenth century. As he indicates in a letter to Scholem which links the foreword to the *Passagen-Werk* to the much earlier foreword to *The Origin of German Tragic Drama*, writing these forewords was a necessary undertaking.[3] Both works brought with them their own 'theories of knowledge' as an integral part of their work.

In Benjamin's case what would seem to jeopardize the – real or envisaged – works that take place after these forewords is that the form which these works will have to take is marked by the difficulty of enacting, if not the potential impossibility of realising, then the project set out in and thus demanded by the foreword. (A similar problem will also be present in Heidegger in the case of 'Time and Being'.) Within Benjamin's work, the complex relationship between allegory and symbol, the use of the monad as a mode of presentation checking the power of representation, the privileging of showing and image over expression, narrative and stories have at least one straightforward consequence: the question of whether the text could ever contain, in the way envisaged, that which the foreword sets up as the project. As has already been indicated, the problem is reducible neither to style nor to genre but pertains to the construal of a task and thus of its present and then to how that task comes to be enacted.

It should not be thought that the question of presentation has to be added to the work of either Heidegger or Benjamin. Benjamin's study of the German *Trauerspiel*, for example, begins by locating the necessity for philosophy of 'representation' (*Darstellung*).

> It is characteristic of philosophical writing that it must continually confront the question of representation [*die Frage der Darstellung*].[4]

In writing to Scholem, Benjamin expresses a doubt that can be seen as touching on precisely this point – the task's possibility, its own effective realisation – in relation to what is there identified as the 'Arcades' project. Of this *Passagen-Werk*, he states:

> I can foresee neither whether it will find a form of representation of its own [*eine selbständige Darstellung*], nor to what extent I may succeed in such a representation.[5]

While this letter was written in 1935, four years before the final drafting of the *Passagen-Werk*, it remains the case that the question of success, let alone the criteria for that success, remains as open after the drafting as it did before.

The foreword's own reiteration of a projected impossibility of completion – of a textual enactment in narrative – will demand a response, a response to the text, a response, perhaps, to the text's own interpretations, that has the intention of distancing both the interpretative and the hermeneutical and their subsequent replacement by experience. It is the presentation of the problematic status of interpretation and the centrality of experience that brings Heidegger and Benjamin into a specific philosophical relation. Despite the problems that will emerge in pursuing it, it is this relation – the relation given within experience – that will be of central importance.

In Benjamin's 'A Berlin Chronicle', the limits of narrative and a certain construal of the politics of memory are advanced. The analogy of archaeological investigation is central to the text's effect since such investigations will demand that the politics of display – incorporating display's time – be taken up.

> Fruitless searching is as much part of [excavating] as succeeding, and consequently remembrance [*die Erinnerung*] must not proceed in the manner of a narrative [*erzählend*] or still less that of a report, but must, in the strictest epic and rhapsodic manner, assay its spade in ever new places, and in the old ones delve to ever-deeper layers.[6]

There are two difficulties with this passage. The first is understanding the claims being made. The second is tracing their consequences. The presentation of Benjamin and the related consideration of the present – the interrelationship between politics and time as constitutive in any attempt to take up the ontology of the present – will continually have to return to these difficulties, returning, perhaps, by readdressing them.

Returning to the present means working with the recognition that the presentation of a task, and, consequently, its writing, take place in time, a time that is complex from the start. Complexity arises because this is a time which, whilst it may occasion a date, at times even enjoin one, is nonetheless to be distinguished from that which is dated. Within the passage of time, the self-conception of the task to be enacted is instantiated. It is this self-conception that will be of concern here, for with it what arises is the time of the task; in other words, the conception of the present in which the task is to be enacted at the present, and with it, therefore, of the present as that which sustains and maintains the task and its self-enactment. The reciprocity here is essential. Presenting these interdependent elements in this way will allow for the possibility of thinking through the nature of the relation between the present and 'now-time' (*Jetztzeit*). Whilst cited in a number of entries, within the framework of 'Konvolut N' 'the present' (*die Gegenwart*) is, for the most part, a term that is still to be clarified. Of course, this lack of clarity should not obviate the necessity of recognising the weight that it has to carry, a weight indicated in the following examples:[7] 'the present' (*die Gegenwart*) is included within the historical task. 'The present' is that which is placed in a 'critical condition' by 'the materialist presentation of history' (N 7a, 5). Moreover it is 'the present' that 'polarises the event into fore and after history' (N 7a, 8). The question that endures concerns what it is that this 'present' is taken to be. In addition, it will have to include a consideration of the link between 'the present' as a temporal moment, the moment within the temporality of the instant and thus a moment which also brings its own ontological considerations with it, and that which is presented, where the latter involves a presentation of and thus also within the present: present instantiation.

The 'present' – in part, Benjamin's construal of what has been designated the epochal present – and presencing are inevitably linked in his work to the presence of critique. Part of the critique of Jung that takes place in 'Konvolut N' and elsewhere concerns how presencing occurs, and with its occurrence what is thought to have been carried over into the present: 'translated into the language of the present' is Jung's own expression, a line quoted by Benjamin (N 8, 2) in order to establish a critical distance from Jung. For Benjamin, Jung's error lies not in the preoccupation with incursions into the present but in the way both the process and the content of presencing are thought. An intrinsic part of the critique of Jung is the effective presence of a construal of the present in which, perhaps for which, Jung's project is not simply vulnerable philosophically but reiterates a politics – the politics of a particular expressionism – that is once again the subject of critique. It is a stance that forms a part of Benjamin's general critique of expressionism. And yet with Jung – with a more generalised preoccupation with Jung in the *Passagen-Werk* – what is involved is more complex. A way of formulating this problem would be to suggest that Jung allows for a present in which what is received from outside of it – the outside as an archaic past, presencing in Jung's words as 'an unconscious animation of the archetype' (N 8, 2) – becomes, despite the appearance of difference, a repetition of the Same.

In less specific terms, it will emerge that in taking up repetition, the present, and hence the differing conceptions of the epochal present, works within the complex of repetition. In other words, repetition will contain the very differences that serve to work the present as a site of conflict. With repetition, even in its complexity, experience is introduced, since experience delimits the stance in relation to repetition and this despite the stance's textual and thus written formulation. Furthermore, forming a fundamental part of what is involved in any consideration of the present is the reciprocal conception of experience that such a present demands. A way into this present will stem from the recognition that, with Benjamin and Heidegger, it is the place and thus the time of 'showing'. With this showing, what remains open is how the experience of showing is to be understood. What is it, therefore, to experience the shown as such?[8]

HEIDEGGER'S PRESENT

While they may lack any predetermined and therefore pre-given presentation, aspects of this initial taking up of Benjamin's work are, in the first place, intended to connect, reconnect, albeit on a general level, the projects of Heidegger and Benjamin. Connecting and reconnecting occur insofar as a constitutive part of each project is the relationship between showing and experience. Nonetheless, it perhaps goes without saying that the specific formulations of that relationship serve to open up an important difference between their projects, thus forcing a consideration of how that difference is itself to be thought. As difference eschews simple positing, its location is paramount. Here it turns on the present. More concretely, this particular point of departure is also intended, in the second place, to take up, again as an example, Heidegger's *Nietzsche*, in particular the final part of the section entitled 'European Nihilism', a text in which 'metaphysics', the history of metaphysics, bears on by bearing the present.[9]

Before pursuing Heidegger's own formulation it should be noted that this presentation is itself intended to take up significant aspects within Benjamin's own philosophical forewords – though, more emphatically, the relationship between the forewords and that which the forewords intend to have follow them. Since it can be taken to harbour the project itself, the foreword inevitably becomes more than a given site – even a preliminary site – within a textual topology. It is the latter component, the inherent complexity of the foreword, which, as has already been indicated, must form a fundamental part of any real philosophical engagement with it. Here the work of Benjamin and Heidegger is such that one tracks and tacks on the other. Neither their opposition nor their similarity can be taken as given. Sails will always have to be trimmed. The problem will always pertain to the nature of the calculation.

Heidegger's final considerations of Nietzsche's metaphysics could be said to incorporate 'today''s location.

'Today' [*Heute*], reckoned neither by the calendar, nor in terms of world-historical occurrences, is determined by the period in the history of metaphysics that is most our own: it is the metaphysical determination of historical mankind in the age of Nietzsche's metaphysics.

(254, 195)

The actual quality of this 'today', its uniqueness, is clarified in the lines that follow.

Our epoch reveals a particularly casual matter-of-factness with respect to the truth of being as a whole.

(*ibid.*)

And yet within the frame of the same formulation, this casual attitude is mediated by the presence of another and greater 'passion'. Again it attests to the age by giving it a specific particularity.

Such an indifference [*Gleichgültigkeit*] to being in the midst of the greatest passion for beings testifies to the thoroughly metaphysical character of the age.

(*ibid.*)

The particular force of this description, one to which it will be necessary to return, is that for Heidegger it is a characterisation that comes from being, one that is sent by it. For Heidegger, the present is, therefore, always already given by the history of being. As such it is, in part, constitutive of that history. It is the precise nature of the given coupled to the mode of access to it that is presented at the end of the text.

The age of the fulfilment of metaphysics – which we descry when we think the basic features of Nietzsche's metaphysics – prompts us to consider to what extent we find ourselves in the history of being. It also prompts us to consider – prior to finding ourselves – the extent to which we must experience [*erfahren müssen*] history as the release of being into machination, a release that being itself sends, so as to allow its truth to become essential for man out of man's belonging to it.

(256, 196)

For Heidegger, the quality of the present resides in what could be described as a giveness that is always more than the simple instantiation of the given. Again, its quality discloses itself in its forming the present, yet forming it in such a way that its 'originality' can always be shown as present. The predicament

33

of human being – a predicament that can be described as the being of human being (identified earlier by Heidegger, in *Being and Time* for example, with the term Dasein) – is given by being; it is part of being's destiny, in that human being belongs to being. In Heidegger's terms, grasping that this is the case will necessitate that 'experience' in which what is proper and original to human being is taken over in its propriety as establishing, though in a sense also re-establishing, the 'original' belonging together of being and human being. The reluctance to separate establishing and re-establishing in any systematic way indicates the extent to which propriety is in some sense already there. The belonging together of being and human being – the latter as the being of being human – has already been worked through in *Being and Time* in terms of questioning. There, Heidegger presents Dasein as that being for which the question of being, and with it its own being, is always, that is, originally, a question. Ontology takes the place of any simple humanism.

The expressions 'indifference', 'casual matter-of-factness' and 'passion for beings' as employed by Heidegger attest to the present epochality of being. Yet they can also be taken as descriptive of the present, the time of writing. Remembering the functional reciprocity between description and task, it becomes a description that demands a particular task. The demand is located in expressions of the form 'we must experience'. In marking the intended elimination of 'indifference', the 'must' brings the inherently actative dimension within the present to the fore. It is this dimension that gives rise to a specific task, a task formulated by the present and thus forming a fundamental part of its constitution. As such, this reciprocity takes the present beyond Heidegger's own description. Heidegger's present is no longer either the 'today', or the 'age', or the current epochality of being. Rather, they are all interrelated with the task they demand (to give one side of the reciprocity) and thus, for Heidegger, form the epochal present. The constitutive elements must be retained and examined within their given reciprocity.

The 'passion' Heidegger identifies is for the other side of the divide within ontological difference. Consequently, while this 'passion' may define the age, it is because of its place within that divide that, at the same time, it gives rise to a task. Present and task are interarticulated. One works within the other. What this entails is, first of all, an overcoming of the given 'indifference' and stemming contemporary 'passion', and, second, thinking being in its differentiation from beings and thus as differentiated from them. The force of the description that presents 'today' as the 'release of being' allows for the recognition of the current epochality of being, that which being 'today' forms and informs, while indicating that it is within the very structure of this presencing, because of what it is, that it becomes possible to consider the conditions of possibility for the thinking of being itself. (The epochal present will always have recourse to a form of the transcendental, since what such a conception of the present will give are conditions of possibility – conditions in which the present is also given.) The latter possibility arises out of 'today''s situation, the present, and is, moreover, predicated upon experience: more significantly, upon an experience that 'we' must have. (Again, a separate though important line of inquiry would concern the identity and thus the ontology of this 'we'; not the question of who we are, but of who is the intended subject of this experience.[10]) The difficulty that resides in experience, in what the term stakes out, pertains to how it is to be understood. It goes without saying that this is a difficulty that arises with the acceptance, as a point of departure, that experience cannot be posited. Perhaps more significantly, however, there is the related problem of how it is that experience's intended effect is to be realised. What is the registration and thus what is it that is registered in the experience that 'must' be had? The recognition of the actuality of such experience, leaving the question of its specificity to one side, is what locates the present as the present. Recognition works to intensify it. And yet the temporality of this intensity is far from straightforward. As will be indicated, it is an intensity that, for Heidegger, is released within an openness and thus within the calm of having experienced. In their link to the future, calmness and the open are given as originally determined by propriety. Present intensity for Benjamin will be significantly different.

Allowing for the present as given by the 'release of being' locates the present as historical. The quality of the present – and thus of Heidegger's formulation of what has already been described as the epochal present – is determined in advance. However, what it is that is determined must be experienced as such, as that determination. It follows that once that experience has taken place and only within the actual terms given by what it is that will have been experienced, it then becomes possible to think, for Heidegger, the condition of the present itself. More accurately perhaps, it is then possible to think at the present that which gives to it – the present – its present determination. Such a thinking is essentially futural in the precise sense that it breaks up the present by taking the present's propriety – that which is proper to the present, namely being – as its own exclusive object of thought. It will be a thinking of the present that takes place at a particular point in time, a date, which will serve to differentiate the present from itself. In the thinking of being the future is possible. While this is to employ terms such as 'present' and 'future' beyond the purview of Heidegger's own specific use, it nonetheless accords with the implicit construal of the future – future possibility – that is at work, for example, in a text such as 'Time and Being', a

text which is of fundamental significance for any serious attempt to understand what it is that a foreword may be and thus to plot the relationship
between time and task. It can be added that the project and thus the strategy
of 'Time and Being', along with, for example, the programmatic claim in the
opening section of 'On the Way to Language' in which the project is advanced
as an 'experience' with language and thus within the distancing of the said
remaining open to the saying, work to reorient the task away from interpretation and the textual and towards experience and action. With any encounter
with Heidegger's text, the precise nature of this experience endures as the
dominant interpretative problem.[11] With it, the question of the status of the
hermeneutic is reopened.

The importance of 'Time and Being' lies in the fact that it is a foreword to a
text that in some sense has yet to be written – there is even the very real
possibility that it cannot be written – and, to that extent, the possibilities that
it holds open themselves open the future, whilst at the same time indicating
the nature of the task that is given. What is meant by doubting the possibility
of its being written pertains to Heidegger's understanding of the 'proposi-
tional statements' (Aussagesätze) that characterise philosophical writing. The
text reiterates the impossibility of such 'statements' doing justice to the task at
hand. The difficulty is stated in the text's opening and is announced again at its
end. In Heidegger's terms, 'statements' is one of a number of 'hindrances' to
the task that is given. The task is thinking being 'without relation to metaphysics' (ohne Rücksicht auf die Metaphysik) (25, 24). It is the 'without' –
thinking 'without' – that is of singular importance here.[12] Before taking it up,
it is essential to examine what the distancing – establishing the limits – of
philosophical writing is going to entail. These entailments work to construct
an important link to Benjamin's foreword. Moreover, they seem to forge a
bridge in regard to presentational method. In both instances they will be
connections which distance.

'Time and Being' was initially a lecture. Responding to it was therefore
intended to be a different exercise than the one demanded by reading. Indeed,
because the very practice of reading means that, within it, there is the necessity of being forced to respond to the movement of statements and
propositions, it is, as a consequence, inherently problematic (again the difficulty of any immediate reconciliation of interpretation and experience).
Heidegger takes up the difficulty of what he is about to present, to say, in the
following way:

Let me give a little hint on how to listen. The point is not to listen to a series of propositions, but rather to follow the movement of showing [*dem Gang des Zeigens*].

(2, 2)

This formulation of Heidegger's recalls the frequently cited though nonetheless still difficult passage from 'Konvolut N' in which Benjamin describes the method of his own work. The possible paradox inevitably generated by Benjamin's juxtaposition of method and montage needs to be remarked upon from the start. What is noted, therefore, is the possibility of holding method and montage together. Were they to fall apart then the way demanded by the foreword would be a way which would always prove to be impossible to follow.

Method of the project: literary montage. I need say nothing only showing [*nur zeigen*].

(N 1a, 81)

Benjamin's showing is, of course, significantly different. What then of Heidegger's showing? What does the showing itself display? Asking what is shown is to recognise – though here this recognition is neither Benjamin's nor Heidegger's – the presence of an ineliminable doubling within showing itself. It should be remembered that the central issue here is the present, the task's time and thus the epochal present (in Heidegger's own formulation). The doubling is the complexity engendered by what the showing shows. It is thus equally, at the same time, generated by it, a reciprocity demanding another take on complexity.

HEIDEGGER'S 'AGE'

Heidegger's concerns at the end of 'European Nihilism' can be read as yielding a construal of the present in which the present has the quality of having been given by being even though the 'age' remains 'indifferent' to the question of being. The nature of the present as that which is constituted by being forces through the present the task of thinking being, thus causing the present to become reconciled with itself (where this becoming brings with it a complex future). The reconciliation is, of course, premised upon the forced actualisation of what was described above as thinking 'without'. The task as formulated in 'Time and Being' turns around the 'without'. Heidegger formulates it thus:

To think being without [*ohne*] beings means to think being without regard to metaphysics.

(25, 24)

The 'without' can be taken, at least provisionally, as the overcoming of 'indifference', the stemming of 'passion', etc. In the end it will involve a similar movement to the one occurring (perhaps envisaged) in what, in the same text, Heidegger describes as 'leaving metaphysics to itself'. And yet, this 'metaphysics' is not just an option for thinking, a way of doing philosophy, though clearly it is that as well. Here, 'metaphysics' is a description of the 'age' and consequently it involves the present. It circumscribes the epochal present. 'Leaving metaphysics to itself' or doing 'without' it is an act in the present which opens the future, but opens it towards a possibility that is there in the present even though by definition it could not occur either 'in' the present or 'as' it. The future becomes the space for the realised possibility of a reconciliation between that which gives the present – the epochal present – its present determination and to which the present is 'indifferent'. In the end, what must occur is a reconciliation with that which is proper to human being; that is, the taking over of the question of being itself. Being reconciled with what had already been there. Nothing will have been rescued, the work of return will have been precluded, the present will have been sacrificed, given away.[13]

The intensity of the present is generated by its being the site of misidentifications (being as 'idea', *energia*, 'will', etc.), and thus the perpetual repetition of irreconcilability; a state whose existence must be experienced, acknowledged and then perhaps even resolutely affirmed. In taking over the present, in taking a stand within it, the present projects a future. The present will never be worked back onto itself. In 'Time and Being', Heidegger is scrupulous in recognising the possible incursion of the retroactive – what will reappear beyond his immediate concerns as the movement of *Nachträglichkeit* (iterative reworking) – and then in attempting to rid those concerns of precisely that possibility. Hence the importance of 'originality', of the already there. The privileging of original propriety over the effective of iteration – iteration's work – is signalled by Heidegger in 'Time and Being' that what is proper to being and time in the sense of 'what determines time and being in their unique propriety' (*in ihrem Eignen*)' (20, 19) is not what he then describes as a 'relation retroactively [*nachträglich*] superimposed upon being and time' (*ibid.*).[14]

The present must – and the 'must' here is the sign of the task as well as the necessity for resoluteness – abandon itself, leave itself behind, do without itself for the future. In so doing, it emerges as the future. 'Time and Being' precedes that which it cannot state and, moreover, that which cannot be stated. It follows, therefore, that the text is almost, in a literal sense, a foreword indicating what is to be done while at the same time not doing it. As a text it identifies what will hinder the effectuation of the task, and in the act of identifying it indicates what might be involved in order that its restrictive and blocking powers be diminished. The present must be differentiated from itself. The problem lies with what sustains the differentiation. In order to be maintained, the 'without' enjoins either forgetting – a forgetting of that which will have been done 'without' – or sacrifice, a task involving metaphysics having been given away: from *Aufgabe* to *aufgibt*, then. Tracing the necessity of either sacrifice or forgetting enables the development of a critical stance in relation to Heidegger's construal of the epochal present. Their necessity becomes an important limit.

Sacrifice and the doing 'without' are necessarily connected. They are tasks demanded by the specific construal of the epochal present. For Heidegger, they enjoin the future. It is this link to the future, a future opened up by the necessity of what is presented, that must be seen as arising out of the project engendered by the text's foreword. The projected impossibility lies in the relation to what it is that must be experienced and the impossible eventuality of its being given within the language of philosophy and thus within metaphysics. It is only with Benjamin that the linkage between experience, future and reconciliation will be sundered. It will be broken up by the necessity of destruction and thus of the caesura. To deploy the phraseology of the final part of the 'On the Concept of History', the future is forbidden precisely because it cannot be thought outside of the twofold possibility of progress and ultimate reconciliation.[15] It is precisely this state of affairs that is captured in the presentation of 'dialectical experience':

> It is the unique property of dialectical experience to dissipate the appearance of things always being the same. Real political experience is absolutely free from this appearance.
>
> (N 9, 5)

BENJAMIN, MONAD, REPETITION

In order both to maintain the difference between Heidegger and Benjamin and so as to give it philosophical force, what must be taken up is the present within Benjamin's own presentation of the term. At the same time, any such move will open up the epochal present in Benjamin's writings (in this instance 'Konvolut N' of the *Passagen-Werk*, its 'foreword'). Here, the presentation of the term 'present' is announced as part of a particular task which is itself located in what amounts to a foreword. In other words, retaining the importance of the actative involves taking up the interplay of ontology and action announced within the recitation of 'the present'; that is to say, positioning another epochal present itself positioned as projecting a task to be completed in writing. At a later stage in the drafting of the notes that comprise 'Konvolut N' – the period 1937–40 – 'the present' is drawn into the consideration of history in ways that serve to highlight 'the present' as a site, while at the same time attempting to distance continuity construed as either sequence or repetition.

> For the materialist historian, every epoch with which he occupies himself is only a fore-history of the one that really concerns him. And that is precisely why the appearance of repetition [*Wiederholung*] doesn't exist for him in history, because given their index as 'fore-history' those moments in the course of history that matter most to him become moments of the present according to whether this present is defined as catastrophe or as triumph.
>
> (N 9a, 8)

A beginning can be made with this 'present'. Here, something becomes a moment of the present; it becomes it because of its introduction into 'the present'. The question that emerges is the extent to which this introduction is constitutive of the present and is thus to be taken, in this aspect of Benjamin's work, as forming an integral part of the construction of the epochal present. Any attempt to take this question up will necessitate considering the status of 'fore-history' in its differentiation from 'after-history' and, therefore, in its being formulated as that which in some sense precludes repetition. It is essential that 'repetition' (*Wiederholung*) be given the specificity that is demanded by the passage, rather than its being assumed to mark out repetition in general (as if there were repetition in general). It will be necessary, therefore, to return to this 'repetition', a return signalling the abeyance of essential thinking.

The distinction between 'fore-history' and 'after-history' figures in a number of places in 'Konvolut N'. Almost invariably it is linked to either 'the present' or the attempt to formulate historical time. For example:

> It is the present [*die Gegenwart*] which polarises the event into fore- and after-history.
>
> (N 7a, 8)

And again:

> The present [*die Gegenwart*] defines where the fore-history and the after-history of the object of the past diverge in order to circumscribe its nucleus.
>
> (N 11, 5)

At a slightly earlier stage, the 'foundation of history' is linked to what is called the 'afterlife' of the object of historical understanding.

> Historical understanding is to be viewed primarily as an afterlife [*Nachleben*] of that which has been understood; and so what came to be recognised about works through the analysis of their 'afterlife', their 'fame', should be considered the foundation of history itself.
>
> (N 2, 3)

The 'foundation of history' is then that which is to be located not beyond the original – as though there could ever have been an original founding moment to which a return could be made let alone a moment of original propriety – but in a present incursion. The continual repositioning, the privileging of the 'afterlife' in the place of 'life', is not intended to be taken as an anti-realist gesture that in some way denies reality by countering the material with the ideal. Rather, reality comes to be invested with a different power, one which will complicate the nature of that reality. The power is, of course, Messianic. As Benjamin states, the method proper to a 'commentary on reality' (*der Kommentar zu einer Wirklichkeit*) is theology. As opposed to philology, theology concentrates on the '*nach*'. With this concentration, however, there arises the inevitable question of limits. Does a *Nachleben* always survive? Is there a limit therefore to this '*nach*' and thus to any *nach*? Can the life of the 'afterlife' (*Nachleben*), the 'afterhistory' (*Nachgeschichte*), come to an end? These are questions for Benjamin's own formulation of time. The problem to which they allude concerns the twofold possibility of fulfilment and reconciliation.

In their varying forms these questions turn around the Messianic, turning in the end towards *the* Messianic question. And yet, what is at stake here is not theology as such – understood as either the language of/for God, or God reasoning – nor the Messiah as the redeemer of a fallen humanity. Here the intersection of time and politics is thought, provisionally, within the framework of the theological in which the Messiah may be present but only as a figure; figuring, perhaps, in the same way as the 'Flâneur' or 'Lumpensammler'. What is intended by this frame is that the Messianic is descriptive of the power that enables the 'event' to have an afterlife; its capacity to live on is explicable in terms of Messianic power. That power is not theological. It is not the consequence of God's word or deed. Indeed, it can be added that a limit to Benjamin's own adventure lay in his having to have recourse to the figure of theology in order to explain this occurrence rather than to the ontology of the 'event' – the limit which becomes, therefore, the limiting of the philosophical within his work.

A significant number of the theological motifs which Benjamin employs

41

turn on time. In a sense this is not surprising, given the contention that theology is the site in which the thinking of time is sustained in his writings. However, the presence of such motifs brings with them a number of attendant problems, not the least of which is the nature of the relationship between motif and motive. This emerges quite clearly with the term 'apocatastasis'. Despite its decontextualisation – perhaps a move evoking another afterlife? – it remains the case that the word is essentially Christian. One unproblematic occurrence of it in the Christian Bible is *Acts* III:21:

> until the time for restoring everything [ἄχρι χρόνων αποκαταστάεως πάντων]

What is evoked is both a fall and a restoration located within totality. (Here πάντων is the Absolute, its having become actual, the giving of the totality gathered in time, given as the place of complete reconciliation.) What is designated in this instance in the Christian biblical context is the restoration of a totality that had come apart. The intended reality of absolute reconciliation is projected. (In this regard, it will be vital to try to differentiate between the Christian concept of 'apocatastasis' and the Judaic or, more properly, Kabbalistic concept of 'tikkun'. While the distinction may not be immediately self-evident, maintaining the difference, it could be argued, is of considerable importance.) Within the Christian framework, the absolute nature of the term is essential, as indeed is the fall from completion. What is restored is that original completion and reconciliation of Man and God. What is restored is that which was originally always already there in Man though retained after the fall, in part in terms of the 'image of God' and, in part, in terms of that image involving a transcendence which in turn denied to the material present the possibility of its own redemptive and, therefore, Messianic possibility. Partiality is excluded as is a possible infinity. In the restoration of the 'all' the necessity for the continuity of any 'afterlife' would have ended. The transformative and continually destructive power of 'now-time' (*Jetztzeit*) – a destruction already indicative of a denial of any impartiality and therefore, in addition, also of a resisted universality – would have become otiose.

What then of Benjamin's use of the term? With this question the problem of the '*nach*' is compounded for the question of the nature – i.e. the ontology – of what it is that is unending. As it does not instantiate the theological, thought as the sacred – the sacred in its disassociation from the mundane – it must follow that in the end the enforced actuality of the Messianic will simply not do. Maintaining theology as the language and reasoning concerning God, were that to be a possible option, would involve thinking its relation to politics rather than taking it as that which provided politics with its temporality.

These considerations, ones which will take Benjamin's concern beyond the limits he has provided for them, come to the fore with the use of a term such as 'apocatastasis'.

In 'Konvolut N', the word 'apocatastasis' occurs as part of what is described there as a 'minor methodological recommendation', concerning the contrasting and then the recontrasting of the putative positive and negative parts of an epoch. The point of this movement was to indicate that one only has value against the backdrop of the other. Retaining the negative – the 'backward' and 'extinct' parts – will involve contrasting them with different 'positive' elements in order that they be positioned anew. Original oppositions are thereby broken up. This breaking is at the same time the critique of historicism – be it Ranke or Hegel – and indicative of the radical nature of Benjaminian destruction. Benjamin concludes this recommendation in the following way:

> And so on *ad infinitum* until all of the past has been brought into the present (*die Gegenwart*) in a historic apocatastasis.
>
> (N 1a, 3)

The value of this recommendation, which repeats the structuring force of the archaeological analogy from 'A Berlin Chronicle' by bringing the past to the present as though to the surface, is that it allows for the effective distancing of oppositions such as major/minor, good/bad, etc., when they are put forward as no more than the constitutive parts of an either/or, especially the either/or given by tradition.[16] Contrasts are to be dialectical and not straightforward oppositional juxtapositions (positing and counter-positing). These contrasts may, Benjamin suggests, be as elementary as 'nuances'. What these contrasts allow for, however, is a continual renewal. As he puts it, 'it is from them that life always springs anew' (*das Leben immer neu*) (N 1a, 41). It is precisely this type of formulation that raises difficulties, since what it demands is a confrontation with the question of how the finality and totality of 'apocatastasis' is to be squared with the continual renewal of life – the continuity of the '*nach*', the 'always new' (*immer neu*) – especially since it is buttressed by the effective presence of the '*ad infinitum*'. (The difficulty of answering this question in part indicates why residues of historicism are thought by some commentators to have been retained by the process marked out and thus enacted by the term 'apocatastasis'.[17])

What arises is in the first place the impossibility of 'all the past' ever being brought into the 'present'. It is not just that the reference to infinity renders it impossible; more exactly, it is that the methodological procedure being suggested is precluded first by this type of finality and second by the 'monadological structure' of the 'historical object' (*des historischen*

Gegenstandes) (N 10, 3). (It will be essential to return to the question of the monad, for with the monad the force of the disruptive nature of Benjamin's construal of time will emerge.) What is wanted by Benjamin is not a continual restoration that intends to restore the original paradisiac site or aims at completion – a completion invoked by the 'all' – but a continual restoration in which each restorative moment is new, in the precise sense of a renewal of life as the afterlife. This particular theological term, therefore, while gesturing toward a state of affairs that is demanded methodologically, nonetheless belies the force of what is wanted. Benjamin uses theology to think the relationship between politics and time. As a consequence, he presents the challenge of thinking time and action beyond the conceptual purview of theology, thereby freeing theology for God.

In the passage under consideration (N 9a, 8), the relationship between 'fore-history' and 'after-history' is given in terms of the present as either catastrophe or triumph. What is located outside of their possible interconnection is 'the appearance of repetition' (*den Schein der Wiederholung*). But what is repetition? It is that which is obviated in the first place by the existence of a dialectical image (the singular insistence and synonymy of Now and Then) and, in the second, by the possible continuity of the always the Same. The use of 'fore-history' intends to rid history of repetition. Yet, even with this twofold exclusion of repetition, the question that still endures is the following: How is the 'after-history' or 'after-life' to be thought? In terms of what concepts and categories is it to be thought?

The question strikes at the heart of this attempted extrusion of repetition since it would seem to be the case that the 'after', the whole strategy of the present constructed by another giving, is itself unthinkable except as a form of repetition. Given this possibility, what will then have to be argued is that what is involved in the distinction is a reworked concept of repetition. What this will entail is a repetition that has been subjected to the process marked out by the distinction between 'fore-history' and 'after-history'. It is only the inter-polation of such a construal of repetition that will allow further insight into Benjamin's response to Horkheimer's insistence of a dialectical formulation of incompleteness and completeness and why Benjamin's introduction of 'a form of memoration' (*eine Form des Eingedenkens*) checks the dialectical presentation of history via the introduction of memory, but in so doing maintains the dialectical image as the ground of the historical itself.

The problem of repetition can be taken a step further by taking up the reference to Benjamin's already cited insistence on the 'monadological struc-ture' of the 'historical object'. Leaving to one side Benjamin's examples, as well as the question of the continuity of references to monads throughout his work, the passage in question positions the object, 'the historical object', in relation to its 'fore-history' and 'after-history' in the following terms:

> If the historical object is blasted out of the historical process, it is because the monadological structure of the object demands it. This structure only becomes evident once the object has been blasted free. And it becomes evident precisely in the form of the historical argument which makes up the inside (and, as it were, the bowels) of the historical object, and into which all the forces and interests of history enter on a reduced scale. The historical object, by virtue of its monadological structure, discovers within itself [*findet es in seinem Innern*] its own fore-history and after-history.
>
> (N 10, 3)

Present here is an ontological formulation of the 'historical object'. The 'demand' that it makes is not a contingent possibility. On the contrary. It is a demand that stems directly from the mode of being proper to the 'historical object' in its being a historical object. What must be questioned, therefore, is the nature of this monad. What, in the above, is the monad in question? It is the enormity as well as the centrality of this question that suggests an approach which, while maintaining history and acknowledging the importance of memory, is concerned nonetheless with the nature of the 'object' and thus with ontology and time.

References to the monad inevitably raise the possibility of a relation to Leibniz's own formulation of the monad in the *Monadology*.[18] What must be sought here is that which in Leibniz's own philosophical writings offers a type of illumination. (The possibility of a historical continuity, or the attempt to establish the same, even the continuity of influence, must be recognised for what it is.) As what is involved is the internality of the 'historical object', the obvious point of entry is Leibniz's own construal of the internality of the monad. In section 11 of the *Monadology* Leibniz argues that:

> the natural changes of the monads come from an internal principle, since an external cause could not influence their inner being.

Slightly later, at *Monadology* 15, this 'internal principle' is described as 'appetition' and then further clarified as what 'causes the change or passage from one perception to another'. What is significant about these descriptions is that the monad's change or development comes from within the monad itself. Change – and change, if it is translated into a different idiom, is going to involve the monad's 'after-life' – will be an 'after-life' that is itself already part of its life in the strict sense that it is a possibility that is already within the monad.

Furthermore, when Leibniz argues that the monad reflects the totality and thus, in some sense, contains all of its possibilities within it, it looks as if Leibniz as well as Benjamin construe monads in a similar way. However, there is a fundamental difference. In this instance it is a difference involving time; not the temporality of the monad as such, but the temporality of that in which the monad plays a constitutive part. Constitution here means that time brings ontological considerations with it.

The time in question pertains to what Leibniz identifies within his writings as 'pre-established harmony'. In other words, time here pertains to the time of this harmony. It will be a time that precludes a straightforward singularity. In *Monadology* 59, the 'universal harmony' is presented as that according to which

> every substance exactly expresses all others through the relations it has with them.

For Leibniz, this mutuality of infinite relations expressed in the monad opens up the need to distinguish each monad from God since, if this infinite – the infinite of both 'division' and 'subdivision' (*Monadology* 65) – were clear to each monad and, in addition, the necessary presence of distance did not introduce a type of confusion, it would then follow, as Leibniz himself suggests at *Monadology* 60, that 'each monad would be a deity'. (This is an identity established and secured by Leibniz's own law of the identity of indiscernibles.) The relation of monads to the infinite is more complex and explicable in terms of 'appetition'; in terms, that is, of the monad's internality, and thus of the ontology of the monad. The interpretative difficulty within this explication stems from having to recognise the abeyance of stasis and with it the centrality of the ontology of becoming.

> In a confused way they all go after/towards (*vont à*) the infinite, the whole; but they are limited and differentiated through the degrees of their distinct perceptions.
>
> (*Monadology* 60)

The movement is harmonious. Moreover, it follows from Leibniz arguing in *Monadology* 7 that, because the source of all change is internal to the monad, all changes have to be reflected in the whole, such that the totality accords with itself. Again, this is possible only for ontological reasons. In sum, it is only because the monad, as Leibniz writes in the opening line of *Principles of Nature and of Grace*, is 'a being [*un être*] capable of action'.[19] Action is not a contingent predicate of substance. The actative is, in part, constitutive of the monad itself. The internal and complete accord – an accord *in toto* – is 'pre-

46

established harmony'. The difficulty here is God. It is, however, a very precise difficulty. If the totality is present in God then, in some sense, the infinite toward which all substance moves – a movement which, as the consequence of desire, is itself explicable in terms of the monad's inscribed desire for completion and thus, in a sense, to be God – is already present for God. In being present for God, and even if appetition provides the continuity of completion, it remains the case that for God the completing harmony is in some sense already complete. (While there may be an ambivalence in Benjamin's work with regard to how reconciliation is to be understood, Leibnizian teleology would, nonetheless, be an untenable proposition.)

While the ontologico-temporal considerations proper to God raise important problems for any sustained interpretation of Leibniz, it is nonetheless also directly relevant for understanding the time of 'pre-established harmony'. (It is the time proper to this harmony that will establish and maintain the significant divide between Benjamin and Leibniz's respective conceptions of the monad.) The harmony is continued and continuous self-completion – completion, as it were, to infinity – it is always already enacting the completing that is proper to it (thereby establishing a necessary link for Leibniz between ontology and the actative). While this does not preclude free will, what it does render impossible is the existence of that act in which the time of completion and thus with it both the ontology and the temporality of harmony – an always already pre-existent harmony – could be subverted, destroyed, let alone blasted apart. Of course, it is precisely this possibility that, Benjamin argues, can occur precisely because of the monadological structure of the 'historical object'.

It is possible to argue that for Leibniz, what could be described as the temporality proper to freedom – the time in which, for example, evil and good acts are committed – is historical or chronological time, while the temporality of 'pre-established harmony' is the time of the universe held in infinite time with God and as such is not a time in which actions with determining results can occur. The reason for this impossibility is almost definitional insofar as the implicit Leibnizian conception of the universe and the temporality proper to it are such that they incorporate the totality of substance and therefore the totality of actions. With Benjamin, however, the temporal structure is importantly different. If there is any connection to 'pre-established harmony' within a philosophy of history, then it would lie in the move that would turn the past into a given historical continuity that remains impervious to intervention or disruption. It would be as though the historical past created an accord that determined the historical task as the necessity to reproduce that founding and already existent accord, such that the reproduction itself accorded with the past. The historical object, the object of/in history, would therefore only reveal itself – reveal itself as it is, a revelation demanding the effective presence, *contra* Leibniz, of the ontology of stasis – in that founding accord.[20]

BENJAMIN'S REPETITION AGAIN

Even though there is an important difference between them that arises here, it is at this point that the complexity of Benjamin's debt to Leibniz emerges. It is precisely the status (the ontology) of what Benjamin calls the 'historical object' that, in allowing for that founding accord – the putative naturalising of historicism – at the same time occasions the object being 'blasted out' of that pre-given continuity in order then to reveal itself – and thus to reveal that which is reflected in it – in another setting. The revelation in another setting, a revelation constructed by that setting, is the explosive 'now-time', the instantiation of the present by montage; by the movement of montage (a montage effect whose determinations are yet to be fixed). It will be a montage that involves temporality as well as objects and images. Consequently, it is not just that this present remains complex; there is a more insistent problem, namely whether montage could ever be provided in a sustained and intentional way such that it avoided being simply arbitrary and, as such, no more than a weak imagistic flutter. In other words, could there be a 'method of montage' that worked to preclude any response other than 'dialectical experience'?[21]

It is with these questions that the problem of the foreword, as the site where the task is announced such that what proceeds from it is the task's enacting, returns. Again, this is not a state of affairs simply added on to Benjamin's concerns; indeed, the framework in which a return can be made is provided by Benjamin (N 1, 9) by bringing 'project' (*Arbeit*), 'theory' and 'montage' together in order to provide a formulation of the undertaking, as a foreword:

> This project must raise the art of quoting without quotation marks to the very highest level. Its theory is intimately linked to that of montage.

If the approach indicated in this passage is taken up, what remains problematic is the relationship between 'quotation' and the monad. A way of addressing this is provided by thinking through the difference between quotation and 'quoting without quotation marks'. While allowing for its being descriptive of images and pictures, montage is, in the end, not merely descriptive of images or pictures. In moving from images and pictures whilst at the same time incorporating them, it will have become a description of time. In other words, independently of actual montage, Benjamin's 'montage' will be a way of constituting the present (the epochal present rather than the instant, the dated present). It will awaken a possibility in which the present as temporal montage will reorient itself in relation to the given and thus to that which is given to it. It is this eventuality that can be identified as present at the beginning of 'Konvolut N'.

> Comparison of others' attempts to setting off on a sea voyage in which ships are drawn off course by the magnetic North Pole. Discover that North Pole. What for others are deviations, for me are data by which to set my course. I base my reckoning on *the differentia of time* [*den Differentialen der Zeit*] that disturb the 'main lines' of the investigation for others.
>
> (N 1, 2; my emphasis)

The possibility gestured at here is that the 'differentia of time' could be temporal montage, the copresence of different times. (If this state of affairs can be maintained then there will be no necessary link between temporal montage and the specific art form of imagistic montage.) The link between montage and time – temporal montage – will have to be taken up at the same time as returning to the foreword and attempting to plot the effect of the presence and absence of 'quotation marks'.

These three elements combine in an important way. The 'quotation marks' raise the problem of repetition. The 'differentia' gesture towards a complex time at/as the present. While the foreword instantiates the methodological and thus projective problems that are sustained by one take on 'quotation marks' and 'differentia', these problems are overcome by another take. With this other take, the problems will come to be distanced by the repetition of what is marked by 'quotation marks' and 'differentia'. As the term which is to be restricted if not dismissed as long as it remains in quotation marks, 'repetition' will turn out to play a redemptive role within the project, projected and projecting beyond its given confines, though only once the quotation marks are removed. Moving from 'repetition' (N 9a, 8) to repetition crystallises the general problem of understanding the loss of 'quotation marks'. To juxtapose images, it may be that the crystal works as a *mise-en-abîme*. The radical consequence of this opening up of repetition, presented within the play of quotation marks, the continuity of their own oscillation, is that, again, though now for slightly different reasons, merely rehearsing Benjamin's own undertakings should not be assumed, in any real sense at all, to be continuing the project of the *Passagen-Werk*. Moreover, if they are repeated then their viability will not be able to be assessed in straightforwardly Benjaminian terms. Once more, it is not that Benjaminian montage amounts to the sustained juxtaposition of chronologically separate images; rather, it is that montage is a term that pertains to time. The importance of montage lies not in the chronologically disparate nature of the images but in the presence of the chronologically disparate being present.

The possibility of 'quoting without quotation marks' is another formulation of Benjaminian destruction. A movement that as has already been noted involves blasting 'the historical object . . . out of the historical process' (N 10, 3). Here, in opposition to either Cartesian destruction, which is the attempt to differentiate the present from itself in an absolute and all-encompassing manner, or Heideggerian sacrifice, in which the present ('metaphysics') is given away for a specific end (the thinking of being), Benjamin's 'destruction' will necessitate the centrality of relation and with it of repetition. For Benjamin, destruction, it can be argued, is maintained by relation. Both the dialectical image and 'now-time' are relations. And yet they are more than mere simple relations. In part, the departure from simplicity pertains to time and, in part, to repetition. It goes without saying that these two parts are related. Opting for the distinction within quotation – the absence and presence of marks as always signifying more than that which is given by the either/or of absence/presence – will capture these two interrelated parts. What has to be taken up, therefore, is quotation, to be understood as a form of repetition.

In its most general sense, to quote means to restate what has already been stated. Any citation, therefore, must also re-site. And yet, with citation there is a convention; this is the presence of tradition. Apart from introducing the continuity of convention, the use of quotation marks works, conventionally, to mark the act of recitation and hence of what could be described as a re-situation. What the convention brings with it, in addition to itself, is a form of continuity. The quotation marks indicate that what is cited (and re-sited) is not new but is the reiteration of what has already been; an intended repetition of the Same in which the singularity of the past's content is itself maintained. (As will be indicated, it is Benjamin's description of the 'historical object' having a monadological structure that will render this singularity impossible. It should be added that this is an impossibility derived from ontological considerations.) The absence and presence of quotation marks within a given narrative indicates the presence of different moments of historical time – chronological time – which are made present as continuous and thus as part of a more general continuity within narrative. Benjamin can be taken as addressing precisely this possibility – the effective presence of enforced continuity – at N 19, 1:

It could be that the continuity of tradition is only an appearance. But if this is the case, then it is precisely the persistence of this appearance of permanence that establishes continuity.

The force of this description is that it gives to tradition the structure of narrative, namely a structure in which tradition is present as a continuous and therefore unfolding sequential temporality. It is in this sense that tradition incorporates progress, albeit its own progress. The intricacy of the link between tradition and progress is that their reciprocity provides further constitutive elements of Benjamin's construal of the epochal present. Here, both progress and tradition are themselves part of the necessary interarticulation of time and task.

The use of quotation marks sustains the continuity of tradition – its 'permanence' – while allowing, as has been indicated, the intrusion of the discontinuous. It is, however, a discontinuity that is absorbed and, as such, becomes part of the 'permanence'. Another type of discontinuity – itself discontinuous with the type cited above – is present in 'quoting without quotation marks'. In this instance, the discontinuity is intended to endure. (It is thus that narrative and monadological structure are in a fundamental and effective opposition. Each will demand a different time and, with this different time, a different ontology, such that their difference is really only explicable in ontologico-temporal terms.) The absence of quotation marks signals the disruption of context. And yet, on its own the interplay of absence and disruption is far from sufficient as a description. The absence of quotation marks is not the only determination. Despite this absence, there is still a quotation and thus a form of presence. All that is missing is that which maintains the quotation as a quotation, namely the quotation marks. In this context, absence and presence are not mutually exclusive. What this means is that the contrast – the absent and present quotation marks, coupled to the continuity of quotation – is between two fundamentally different forms of repetition. What is emerging, therefore, is that, far from providing either a false path or the simply peripheral, repetition, though more significantly the anoriginally present divisions within repetition, can be taken as central to any understanding of Benjamin's construal of the task at the present, a construal which demands the recognition of the ineliminable presence of reciprocity. The centrality of repetition plus repetition's constitutive divisions will allow the larger problems raised by Benjamin's use of such terms as 'apocatastasis' to be redressed with greater precision. The problems are inevitably linked to the unstated and therefore unacknowledged presence of repetition. What remains, however, is to set up the differing types of repetition and their enacted interrelation with time and the announced task (the site of the foreword). Enactment here is intended to mark out the ineliminable presence of the actative. Action will always be part of the present's weave.

Once thought beyond the purview of the Same, repetition opens up the possibility that what is given, repeated, is presented in such a way that its occurrence may be the result of a working through or a reworking that is itself no longer contained by the Same. What is given is given again. This re-giving is neither simple iteration nor a repetition of the Same. Work is the divide. The re-giving therefore needs to be thought as an iterative reworking. The process of reworking re-presents the given in such a way that other possibilities that are in some way already inscribed within and thus brought with it are, as a consequence of that work – and thus also as constitutive of the work – able to be revealed. It is this possibility that is based on the 'monadological structure' of the 'historical object'. The affinity here is, of course, with Freud's conception of 'working-through' (*Durcharbeiten*) and the way in which the temporal structure of *Nachträglichkeit* is incorporated as the temporality of 'working-through'. Perhaps the most important way of examining the prospects held open by iterative reworking (the other repetition) and the monad is by reintroducing the concept of the foreword and, with it, the relationship between foreword and repetition.

With Heidegger, the foreword presented that which could not be followed. This has to do with the language of metaphysics and the way in which experience in opposition, and thus in contradistinction to writing and language, functioned in his formulation and presentation of philosophical work. For Benjamin the problem of the foreword, while different, still raises problems touching on the possibility of the realisation of the task demanded by it. In Benjamin's case, this will be linked to the nature of montage and with it to the possibility of methodological montage. Again, experience will play a pivotal role in any understanding of this complex set up. In both Heidegger and Benjamin, the present is to be differentiated from itself. In Heidegger's case this differentiation will be necessary since the present is taken to be metaphysics – the 'age' – and therefore the task involves 'leaving metaphysics to itself' and thus thinking 'without' it. Here there is a differentiation that necessarily eschews relation. With Benjamin the differentiation occurs by an act of repetition, a repetition that can be thought and thus presented in a number of different ways: as 'memoration', as 'quotation', as 'awakening', for example. In each instance there is a juxtaposition or constellation that breaks the effect of continuity.

If what has been identified as temporal montage, taken in conjunction with 'quoting without quotation marks', and formulations of a similar nature are themselves all linked – a linkage that, in the end, will come undone for reasons both ontological and temporal – to the 'dialectical image', then that constellation can be pursued in order that constitutive elements be taken both together and in their sundering. Of central importance here are the methodo-logical components provided in the formulation of the image. The significance of this particular adventure is that it highlights the problem of the interplay of method and experience.

> The dialectical image is a lightning flash. The Then must be held fast as it flashes its lightning image in the Now of recognisability. The rescue [*Die Rettung*] that is thus – and only thus – effected, can only take place for that which in the next moment is irretrievably lost.
>
> (N 9, 7)

The epochal present for Benjamin comprises, therefore, the unfolding of a continuity that can be blown apart at any moment. Coupled to loss, the irretrievable loss, the flash of lightning harbours that residue of apocalyptic thinking that also inhabits the use of the term 'apocatastasis'. The question is whether Benjamin is only an apocalyptic thinker. Answering the question necessitates attending to a divide in the work. To the extent that this conception of the 'dialectical image' is retained, then there can be no text, no enacted writing, that follows from this 'image' presented and thus serving as a foreword and thus not presented as itself. The apocalypse is not method-ological. Not even the presentation of forced and enforced juxtapositions can rehearse the potential of 'lightning'. Irony is too strong to allow this rehearsal – the forced enforcement – to function unproblematically. On the other half of the divide, however – a divide in which the elements present in each half will always inhere in the other – there is the potential inherent in the 'historical object'. Potential pertains to the ontology of the object. It goes without saying that the 'historical object' and the 'dialectical image' are not the same. The latter pertains emphatically to experience, while the first brings different ontological and temporal considerations to bear. It is the 'monadological structure' that can be taken as allowing for the 'dialectical image' and yet – this will be the point of greatest significance – it does not have to have that result. The 'monadological structure' will allow, equally, for another repetition: repetition as iterative reworking. (Here repetition has come to be subjected to the process that it names.) This time it will be a repetition in which, to redeploy the same language, continuity has been 'blasted' apart because of the presence of a quotation which, while referring to its context and thus while bringing its context with it – a bringing to be thought as a reflection to be released – comes to be released at the present.

Its release is, therefore, at the same time, an integral part of the present. This other repetition arises because of the ontology of the monad, Benjamin's monad.

While there can be no foreword and thus no afterword to the apocalyptic, there can be nonetheless a foreword that incorporates and acts out the rescue and thus the redemption of repetition. With repetition, the present will always be characterised by the 'differentia of time'. It will be repetition that, whilst eschewing prediction, will give the present as the site that is given in being worked through. Benjamin's construal of the epochal present can, therefore, be taken as bearing on the present, bearing it.

In sum, therefore, and returning to Benjamin's initial formulations, it is the 'present' as that which 'polarises the event into fore- and after-history' that becomes a site sanctioning its own constitution, though always as a further and furthering reconstitution, taking place and thus having a place through repetition. It is thus that the future is forbidden. This constitution, the act of constitution, not only introduces the primordiality of conflict, the flight from the homogeneous into the present, it allows at the same time the present – the present's potential – to stand apart from the homogeneous passage of time. There are two levels of destruction. Both are necessary if conflict is to be maintained and simultaneity sundered. Both enact the departure from the pre-established. It is the twofold nature of destruction that is announced in N 9a, 6. It is a destruction that is the province of historical materialism, the other name, for Benjamin, for the copresence of politics and time.

> Historical materialism has to abandon the epic element in history. It blasts the epoch out of the reified 'continuity of history'. It also blasts open the homogeneity of the epoch. It saturates it with ecrasite, i.e. the present [Gegenwart].

Even recognising the intrinsic difficulties of its formulation the present – the epochal present – is the site of an action connected to experience.

What then of showing? Remembering, if only as a contrast, that Heidegger's showing pertained to the presence of that which had already happened; showing was linked to the already there. The refusal of the retroactive was intended to maintain that 'originality'. Its refusal can be understood, if only initially, as the attempt to rid the historical and experiential of that form of repetition identified by the term Nachträglichkeit. Having cited part of the section concerning showing (N 1a, 8), its complex mediation needs to be introduced. The extract is completed in the following way.

> Only the trivia, the trash – which I do not want to inventory, but simply allow to come into its own the only way possible; by putting it to use.

The reference to the marginal brings back not simply the allusion to archae-ology and the need to investigate the castings but the whole – if the use of such a term is not here oxymoronic – of allegory (the whole being both the ontology as well as the temporality of allegory). At this stage, this is not the central point. Rather, it is the contrast between something obeying its own law 'coming into its own' and being 'put to work to use'. The contrast here is stylistic. The opposition vanishes with the recognition that one is the other. The propriety of what is, is its being used. Showing is use. The doubling of showing, in showing, to which allusion was made above, is now affirmed. Showing cannot eliminate reworking and can never obviate the process of a retroactive and thus iterative reworking. The recognition of this ineliminable possibility will occasion another reworking of experience. The present is partial and intense because it is the site of repetition, the place continually structured by repetition as a working through, iterative reworking, and thus as the potential site of its disruptive continuity. In other words, the present maintains, by articulating, the structure of hope. This is Benjamin's potential. The 'without' – the philosophy working with without – founders, yielding its place to the inevitability and ineliminability of the other repetition, as that which works the present.

SHOAH, REMEMBRANCE AND THE ABEYANCE OF FATE

Walter Benjamin's 'Fate and Character'

OPENING

Any attempt to begin will always mark out an opening, giving rise, within it, to a site, a further opening that is still to be completed. It thus remains open. It will be here that the subject in question intrudes. In this instance, there are three beginnings. They are connected and thus admit a complexity of subject and a complex of sites. It is the character of this occurrence, namely the Shoah, that is of concern here. The problematic element lies in the extent to which it − the occurrence in question, its character − can be stated. As an approach, the enduring problem is one of thinking this occurrence, allowing it − and in using 'it', acknowledging, without hesitation, the poverty of any form of generality − to arise as a demand for philosophy. This demand will, in this instance, be taken up in relation to Walter Benjamin's 'Fate and Character'. The twofold nature of the demand will already work to situate the present. As beginnings, therefore, they will cross.

THE FIRST BEGINNING

Apart from factual detail and the detail, the plethora, of facts (with their absolutely necessary and thus obligatory accumulation), what can be known of that which occurred? Of the Shoah's occurrence, what can be known? What is being questioned here, as a beginning, is neither memory nor the project of remembrance, but knowledge, and with it the envisaged, given, relationship between epistemology and memory. What does memory know? The language of knowledge and thus the possibility of knowledge will always reach a limit. However, this limit is not located within the realm of the purely epistemological; in other words, it does not pertain exclusively to what can be known. Rather, it is the limit established and thus delimited by the work of representation, since any epistemic claim will always be enacted within the general problematic of representation. It does not just always have to appear as a representation. Rather, it is *constrained* to appear as one. (What is opened here is the complex and ultimately conflictual relationship between epistemology and judgement.) The question – the question of knowing what took place – therefore concerns the representation of what is known. Representation presents the known. (Fiction's parasitism, a self-given site, is included therein.) The situation is more complex since the connection of representation and knowledge has already been and will already have been reworked by memory. The tense interplay at work here has consequences. Indeed, the inability of classical epistemology to deal with memory because of the former's failure to take up and thus to re-present the inéliminable link between memory and repetition – a link opening the move from memory to remembrance – will need to be noted. Initially as memory, the work of remembrance operates as the already present mediator of the present. Even though it cannot be reduced to it, the mediation involves memory. Here, memory comprises that which, in part, gives the present itself. Furthermore, it will be the work of memory in the present, working to maintain the present, that will inscribe hope. However, rather than providing an opening to the future and thus only ever being of the future, hope will form an integral part of the present's constitution. In marking an inéliminable spacing within the present, a productive caesura, hope will as a consequence be of the present. Given the inherently limited power of dating, of temporal markers within chronology, the question that endures concerns the nature of this present.

THE SECOND BEGINNING

Benjamin's text, 'Fate and Character', was written in 1919 and first published in *Die Argonauten* in 1921. Both of these dates predate the Shoah; they predate its historical occurrence. They take place before it. This 'before', however, raises the problem of time and thus the situation of any occurrence, including its site, and of how it can come to be dated. But does not the presence of an immediate chronological difference, the before and after, entail that a different set of questions must be asked of this text and, thereby, of its representation? Different, that is, from those brought to bear on any thinking of the Shoah? Maintaining difference may involve both the sundering of continuity and the possibility of another thinking. (The centrality of thinking and that within which thinking is envisaged as taking place, as having to take place – itself a happening that marks out by having to enact the constraint of tradition – must endure.) If this were the case, it could only be so because of the restriction imposed by its date. An important element of the task at hand therefore involves trying to determine to what extent dates and the relationship between dates, knowledge and representation could delimit the activity of interpretation and thus of understanding. It may be the case that the time of memory, if not the temporality of the present, eschewed the temporality of dating while also maintaining the mark of chronology.

Might it not be the case, moreover, that despite the presence of different dates – a before and an after which in being identified and thus accepted then come to bear the mark and enact the necessity of chronology – such dates demand, nonetheless, a conception of time that would ultimately be as inappropriate to Benjamin's text as it would to any thinking of the Shoah? There is more at stake here than the ontology and temporality of occurrences. In addition to the problem of the relationship between any occurrence and the occurrence of the Shoah, there is also a more general problem of the relationship between time and memory. What is the time of memory? How is its location as a continual relocation in the present to be understood? Answering these questions will demand the repositioning of remembrance.

THE THIRD BEGINNING

In 1919 what could have been known? What, *then*, could have been predicted? Predictions always take place in the present. Moreover, the act of prediction works to define and thus to locate a specific present, a present whose specificity is identified here by the 'then': what, then, could have been known? Furthermore, a prediction opens up the future in which it will come to be realised. It should be added, of course, that this is not the future marked out within chronological time, even though it is situated within it, but the predicted future which is the future of the prediction. (This distinction between natural time and the time of redemption will figure in an important way in Benjamin's own text.) Equally, prediction constructs its proper past not just in terms of the time prior to prediction, but as the temporality both deployed and implicated within prediction and thus in some way furnishing it. (Prediction, therefore, is not without its correlates amongst possible philosophies of history.)

The temporality of prediction is assumed to be fundamental to any understanding of fate and character because it constructs a totality by unifying time, albeit chronology's time. The predicted has, in some sense, already happened; this is the happening of inevitability. Within it, the known has already been acknowledged as such and the future incorporated in terms of the prediction of what will be known. Understood in the precise sense of that which comes to be understood, the future will never work on the present. On the contrary, the future will only ever be the work of this present – prediction's present – on the basis of the continuity that it reinforces. It is this conception of the relationship between past, present and future that is the implicit critical point of departure for Benjamin. The assumption concerning the link between the time of prediction and fate and character provides Benjamin's text with its opening. What opens Benjamin's text is an opening concerned to break the link between, on the one hand, causality and, on the other, fate and character. In a direct sense, therefore, it is an opening that defies prediction. Within it, fate and character come to be re-presented in the abeyance of the hold of their traditional image. (Abeyance will mark its own inevitable demand.) The question that must be asked, therefore, is the following: To what extent does such a reformulation or presentation allow for an approach to the Shoah? What this question involves is the general problem of thinking it as an occurrence. Thinking its occurrence will always be a thinking in addition to that which is given by history. Furthermore, this thinking should not be identified with an elementary formulation of cognition and, by extension, psychology. What is at stake is far more significant, since it pertains to the use or deployment of the concepts and categories of thought itself. It is precisely this position that has been noted by George Steiner. While he is not alone in making such a point, the full import of his position warrants detailed attention, since it questions the possibility of retaining that which is given to determine thought.

> It may be that the Shoah has eradicated the saving grace, the life-giving mystery of meaningful metaphor in Western speech and, correlatively, in that highest organisation of speech which we call poetry and philosophical thought. There would be a just logic and a logic of justice in such an eradication.[1]

It may also be that Benjamin's work – itself the reworking of fate and character – can be read as that which provides the possibility of a response to Steiner's supposition, a response after its happening. There is a problem here posed by the sense of this 'after'. The problem is simply that, within one possible determination, nothing should have happened after it. However, by allowing 'after''s other determination, what occurs after 'it' will have to have been determined by it. (The question of thinking through this other determination endures.) Here, there will be a necessity that refuses the charge of dogma. Resisting this determination and, therefore, turning from a form of necessity, would consequently become a form of active forgetting (the latter being modernity's own nihilism, the moment of forced failure and affirmed complacency within the present – the present, that is, generated by the banality of scepticism). The response envisaged in this instance will involve a conception of singularity. As will emerge, it will be the singular that obviates singularity. In other words, what comes to be given – given as the demand of any thought of the Shoah – will be its insistent presence. Singularity will be defined by the absence of any pregiven relation. This apparent paradox only works beyond the work of fate. What must be resisted, however, is that possible aestheticising of the Shoah in which it takes on the character of the sublime.

The difficulties that are encountered here return to the problem of the simple beginning. Of course, all these beginnings, though here from a different site, merely begin once again further meditations on the occurrence of the Shoah. And yet, it should not be thought that the approach to the Shoah could ever be the same as any other. What this will mean is that the approach – the universality of approaching, the way of the universal in other words – is what must be questioned, a questioning which, with these beginnings perhaps, occurs in the approach itself.

TO BEGIN: 'FATE AND CHARACTER'

Benjamin's difficult and at times 'hermetic' text takes up the problem of the temporality of history once the dominant directional determining forces of chronology and teleology have been discarded. In being discarded, what is displaced is their explanatory force and thus their inclusive nature. Benjamin's is a destructive text. It shakes the continuity of interpretation in order to arrive at that conclusion which is the shaking of interpretation. The shaking of continuity will allow for that occurrence or, perhaps, that 'emergence' in which what comes to be demanded is the necessity to think the relation that is enjoined by the demise of totality – the totality of the all – and thus with it, in its path, the generation of difference outside of the pregiven and thus predetermined confines of the either/or. In 'One Way Street', Benjamin expresses this break in relation to the startling of truth.

> Truth wants to be startled abruptly, at one stroke from her self-immersion. whether by uproar, music or cries of help.[2]

In a manner prefiguring this need, Benjamin's 'Fate and Character' opens with a series of distancing manoeuvres that may, in the end, startle.[3] Not only is there the attempt, to which reference has already been made, at undoing the given relationship between fate and character; there is also the move to rework the connections – the pre-existing connections – between, on the one hand, character and the ethical, and fate and religion on the other. What is essential in this instance is to trace the presuppositions at work in Benjamin's own formulation and then their subsequent destruction. As a consequence, the already prefigured problem of relation will be seen to underpin the nature of this destruction: the specificity of Benjaminian destruction. Destruction already complicates time, and in so doing checks the given continuity within fate (a continuity enjoined equally by fate). The sundering of this fate for another fate is the redemption of time. Benjamin argues in a later text, 'The Destructive Character' (1931), that

> [t]he destructive character . . . because he sees ways everywhere, he always positions himself at crossroads. No moment can know [*Kein Augenblick kann wissen*] what the next will bring.[4]

Here, the centrality of the given site, the moment (*Augenblick*) falls beyond the hold of prediction. It falls, moreover, beyond the dominating and encompassing hold of epistemology. The emphatic moment will demand a more complex thinking. With the abeyance of prediction and thus with the restriction of universal history, the 'moment', and with it the present, will be reinvested. It will be this moment and thus another present that will become the site of hope.

Benjamin's first move in 'Fate and Character' is to note the connection that pertains between both fate and character and a signifying system. Neither can be approached as though they existed in themselves, as if they were outside of such a system. Fate and character are always read through the medium of signs; moreover, they generate signs to be read. This shift to reading and its concomitant repositioning of the natural is of singular importance. Benjamin's interest in relation to these signs is not with their own content as signs, but with what the existence of 'such a system of signs . . . signifies' (172/125), in other words, with what the necessity for a secondary signification reveals about fate and character. One is always 'read' through the other.[5] It will be essential to return to this question since what it opens up is the possibility of a reconsideration of the site and the temporality of the given, that which is always predetermined and therefore is always pregiven.

The text's initial object of critique is the posited definition of fate and character where one is defined in terms of the other. In sum, Benjamin's position is that the success of such definitions must be premised upon always being able to distinguish between the inner person, which in some sense is character, and the outer person who is in the world and thus lives fatefully in relation to that world. Benjamin's argument is that it becomes impossible to hold these positions apart because one side of the person can always be reduced to the other.

Consequently, the definitions tend to collapse into each other and thus into confusion. As Benjamin argues:

> it is impossible to determine in a single case what finally is to be considered a function of character and what a function of fate in human life . . . the external world that the active man encounters can also in principle be reduced, to any desired degree, to his inner world, similar to his outer world, indeed regarded in principle as one and the same thing.

(173/125–6)

The way out of this difficulty will involve a process of redefinition and, therefore, a separate consideration of fate and character. It should be added that this reconsideration will involve taking into consideration what was at work in the earlier definitions. Relation figures in the process that incorporates a reworking rather than the abandoning of the definition already given. The gift eschews any absolute giving up: the task of surrender. Once again, this necessitates releasing the hold over them that had been established by their having been inextricably linked to either the ethical or the religious. Benjamin's methodological move is encapsulated in his claim that 'We must banish them from both regions by revealing the error by which they were placed there' (173/126). In the case of fate the error emerged not because of the relation between fate and guilt as such, but because of how that relation was understood. The misconstrued position stems from the common supposition that 'fate-imposed misfortune is seen as the response of God or gods to religious offence' (173/127). (It is due to the enduring force of such ideas that the present relevance of these concerns is revealed.) The argument against this position is premised on the absence of any corresponding relation of fate to innocence. Once the argument is taken a step further by the consideration of a possible connection between fate and happiness, then the position of releasing fate from the hold of religion is strengthened. In sum, the assumption of a link between fate and guilt presupposes one between fate and happiness. It works out that the opposite is the case. Using Benjamin's own imagery it could be said that the continuity of connection is blasted open. The fate of continuity is now fated since, for Benjamin, it is precisely happiness which 'releases the fortunate man from the embroilment of the Fates' (174: 126). In cutting continuity, happiness gestures towards a redemptive illumination. Guilt and misfortune are not dismissed, however, as elements of fate. Rather, they are relocated, moved by their having been repositioned. The movement here is from religion to law (Recht). Not law in the sense of justice, as though this latter were divested of fate, but law in the more profound yet transformative sense of both the inevitable and inescapable laws of fate and its subsequent abstraction that takes the form of justice (this is, perhaps, an ineliminable doubling of law, necessity's complexity). For Benjamin, law is 'a residue of the demonic stage of human existence when legal statutes determined not only men's relationships but their relation to the Gods' (174/127).

The confrontation with the Gods is the site of tragedy. Here it reaches beyond this restriction since Benjamin interprets Attic tragedy as the site in which fate is subdued and the web of continuity destroyed. Its having been subdued emerges as symbol. With this confrontation, the tragic hero is reduced to silence. It is this silence that reinscribes the tragic hero in another fate.[6] For Benjamin no voice can be given to this overcoming. Nonetheless, tragedy is where fate is limited and its hold delimited.

> It was not in law but in tragedy that the head of genius lifted itself for the first time from the mist of guilt, for in tragedy demonic fate is breached.
>
> (174/127)

This breaching, the tear in the continuity of fate, is, in the language of Benjamin's *Trauerspiel*, the place where the 'transfigured face of nature is fleetingly revealed in the light of redemption', perhaps the startling of truth where the reign of similitude is subverted by a repetition yielding the intensity of the present. Fleeting presence is the temporality of the symbol. No longer is death the only response to fate; there is now the possibility of a release from fate by the transformation of the natural and thus by the subversion of continuity. The Messianic takes the place of the historical by its emergence within it. This moment and movement of revelation is the *Jetztzeit*.

There are two important additional elements here. The first is the reworking of fate into the 'guilt context of the living' and not of the individual. The second is the introduction of 'genius' as that which provides the way out of the determinations of fate. It is essential to note that causality is being reworked in terms of human practice since guilt here is not opposed to 'purity'. Even if, as has been suggested, 'fate is the guilt context of the living', this should not be understood as suggesting that fate belongs to humanity or that it is the possession of a single individual. Rather, it is that fate is in human being. It is part of the historical and temporal being of being human. Fate pertains to the 'natural condition of the living', but in terms of an illusion. It is the illusion of continuity and myth. In Benjamin's argument, fate becomes 'that part involved in the nurturing of guilt and misfortune by virtue of an illusion' (175: 128). Here, illusion can provisionally be understood as the forgetful turning away from happiness where experience becomes no more than the re-experience of the already experienced. It is important to note that what is at stake here is a particular construal of repetition – one in which forgetting may come to play a constitutive role.

It is in relation to this description of fate that Benjamin deploys the example of the clairvoyant's activities. With them a connection is drawn with the temporality that Benjamin implicitly links to tragedy, the time when fate is wrecked. The clairvoyant 'discovers in signs something about natural life in man that she seeks to substitute for the head of genius' (175–6/128).

The one who visits her gives way to fate, i.e. the guilty life within him or herself, by allowing for the substitution. Yet her activities contain something else. Benjamin concludes his treatment of fate with a complex reference to time. What he describes as 'the guilt context' (*der Schuldzusammenhang*) has an inauthentic temporality and, as such, differs markedly from the 'time of redemption, or of music, or of truth'. This posited authentic temporality involves a specific relationship between the present and the future. The fortune-teller and palm-reader bring the future into the present such that while it is present the future is never copresent. It is always mediated by a sign system yet not itself mediating the present. Time opens up another series of problems to which it will be essential to return. (As with any return, what it signals is the effective presence of the temporality of interpretation.)

Benjamin introduces his discussion of character by noting that it, as well as fate, concerns 'natural man'. He starts by freeing character from its already posited relation to the ethical. The same type of argument will be used here as was deployed in the case with fate. There guilt was removed from what appears to be a simply theological context and placed in the material world of human existence. This link with materiality is fundamental to Benjamin's understanding of the Messianic and thus of redemption since for Benjamin the Messiah is the figure in which politics and time come to be thought together. (The Messiah figures in the interruption of continuity.) For Benjamin, the moral terminology developed in relation to character will be retained only in its having lost its 'moral valuation'. Again, he identifies another error that worked, initially, to join fate and character. He formulates this connection in terms of the weave or construction of a fabric. 'This connection is effected by the idea of a network that can be tightened by knowledge at will into a dense fabric, for this is how character appears to superficial observation' (176/129).

It is in this cloth that the moral is thought to obtain, for in it a quality can be read to which moral estimation can be given. For Benjamin the mistake here is the conflation of actions and qualities. It is only the former that can have true moral significance. The metaphor of cloth must endure independently of morality. This is brought about by the process of abstraction.

This abstraction must be such that valuation itself is preserved; only its moral accent is withdrawn, to give way to such conditional evaluations, in either a positive or negative sense, as are expressed by the morally indifferent descriptions of qualities of the intellect (such as 'clever' or 'stupid').

(178/129)

It is in comedy that actions appear independently of moral judgement. Within Benjamin's general argument comedy is the site where actions only 'reflect the light of character'. In this sense, character has no deep structure which could be read. It is a surface in which a simple individuality presents itself. This is why Benjamin will argue that nothing can be learned about hypochondria and miserliness from Molière's characters in *Le Malade Imaginaire* and *L'Avare*. There is no hidden world to be presented. In Benjamin's own terms, 'character is unfolded in them like a sun in the brilliance of its single trait'. Character, therefore, is freedom: a will freed to act as pure individuality within and against the terms set by tragedy. Here is the link to fate. It is a subsequent and perhaps redemptive connection. Benjamin formulates this connection in the following way:

While fate unfolds the immense complexity of the guilty person, the complications and bonds of his guilt, character gives this mystical enslavement of the person to the guilt context the answer of genius.

(178/130)

Such a formulation works, as Rodolphe Gasché has argued, to identify and sustain the specificity of a given character and, at the same time, to provide it with whatever is necessary such that 'the knots of fate are cut apart'.[7] This means that human being is never reducible to its insertion into the work of fate. (Human being will have to work through its insertion into fate.) Furthermore, it is via character that the reduction of the human to the natural is effaced. Once again there is a break with prediction such that emerging in the fissure is the generation of difference out of indifference. What is at play here is not comedy *per se*, but the character of the comic figure as itself a figure. In Benjamin's terms, the first figure is 'not the scarecrow of the determinist; it is the beacon in whose beams the freedom of his actions becomes visible' (178/130). The second figure is the reading of character. Its figuring. It is with this final sundering of continuity – 'the blows of fate' – that another possibility will emerge.

This summation presents the constitutive elements of Benjamin's complex text and, with it, the arguments which work to reposition both fate and character. Depth does, however, need to be given to certain of these arguments.

But this is a task that can only really be undertaken once there has been an attempt to clarify the description of fate as involving the 'guilt context of the living'. It should be remembered that the specific, though initial, question guiding these moves to illuminate this adumbration concerns the problem of thinking the Shoah. What will continue to be taken up, therefore, is the nature of the connection between Shoah, fate and character. The magnitude as well as the seriousness of this question necessitate that care is taken.

If fate is no longer proper to the individual or even to a universalised individual, then the guilt in question is not the consequence of original sin. Guilt appears in its being forgotten, in its being that which emerges in its transcendence by the work of character. What this means is that guilt is not part of either history or temporality as the merely given, a posited provision. Rather, and more emphatically, it is that guilt is the expression of a history and a temporality. It has already been noted that the 'guilt context' is described by Benjamin as having an inauthentic temporality. One initial way of grasping the stakes of this inauthenticity, and therefore of guilt, is within the terms provided by a note to Benjamin's last work 'On the Concept of History'. The note also indicates the banality, if not the potential profanity, of prediction:

> We know that the Jews were prohibited from investigating the future. The Torah and the prayers instruct them in remembrance, however. This stripped the future of its magic, to which all those succumb who turn to the soothsayers for enlightenment. This does not imply, however that for the Jews the future turned into homogeneous, empty time. For every second of time was the straight gate through which the Messiah might enter.[8]

The future is always a present possibility and, as such, a condition of the present. The move that takes place here, therefore, and which repeats the one already noted in 'Fate and Character' has the effect of altering the order of — while at the same time retaining the presence of — past, present and future. In the earlier text, the positive example concerns that which is to be learned from the fortune-teller and palmist. The first thing to note is that it is not derived from their status as those who have access to the future. It is rather, as Benjamin indicates, that they 'teach us at least that time can at every moment be made simultaneous with another (not present)' (178: 130). The simultaneity involves a parasitism on another life, 'a higher less natural life'. The allusion to the diminished power of nature is a reference to the possibility of Messianic time intruding into the continuity of history, the latter being the natural life of time. This other time 'has no present' (*hat keine Gegenwart*). And yet, of course, it is present as simultaneous with the present, even though one temporal domain can never be reduced to the other. It will be precisely this present, the present that is denied, that will be of central interest, for with it what must arise is the question of the site and the time of its denial, and as such, their present. What will figure here is the present's anoriginal complexity.

However, there is still more than can be learnt from the fortune-teller. Other considerations endure. While the time to which they gesture opens rather than precludes the possibility of the Messianic, the fortune-teller also wants to incorporate the future into the present and thereby to make the two radically distinct times not just simultaneous but copresent. (Here copresence would be both ontological as well as temporal). Ironically there-fore, fate becomes a pure ground. What present means, however, is the present as the time which is dated and thus the continuity of its being present. This continuity – the persistence of a present yet to be breached – is that out of which the head of 'genius' comes to be lifted. It is remem-brance that in opening time, works in contradistinction to this reduction to the present. The approach to the future, as with the relation to the past, are both enacted as a remembrance, insofar as it is this construal of the work of memory that provides the model in terms of which the relation to any puta-tive past and future is to be thought. The reality of the past and the future will no longer dominate as questions; they will cede their place to the nature of the 'historical object' and the place of its presence. Neither the fortune-teller nor the palm-reader can be said to remember. They predict within the life of fate. Their predictions form and inform the time of continuity, the pure presence of fate.

Character disrupts this continuity. It should not be thought that fate and character are absolutely distinct, for, to use Benjamin's own setting, comedy works within tragedy. Here Benjamin acknowledges his debt to Cohen with the reference to Cohen's argument that 'tragic action . . . casts a comic shadow' (178: 130–1). The casting of shadows enjoins its own play of adum-bration; perhaps uniquely, remembering is linked to disruption. Here, the larger question will be the remembering of that whose disruption precludes any simple reiteration of continuity. It is only refusal – which will work as a type of forgetting – coupled to actual forgetting, that will allow the effect of the Shoah to be effaced. As its effect would involve thought and thus the possi-bility of thinking, refusal and forgetting would combine in sustaining continuity's reiteration. The disruption, the break-up of that seamless present, is to be undertaken in order that it be remembered and, therefore, that the Shoah's consequences for thinking come to work through the demand that it be thought. As such, memory and work will be part of what constitutes the present. Part of tracking this movement demands holding together both the necessity of the task as well as that which makes it possible. The latter is the necessary yet complex interrelation between thinking and remembering.

Therefore, what must be undertaken – the task that will have already been demanded – necessitates building upon the other possibility for memory, namely remembrance. Prediction will always be trapped by the conception of temporality that it demands and the conception of occurrence – an occurrence eventually opening up the event – that it envisages, the interplay of time and task that marks the epochal present. The latter is that present in which the reciprocity between time and task maintains and establishes the contemporaneity of philosophy by setting up a mutual reciprocity between the conception of the present (the 'now' that is the time of writing, writing's time) and the task demanded by that conception. The suggested way ahead here will involve taking remembrance as opening the present to both the future and the past. In this sense, remembrance will be linked to vigilance and, as such, it will take on a different form than that usually staked out for it. Remembrance will no longer be simple memory since with the advent of vigilance – once placed beyond the realms of loss – it takes on a political and ethical dimension. Moreover, remembrance, because of its location, means that hope will no longer be trapped by either mourning or melancholia.[9] Distance, maintaining distance and hence relation, will come to be affirmed.

The difficulty in trying to present what is at work here involves avoiding the trap of the either/or. Mourning will always be linked to a necessity. What will be necessary, however, is holding to its pathos. This possibility for mourning will have to be maintained. Mourning will nonetheless only emerge as a type of remembering if incorporation and resolution are precluded and with their being precluded, almost as its announced mark, the relation of distance is allowed; its ineliminable presence maintained by being affirmed. And yet, of course, mourning cannot be retained simply as pathos. With the primordial presence of distance there emerges a spacing and thus the given necessity to negotiate the insistent presence of relation (one response will have to be the two poles of contemporary nihilism, namely active forgetting and scepticism). What this means is that mourning is no longer appropriate to delimit, perhaps, to name, *in simpliciter*, the active participation within relation. On the contrary. It will be a participation that affirms not only the presence of relation, but its necessary irreducibility, opened as marking the continual opening of the site of vigilance. Again, it is this irreducibility that will have to reposition mourning in relation to vigilance; consequently mourning can no longer be taken as an end in itself. The shift in the register of mourning means that while it is not the direct consequence of vigilance – in the strict sense that it would only be possible and therefore only allowed because of the presence of vigilance – the same maintained opening must be sustained in each. Giving way to remembrance, memory causes the former to emerge as an insistent question. The necessity of remembering will never have been in question.

It is rather that the question pertains to what it is that remembrance is taken to be. In this context, the full weight of the question must endure. Mourning will have become an affirmative remembering which, in the absence of its self-enclosing finality, maintains hope in the present since hope will have become linked to securing remembrance, securing it in and as part of the present. Hope, therefore, will be inevitably connected to the maintained presence of the possibility of present remembrance. (Again the present is maintained.) If hope is to involve the future, then the future in question is not that which is there for the present. This concept of the future would eliminate the present. In other words, the future in question is not that into which the present – chronology's present – is given. Not only will such a present no longer be apposite but, in addition, in being won over from chronology's future, the future will be there as a possibility within the present. What this 'within' means, however, is not that the future is there as an addition, but that it is present as a constitutive part of the present itself. Hope is sustained by the affirmed sundering of continuity and is thus present with the affirmation of the incomplete. However, in forcing the thinking of that which works beyond the confines of an inclusive and therefore predictive history, and thus eschewing continuity, the Shoah is not hope. What after all would be continuous with the Shoah? Within what universal would it form a part, even diremptively? Yet hope does exist in relation to the Shoah. What this relation entails is that, in its having to be thought, in the demand to think it, there lies the possibility of thinking hope. There is an odd and disturbing dimension of this hope – of how it comes to be thought – to which it will be necessary to return. Part of the difficulty is that what is being argued for here is hope as an ontological category. Reworking hope such that what is central is the hold of time and its interarticulated mode of being entails that its presentation no longer has an automatic and unequivocal ethical or moral dimension, one which would, by its very nature, necessitate approval.

REMEMBRANCE'S OPENING: SHOAH

What is hope for? How is remembrance to be approached? The force of these questions lies in the recognition that there are neither monuments for nor ones which mark out what has already been identified as present remembrance.[10] As Benjamin's reworking of fate and character makes clear, there can be no straightforward tradition for the emphatic interruption of fateful continuity (the latter, perhaps, being another name for tradition). A way of giving greater depth to what has been identified here as present remembrance will emerge from looking briefly at the problem of connecting not simply Benjamin's thought, but thinking itself, what Steiner identifies with the terms 'poetry, philosophy, logic', to the Shoah. The problem will exist in and for any body of writing or philosophical thought. This is the challenge of Steiner's position to which reference was made earlier. In the case of Benjamin, there could have been no explicit reference. Yet the problem itself is raised within the actual formulation of another attempt to link the present and the past.

What is involved here, at least initially, is an occurrence that seems to demand the description of a singularity that checks any simple formulation of the mechanisms of history, for example, the 'cunning of reason', the continuity of progress. It will be seen that it is in the work of this singularity that the further reduction to absolute singularity is rendered impossible. The trap of the absolute is exposed by the necessary presence of the relation of non-relation. Furthermore, pure singularity, because of the relation between positing and existing, will always lend itself to occlusion or absorption. The problem of absorption that threatens is more complex than it seems. Not only is there the necessity of maintaining a remembering excluding absorption; there is also the real possibility that it is the faithful who may forget. For the faithful, however, the forgetting in question would be complex since it would involve that modality of absorption in which continuity was maintained, tradition allowed to hold sway and identity to remain homogeneous. There would be a monument but not one that demanded its own thinking. Monuments will never be sufficient for remembrance. In general terms the problem of tradition and its relation to memory (accepting the initial generality of these terms), as it pertains to both philosophy and theology, emerges at this precise point.[11]

The passage in question comes from the fifth of the sections that comprise 'On the Concept of History'. Here the 'present' – the cited 'present' – is given a specific concern in relation to the past. As the passage opens, what must be noted immediately is that the connection – and hence the basis for any possible relation – between the past and the present is itself not given. The absence of such a posited connection and, with it, the elimination of any constitutive role for chronology, means that establishing it – taking up the 'concern' – will involve the necessary sundering of any subsequent continuity thought within the field bordered by fate and progress.

Rather, being given, 'concerns' are made. The process of making, therefore, is central to Benjamin's project. The ineliminable presence of action and, with it, of the inscribed presence of the actative in this formulation, should not pass unnoticed:

> every image of the past that is not recognised by the present as one of its own concerns threatens to disappear irretrievably.[12]

In the specificity of their formulation, these lines pose three initial and inescapable problems. The first is the nature of the recognition; the second is the meaning of 'concerns'; the third is that they are present as the possession of 'the present'. (Again, the insistent question is the nature of this 'present'. The question insists because of the irreducibility of this present to the time held by dates and thus to either chronology or the historicism of universal history.) In relation to the Shoah, while the threat appears to take the form of its projected disappearance from memory, its being forgotten, what is actually at stake is both more significant and complicated. There has already been allusion to this founding difficulty. Indeed, it will arise from having to allow for the absence of a necessary link between the monumental and remembrance; in other words, it is given by the absence of an already given foundation. The latter will always be more than memory. With regard to the Shoah, it is the relation to thought that must endure since what will always have to be retained is the question of the Shoah as an occurrence for thinking. Remembrance is inscribed, therefore, in the very process of which its own formulation – its being in/as the reworking of memory – forms a part. It is precisely the impossibility of an outside that implicates philosophy in the practice in which it takes place. What is involved here is twofold. In the first place, there is the question of what conceptions of time and memory will allow for 'the images of the past' to be recognised at the present and as part of the present. Regardless of the answer given to this question it remains the case, as was indicated above, that it will always be more than just a memory. In the second place, there is that state of affairs already noted by Adorno in which the 'effacement of memory' may be the result of what he describes as 'an all-too-wakeful consciousness'.[13] Both points indicate why the injunction: 'remember' is, on its own, far from sufficient.

In the different domains of the political, philosophical and theological, the sense to be attributed to such a demand is neither singular in content nor generative of a single action. In relation to the Shoah and therefore to the demand that it be remembered, the injunction opens up the presence of already inscribed divisions. Each one marks out different and at times incompatible responses to the demands of memory. The existence of such conflicts cannot be accounted for as though the issue were simply that of differing responses to the 'same' occurrence. On the contrary; they are only really explicable in terms of conflicts concerning the specificity of memory in relation to any thinking of the Shoah, and thus of conflicts concerning the work of time that positions the complexity of memory. What this means is that conflicts concerning how the task of memory is best served are in fact conflicts that concern the present. The present in question is the epochal present, namely that present that is given by the reciprocity of time and task. Opening up the present will mean staying, initially, with the actual formulation of the passage.

What then is 'recognition'? At one end, recognition is, in terms of function and etymology, part of the process marked by understanding and knowledge working within the ambit of representation. In general terms, it pertains to representation since what is involved is the taking over of the object such that what is taken over can be presented as taken over and thus as itself: the literal move of re-presentation. It is the move that takes place within epistemology and this is the case even when taken as that which brings epistemology into play. The fulfilling of these two conditions of presentation is the operation of representation. As such, it poses the general transcendental question of the conditions of possibility for any recognition. However, generality is not the issue here. Indeed, as is clear from the *Passagen-Werk*, in strictly Benjaminian terms it would be that the monadic structure of the 'historical object' would work to preclude any sustained attempt to understand 'recognition' as re-presentation. In this instance, however, it is the particular recognition of the Shoah that is of concern. While it may be possible to address the conditions of possibility for knowledge and even recognition within the framework handed down as tradition and thus as that within which such problems are constrained to be confronted, the viability of such a response still remains an open question as regards the Holocaust. If it were not then the Shoah would be no more than an extreme, breaking certain bounds by figuring the sublime, by being taken to be beyond any given determination or incorporation. With such a formulation the question: 'Why the heavens did not darken?', would have to be taken seriously as a question rather than as a symptom. Not only is this a misconstrual of the sublime (it overlooks the role of the faculty of the supersensible); it conflates two possibilities. One is that nothing can be said because a limit is both reached and transgressed. Such a position is inherently inadequate because of its necessarily parasitic relation to representation. The other is that what has arisen within thinking is a task that will, in being taken on – in the very movement of its being taken over – come to determine philosophical activity itself. It will be a determination, however, whose specificity cannot be delimited by prediction. It is this latter possibility that is captured by the procedural eventualities in the following questions. Has the possibility of 'recognition', of knowing what it is that recognition would be, been determined by the reality of the Shoah such that its actual determination remains as an open question? Is this set up one of the factors structuring the contemporary?

If the dilemma concerns the way in which recognition leads inexorably to cognition and thus the incorporation, absorption and eventual forgetting of the object (the epistemological equivalent to mourning, whose effective presence effaces the structure of hope) then perhaps the engagement with recognition that will retain the possibility of hope by holding open the site of remembrance and thus maintaining the demand for active participation as vigilance, would be to hold recognition apart from cognition. The distinction is not gestural. What it would mean is that while a relation would be possible, it would be a relation of distance. Distance and relation are not to be understood as though they formed no more than part of a conceptual geography. There is also a dynamic involving repetition. The repetition would involve a continuity that worked beyond the confines of mourning. And yet, held by the limit of epistemology, mourning will always need to allow for another mourning. Even though the necessity for mourning loss and incorporation would be distanced by a vigilance working against the forgetting that would be introduced by incorporation, mourning will have been subject to its own inevitable reworking. Hence the necessity of allowing its own pathos to endure.

The relation of distance would become a site of tension: the impossible possibility of resisting what would otherwise be inevitable, namely the formulation of recognition in terms of cognition. The move here described as a holding apart, or a relation of distance, derives its necessity from the nature of cognition as being that which demands the presentation of an absolute insofar as cognition is contingent upon such a presentation. In more general philosophical terms, the absolute in question is, by definition, as much epistemological as it is ontological. It has to incorporate the latter since epistemological certitude is itself dependent upon the presentation of the object in its totality. (It would be this dependency that works to situate the opening question of this chapter: Of this occurrence, apart from factual detail and the detail of facts, what can be known?) It is, of course, this absolute which provides the way into representation because representation is the re-presentation of that which has been cognised. It comes to be presented as such. There is an inevitable logic at work here. The relation of distance will allow for presentations, and thus for knowledge, but these will work at a distance from the structure of representation and with it the logic of identity. Not only, therefore, does the mimetic presentation of images cede its place to a presentation within becoming; classical epistemology gives way to judgement. This double movement has a critical effect on claims to have recovered and to have represented the past. It opens up its own site of judgement.

The relation of distance is neither formal nor descriptive. It is present in Benjamin's reworking of remembrance as pertaining as much to the future as it does to the past. It also signals the reworking of historical time, ridding it of teleology and thus of the possibility for prediction. The sundering of fate in Benjamin's destructive move announces its actuality – an actuality only there *après coup* – because of that which is demanded of the present. Remembrance needs to be situated within the relation of distance, a relation at the present and thus working to sustain present remembrance. Its continuity is provided by the tension that works within and thus provides the work of this relation. Present remembrance involves a continual recognition that is always holding open the possibility of cognition – a cognition that can neither complete nor end – thereby bringing another knowledge into play. In holding it open, it reworks the present as a site of hope. (As such, the possibility in question will remain an insistent and yet impossible possibility figuring the incomplete.) The absence of any closure or moment of completion demands that present remembrance become charged with vigilance. The impossibility of representation, the completion demanded by its project and thus with it the necessarily incomplete nature of cognition, only betrays negativity by being its betrayal. Negativity is overcome by the projected solidarity envisaged by vigilance. It is in precisely this way that the present can make an image of the past 'one of its own concerns'.

Even though it is similar to all other occurrences by bearing dates and demanding knowledge, the Shoah's occurrence is also and at the same time radically dissimilar. It is therefore both unique and not unique. The question of its prediction, its being the work of fate, its having been known in advance reduces it to the status of a moment in historical time, a flicker in the passage of continuity. And yet it is an occurrence, one whose dates are known. The difficulty is thinking its specific impossible possibility. It goes without saying that the horror is having to think it in the first place. Nihilism is the refusal of this thinking. A thinking that once it is undertaken determines the nature of thinking, and as such works to determine the specificity of modernity: the site of contemporary thought.

4

AWAKENING FROM TRAGEDY
Tragedy's present condition

PRESENT TRAGEDY

It is not as though it would ever have been possible to escape the concerns of tragedy. As a word, it is already harboured by the everyday, and as a literary or philosophical term, it can be located at those intersections which chart the interplay of history and humanity. And yet, despite an appeal to the common-place, each of these formulations begs questions. What is the everyday? How is history and humanity to be thought? What would allow even these most tenta-tive of generalisations to occur? Rather than pursue their detail, these questions can be left to one side because they fail to situate tragedy. They fail to allow for its possible specificity because they do no more than provide the implausible security of generality and abstraction. Thus the question to be addressed here will concern the already present place of tragedy and, there-fore, how it — whatever the 'it' of tragedy may be — will come to impinge upon modernity. Here, there will be two initial questions which, in their difference as well as in their similarity, open up the problem of staging tragedy at the present. The questions are the following: Is the present traversed by the work of tragedy? What is tragedy at the present?

These questions already belie their form. As questions, they bring with them the insistent presence of a specific ground. Here, the ground is time. As a beginning, and prior to broaching the question of tragedy as a general problem, prior to focusing on Benjamin's demand to think the specificity of *Trauerspiel* as opposed to tragedy, it is essential to stay with the ground of time. What must be brought to bear upon these questions is their commit-ment to specific forms of temporality. (Perhaps this would mark out the presence of a philosophical concern, rather than one which was properly literary.) Asking about the nature of tragedy at the present, invoking the possibility of its hold upon modernity, perhaps even defining the terms of its own self-description, is already to make a series of claims about the nature of historical time. Time will have already figured within that which structures them as questions. The site of engagement, therefore, is not set by the need for a deliberate calculation leading either to response or description. Engaging with this site will mean allowing the presence of time to have already offered the terrain upon which the question of tragedy is posed. As will emerge in greater detail, any thinking of tragedy will already be a philosophical formulation of the present, and has consequently to be understood as an attempt to formulate the epochal present.

Here, it will be essential to follow a complex and demanding path. Moving between the insistence of tragedy, via Walter Benjamin's own attempt to differentiate the specificity of *Trauerspiel* from tragedy (an attempt that will insist on the particularity of the Baroque, not in opposition to modernity as such, but as that which brings with it its own distinct object), to what may have allowed the hold of tragedy in the present, will allow both the specificity of tragedy and the connection between tragedy and the present to emerge. This latter concern will necessitate a reversion to Benjamin's demand for the particular. Allowing for this particularity will involve noting the way in which Benjamin analyses fascism in terms of the conditions provided by the advent of modernity. (As such, of course, fascism will emerge as neither reactionary nor conservative, but as a version of the mythic within modernity; modernity's other possibility.[1]) Finally, insisting on different forms of particularity will necessitate reworking the distinction, as recently formulated by George Steiner, between tragedy and 'absolute tragedy'. Steiner attempts to bring a conception of tragedy that will bear upon the present; the question, however, must concern the particularity of the present onto which it is brought to bear. The force and importance of his position means that it cannot go unquestioned.

Whether or not it is recognised, to write of tragedy is not to write of a universal human condition. To write of tragedy will become a writing of the present and thus of the formulation of differing conceptions of the epochal present. It will always have been such a writing since claims about tragedy will almost inevitably involve a commitment to claims about the nature of the present and thus will involve recourse, again implicitly or explicitly, to conceptions of historical time. Steiner draws a distinction between tragedy and what he defines as 'absolute tragedy'; the force of the latter is that it will incorporate, unequivocally, the age in which its differentiation from tragedy has itself been staged. Steiner writes that in

> the absolutely tragic, it is the crime of man that he is, that he exists. His naked presence and identity are transgressions. The absolutely tragic is therefore a negative ontology. Our century has given to this abstract

paradox a tangible enactment. During the Holocaust, the Gypsy or the Jew, had very precisely *committed the crime of being*.[2]

This sense of the tragic needs to be set against the more enduring sense of loss that, in Steiner's writings, comes to define his conception of the epochal present. It is the diagnosis of the present that forces upon art and philosophy the role that he will then come to attribute to them. Again, what is at work here is the sustaining reciprocity between time and task. Despite appearances to the contrary, neither art nor time exist in themselves. Within his writings, one is defined by its position in relation to the other:

> It is the capacity of the arts, in a definition which must . . . be allowed to include the living forms of the speculative (what tenable view of the poetics will exclude Plato, Pascal, Nietzsche?), to make us, if not at home, at least alertly, answerably peregrine in the unhousedness of our human circumstance. Without the arts, form would remain unmet and strangeness without speech in the silence of the stone.[3]

In Steiner's writings, the absence of the house – the homelessness of the human – is linked to the death of tragedy. In the book of that name he argues that the impossibility of tragedy's perdurance arises because of the interdependence of tragedy and the divine.[4] With the advent of the secular, God's death is equally the death of tragedy proper. And yet, for Steiner, as Ruth Padel has argued, the estranged human can still find that which generates place.[5] The place is there with the presence of the art work. Its insistent presence is there beyond the work of interpretation and the simple operation of the hermeneutic. What this means is that the predicament of the human in the present will have been given by the work of tragedy. Rather than the age being tragic, it is defined almost by the possibility for a recreation of the conditions of tragedy: not absolute tragedy, but tragedy as given by the relationship between humans and the divine. The rediscovery of the divine – the hold of real presence – reintroduces the conditions under which tragedy could have a place. It may be that, for Steiner, 'we' can be saved by the Gods because it will only be in the resurgence of the divine and thus in the recreation of the tragic that the human may refind its own, now presently lost, sense of propriety.

At work in this formulation is the epochal present. The conception of the age already determines the project and the specific task of writing. Steiner's evocation of 'the unhousedness of our human circumstances' opens up not just one of the perennial literary tropes in which the tragic has been formulated, but a theme that plays an important and constant role in Heidegger. It would be essential in this regard to begin to connect what is identified in 'Building Dwelling Thinking' as 'the homelessness of man' (*die Heimatslosigkeit des Menschen*),[6] to the commentary on Sophocles' 'Choral Ode' advanced in *An Introduction to Metaphysics*. In the latter, 'man's' strangeness, what makes him in Heidegger's translation of τὸ δεινότατον the 'strangest of the strange', is not just that 'he passes his life amidst the strange',

> but because he departs from his customary, familiar limits, because he is the violent one, who, tending toward the strange in the sense of the overpowering, surpasses the limit of the familiar [*das Heimische*].[7]

The place of homelessness cannot be generalised. Heidegger demands something that, at one point within his writings, is a form of spiritual renewal. Steiner, on the other hand, allows for an almost personal redemption through art. The differences are stark and are perhaps best analysed in terms of myth. The similarity and thus their initial significance lies in their presence as signs of the secular, marks of the absent Gods. Steiner argues that to the extent to which 'we inquire of modern or future tragic drama', then

> we are asking ourselves about the internalisation in consciousness and in our culture of the manifold notifications of God's death and the eclipse of religion.[8]

While there needs to be a shift in orientation, the place of the home, and equally of an enforcing fragmentation, will figure within both Benjamin's analysis of modernity as well as his study of the Baroque. What needs to be addressed is the nature of the relationship between the two senses of place, fragmentation and loss.

Heidegger's evocation of 'homelessness' is a description of the time of writing. The present is characterised by an ineliminable 'homelessness'. Homelessness is the predicament of historical Dasein. Rather than taking the predicament as natural or as merely descriptive of a certain chronological conjuncture, it has to be understood as the positioning of Dasein in relation to its own time. It is the nature of that time that determines the direction of the philosophical task. This path needs the setting provided by this description of the present; it is almost unthinkable without it. This is the determining ground of time. Heidegger is a thinker of modernity if modernity is characterised by an emphatic sense of estrangement that can be continually mediated by an insistent dwelling on the 'matter' (*Sache*) of thinking. (The task it generates is, after all, what stems from a repositioning of the *Seinsfrage*.) The importance of insisting on the ground of time is that a detailed analysis of specificity – the conditions of tragedy as opposed to 'absolute tragedy', or the Baroque as opposed to the modern, for example – will reveal that what is actually at stake is a specific conception of the present. What emerges with Benjamin is the demand to think that specificity. With that demand, Benjamin's concern will open up beyond the simple hold of his own writings.

SPECIFICITY: *TRAUERSPIEL*, TRAGEDY

If only as a beginning, it is possible to start with Benjamin's formulation of the relationship between the earlier *Trauerspiel* project and the work that came to be known as the 'Arcades Project'. An integral part of such an understanding involves tracing the nuances of Benjamin's own formulation of this relation. One such formulation occurs in a letter written to Scholem on 20 May 1935. Rather than addressing the letter's detail, two moments of it will be taken up. The first moment plots complex points of intersection and division. Writing of the 'Arcades Project', Benjamin speaks of succumbing

> to the temptations of visualising analogies with the Baroque book in the book's inner construction, although its external construction decidedly diverges from that of the former. And I want to give you this much of a hint: Here as well the focus will be on the unfolding of a handed down concept. Whereas in the former it was the concept of Trauerspiel, here it is likely to be the fetish character of commodities.[9]

It is vital to note that in this passage, Benjamin identifies the difference between the two works in terms of their 'external construction'. While it is tempting to gloss this difference, the distinction between the two modes of presentation nevertheless touches on the central issue, namely the nature of the difference between the projects. While this may seem a concern with mere textuality, it is in fact one in which that textuality betrays the work of time. Moreover, the recognition by Benjamin that what is involved in both projects is the reworking of an already present concept indicates the extent to which the project of 'rescue' demands to be thought in terms of repetition. Arguing that what drives both projects is 'the unfolding of a handed down concept', is already to note the inscription of repetition. It is, of course, a conception of repetition that has already repositioned itself beyond the hold of the Same, while at the same time distancing the nihilistic possibilities within an enacted metaphysics of destruction.

The second significant moment within the letter arises from Benjamin complaining – quite justifiably – of his own circumstances. Despite his difficulty, he relates the following 'thought'. It is one on which he 'enjoys dwelling'. Here the comments only refer to his later work. Dialectics will become the place of differentiation.

How much of the dialectical synthesis of misery and exuberance lies in this research, which has been continually interrupted and repeatedly revived over the course of a decade, and which has been driven out into the remotest regions. Should the book's own dialectic prove to be just as sound, then it would find my approval.

(*ibid.*)

What is being suggested in these extracts is the interrelated nature of the concepts specific to the projects in question and their subsequent formulation or expression. What cannot be generalised is a method that ignores the nature of the concept. And yet what holds these moments together is the presence of dialectic. It is worth noting – and this despite its formulation in a letter written to the non-Marxist Scholem – that the dialectic of misery and exuberance is used by Benjamin to describe not only his own life during the period of the 'Arcades Project''s own construction, but also the research involved. He holds back, however, from the claim that this is the dialectic that figures in the book as such. References made by Benjamin to the dialectic are far from straightforward. There will have to be at least two senses in which dialectic figures. The first pertains to the image and occurs throughout his attempt to formulate the 'Arcades Project'. In 'Konvolut N' (N 2a, 3), this is described as 'dialectics at a standstill'. Furthermore, in the same section, this form of dialectic is connected to the authentic:

Only dialectical images are genuine [*echte*] (i.e. not archaic) images: and the place one happens upon them is language. Waking [*Erwachen*].

Here, since what is involved are different conceptions of the image, the important distinction is the one between the dialectical and the archaic. It will be essential to return to it. It will be of no surprise to realise that the nature of this distinction is temporal; it does not have to do with the image itself. There is, however, another sense of dialectic, which while related, has a different force. Noting its distinctive trait will allow a return to be made to the precise nature of what Benjamin has already identified as 'the dialectical image'. The key to the latter may inhere in the complex qualification that what is at work in this instance is dialectics at a 'standstill'.

In the work on *Trauerspiel*, part of the real force that is harboured by the project is the recasting of the nature of symbol and allegory.[10] At the beginning of the section on 'Allegory and *Trauerspiel*', this reworking initially occurs because of the inadequacy of the conceptions of symbol and allegory that had been held hitherto. As regards symbol, it was because there was thought to be a unity between form and content – a unity that had to have been present despite the difference between form and content – that the actual specific

80

presence of both form and content failed to be taken up. Benjamin describes this state of affairs arising because of 'the absence of dialectical rigour' (337/160). A further consequence of the failure of rigour is that

> the unity of the material and the transcendental object, which constitutes the paradox of the theological symbol is distorted into a relationship between appearance and essence.
>
> (337/160)

In other words, the failure to allow for the irreducible nature of the symbol's components gives rise to a situation in which what is given is traduced by its having been transformed either into a form of unity or at least a type of non-dialectical totality. As Benjamin puts it, this 'abuse' occurs whenever the 'appearance of an idea is called a symbol' (337/160). What is not being denied here is the incorporation into the work of the symbol of the instant. Benjamin reads the development of the symbol within the Romantic period – while acknowledging that its history is far older – in terms of this transformation. In the case of the Baroque, that which counters this formulation – and it is a formulation which is above all else the articulation of time, time's presence – is allegory. Allegory resists the permanent, the latter yielding the interarticulation of beauty and the transcendental by its linkage to the ruin. As Benjamin writes:

> Allegories are, in the realm of thoughts, what ruins are in the realm of things.
>
> (354/178)

What, however, is a ruin? Again, it must be remembered that what is at work in this question is the specificity of the Baroque. As a beginning, an answer to this question is that, with the ruin, history is given a specific location within a more generalised ordering of the world. (Once again, this should be understood as part of the process of stripping time of any potential naturalisation. History will always involve a conception of time within which history comes to be articulated as history.). Rather than marking an incorporation within the permanent, history is present with what has decayed and is thus part of a more generalised process of decay. It is as though history and nature abut to the extent that the latter is taken as the perpetual movement of decay. No longer is it the nature given by God but, to use Benjamin's formulation, 'it is fallen nature which bears the imprint of the progression of history' (356/180). The copresence of the ruin and its setting – almost the ruin's absorption into its setting – sets in play a relationship between part and whole that marks the presence of a connection that has to be thought beyond the hold of the simple opposition between particular and universal. This other relation occurs when what has already been named by Benjamin in the Prologue as '*Platonische Rettung*', starts to hold sway. It is worth noting the passage in its entirety as it provides the ruin within an integral part of its philosophical force.

> When the idea absorbs a sequence of historical formations, it does not do so in order to construct a unity [*Einheit*] out of them, let alone abstract something common to them all. There is no analogy between the relationship of the individual to the idea, and its relationship to the concept; in the latter case it falls under the aegis of the concept and remains what it was; an individuality; in the former it stands in the idea, and becomes something different; a totality. That is its Platonic 'redemption' (227/46).

It is this position which is reiterated throughout the study of *Trauerspiel*. It is read by Benjamin in Goethe's formulation of that hold on the 'vitality' of the particular that brings with it the general. It figures, furthermore, in the extraordinary claim that with the breakdown of the eternal and thus with the decay of transcendence, 'allegory declares itself to be beyond beauty' (*jenseits von Schönheit*) (354/178). The next line reintroduces the ruin by setting up the analogy between allegory and ruin. What is meant by ruin, perhaps the key to the whole analogy, itself lies in the thinking demanded by the word 'beyond' (*jenseits*). Here, the beyond is not an element in the realm of the aesthetic; it is an occurrence with time.

What does it mean to be beyond beauty? This question has to be answered in relation to the Baroque. Indeed, its answer should yield that which marks out the Baroque itself. Here there is the dialectic of transience and permanence. Echoes of precisely this dialectic mark the movement bringing with it the question of legitimacy in Shakespeare's *Richard II* and *Henry IV* parts I and II.[11] While it may seem both to involve an unnecessary detour and perhaps to repeat procedures that already have a significant currency, it is useful to pursue this point within Shakespeare. What will emerge is that while the Baroque gives rise to a world in ruin, that ruin can itself yield a singular subject position, the view generated by the melancholic gaze. The process of decay can be seen and thus held as a discrete object. However, decay is not dislocation. Moreover, the singularity of the subject position within the Baroque is impossible within modernity because dislocation is only present within it – within and as the founding of modernity – in its being effaced.

With Richard's death and Henry's acquisition of the crown, the question of legitimacy can no longer be answered by an appeal to linear progression. What conception of linearity there was prior to these events lay within a world in which kingship had become indissolubly linked to political power. Political legitimacy can no longer have recourse to nature but is only to be found in the attempt to hold on to power itself. Within this world, a world that has fallen apart, rebellion is not only a dominant motif, but demands to be understood beyond the hold of a transcendent realm that would serve to legitimise it. The world of the transcendent, of nature and thus of the divine itself has fallen apart. Such a world remains, but only as ruined. While the ruin endures as an indispensable part of the Baroque, it occupies this position because, as with allegory, 'it fragments the illusion of wholeness'.[12] With modernity, allegory may be necessary to fragment the whole but only because the whole is continually given as whole. What is given in these moments from Shakespeare's history plays is presented as the already fragmented.

In the opening scene of *Henry IV Part I*, Henry contrasts Hotspur to Hal in a way that is far from favourable to the latter. Here Hotspur is described as

> A son who is the theme of honour's tongue;
> Amongst a grove, the very straightest plant;
> Who is sweet Fortune's minion and her pride;
> Whilst I, by looking on the praise of him,
> See riot and dishonour stain the brow
> Of my young Harry
>
> (Act I, Scene 1)

These lines rehearse the problem of legitimacy and of Hal becoming the rightful heir because the lines themselves create the need for Hal to legitimise himself. It is precisely this possibility that is set in motion by the soliloquy at the end of Act I, Scene 2, the last lines of which indicate the force of the secular world of appearance: 'I'll so offend to make offence a skill, / Redeeming time when men think least I will'. Legitimacy is further rehearsed in *Henry IV Part II* when Hal, seeing his father asleep and thinking that he is dead, places the crown on his own head. His language is an attempt to reinscribe continuity into and onto a world in disarray:

> My due from thee is this imperial crown,
> Which, as immediate from thy place and blood,
> Derives itself to me. Lo where it sits –
> Which God shall guard; and put the world's whole strength
> Into one giant arm, it shall not force

This lineal honour from me. This from thee
Will I to mine leave as 'tis left to me.

(Act IV, Scene 5)

It is the very presence of disarray that causes Hal to reinscribe the order of succession back onto it. Allegory is beyond beauty in the precise sense that just as the ruin marks the presence of a structure that eliminated the possibility of unity whilst neither yielding nor representing a whole, allegory cannot gesture to a world in which elements would be held in a synthetic whole. With such a world, the attempt to unite these elements through a reversion to a transcendental realm that would legitimise particulars is also precluded. Within allegory – within the process that marks both the necessity for as well as the practice of allegory – it is as if particulars – perhaps particular instances of beauty – can no longer be legitimated by the form of beauty. Allegory is 'beyond beauty' in the precise sense that it is beyond the ontologico-temporal structure in which beauty functions. Allegory abounds with figures that mark the inscription of transience in a world that eschews its own redemption. It is this which, for Benjamin, marks the end of universal history. Equally, it marks the end of a redemption though in terms of an incipient or coming totality. Henceforth, with the Baroque, history has fallen.

> Everything about history that, from the very beginning, has been untimely, sorrowful, unsuccessful, is expressed in a face – or rather in a death's head.

(343/166)

With the world in disarray, perhaps only held in place as an impossible whole within the melancholic gaze, transience becomes eternal. This is the work of legitimacy but, equally, it is the potential idealism within *Trauerspiel*. Allegory will have worked against the movement that seeks to locate an interrelationship between the transcendent, the permanent and the instant. The symbol, one given within 'profane' thought and thus taken as providing a type of unity of the work of the instant in which the permanent is figured transcendentally, will have been jeopardised by the hold of allegory. It may be that allegory reveals the truth of symbol. (Here, what the revelation of truth entails is the symbol's fall from the theological to the profane and thus from the possibility of its rescue. Rescue would not return the symbol to its original place, as though there had been an unproblematic origin. On the contrary, it would reveal it as having fallen.)

While it will always be necessary to return to the force of allegory, Benjamin's final formulation reconnects allegory to the ruin and in so doing reintroduces the image (*das Bild*):

84

In the ruins of great buildings the idea of the plan speaks more impressively than in lesser buildings, however well preserved they are; and for this reason the German *Trauerspiel* merits interpretation. In the spirit of allegory it is conceived from the outset as a ruin, a fragment. Others may shine resplendently as on the first day: this form preserves the image of beauty [*das Bild des Schönen*] to the very last.

(409/235)

The contrast enacted here in the last line is both difficult and elusive. It is as though two conceptions of beauty are at stake. There is beauty as the eternal which has then been written into the place of the fragment or ruin. In this instance beauty becomes linked to appearance, the shine of the eternal in the place of the particular. Here what endures has a transfigured permanence. And yet, rather than the Platonic conception of beauty, it is the image of beauty that is here at stake. It is this set up which is articulated in the Prologue in the following terms:

The mode of being in the world of appearance is quite different from the being of truth, which is something ideal. The structure of truth, then, demands a mode of being which in its lack of intentionality resembles the simple existence of things, but which is superior in its permanence. Truth is not an intent which realises itself in empirical reality; it is the power which determines the essence of the empirical reality.

(216/36)

Moreover, it is precisely this set up which forms the dialectic of transience and permanence, a dialectic that holds itself within a tension beyond synthesis. It is at this point that it would become possible to differentiate between Benjamin and Hegel. Pursuing this undertaking would involve having to show why neither the presence of the particular nor the moment of history as formulated by Benjamin can be thought in terms of the relationship between universal and particular charted in Hegel's logical writings (cf. §165 *Shorter Logic*) nor in terms of the movement of history presented in the *Phenomenology*. The latter is that movement which will always have attempted to overcome the place of tension in the service of the actualisation of the All. What tensions remained have to be located within the framework of the realisation of the Absolute, and therefore could only ever be seen as no more than its after-effect. What this means is that while the Absolute does not complete in the sense that its realisation precludes activity and development, what it does entail is that particularity, and thus the determinations of the present, are

85

only available as components to be incorporated into the realisation – both formally and experientially – of the All.

The specificity of the Baroque becomes the work of a particular dialectic. The viability of that term cannot be a central concern here. What is fundamental is that what it marks out is a state of tension. Moreover, this tension is one that insists by its having obviated the possibility of an encroaching continuity that would subdue the disarray. Shakespeare's history plays form but an example of what is being staged. *Culture of the Baroque*, José Antonio Marvall's study of the seventeenth century, allows the point to be made with great historical clarity:

> In the first half of the seventeenth century, the social consciousness of crisis weighing upon human beings provoked a world view wherein the minds of the epoch felt overwhelmed by an innermost disorder.[13]

Disorder and disarray mark the world. They explicitly structure experience. The disorder to which Marvall refers is effectively present in Baudelaire. The question, of course, is whether or not it is there in modernity. (And here there may have to be a departure from Benjamin in order to return Benjamin's larger concerns.) To be precise, with the Baroque, with the world of *Trauerspiel*, this chaos was at hand, it marked existence, it informed and formed the great works of literature and art that were organised around the theme of melancholia. Melancholia could not subdue disorder; all it could do was hold it in place.

In his famous 'Le Peintre de la Vie Moderne', Baudelaire brings together the transitory and the permanent:

> Modernity is the transitory, the fugitive, the contingent, half of which is art, and half the eternal and immutable.[14]

The fugitive is a central theme in Baudelaire – after all, in 'À une Passante' beauty is presented – perhaps even personified – as *'fugitive beauté'*. And yet, the force of the juxtaposition of the transitory and the eternal would demand an explication in terms of the inscription of one into and onto the other. The eternal has lost its force. It is thus that with this loss – the wearing away of the eternal's hold – the question of allegory would have to be posed at its most insistent. Baudelaire begins by holding open that which the full force of modernity will close. Modernity will close up the actual dislocation that yields its specificity. It is this difficult set up that needs to be pursued. With it, the specific nature of the modern will emerge.

Given within that type of enforcing presence that denies dislocation, the location of the modern will nonetheless take on the force of a different form of separation. Here the point at issue involves the following constitutive elements. As a beginning, the initial and fundamental element is that part of the process of dislocation that marks modernity. At the same time, this process generates the particular movements of continuity that themselves provide the temporality of progress or historicism. In turn, this yields its own conception of dispersion and a general lack of place. Hence Heidegger, for example, when writing of 'homelessness', writes both of the present, i.e. of a specific formulation of the epochal present, while also evoking a conception of dispersal that will have been given by the structure of conti-nuity. It is thus that in his work both the explicit as well as the implicit critique of historicism – understood in more general terms as a form of continuity – does not yield particularity. It demands a thinking of another sense of continuity, the continuity given by thinking the always present propriety of being. In other words, rather than a philosophical critique of continuity generating a thinking of particularity in and of itself, it generates another sense of continuity, precisely because it is done in the name of such a continuity. Moreover, the presence of historicism understood as continuity will still generate its own sense of particularity and thus of the excluded. With Heidegger, particularity is sustained as that which is unable to belong to a whole. This point is dramatically present in Heidegger in terms of the specific conception of language through which a people speak being. What would count as being part of a people, as being able to belong, would be delineated by the unity given by the identification and the self-identification of a people as a people by the taking over of a particular task. Once there is the move from a people to the specificity of human finitude, it becomes clear precisely what finite individuals have to embrace in order to belong to the people and thus to form part of that process in which the destiny proper to the people is to be realised. Such distinctions find their philosophical force in terms of what Heidegger calls ontological difference.

It is in terms of such a conception of unity or continuity that it is possible to overcome that particularity – either disparate language users forging a community of the disparate, or identifications of being with that which lies outside its proper domain – that marks the everyday. Even though the everyday becomes the site in which the temporality of historicism is played out, for Heidegger, as has already been noted, this takes place in terms of a more fundamental sense of propriety. Indeed, it is this more fundamental sense that provides the link holding together the All by generating that which is positioned outside as well as inside. (There is no point positing the everyday as though it were an instance of that which insisted prior to its being thought. The everyday is a conceptual moment that continues to be positioned by the differing philosophical positions that posit it as other than the abstract, conceptual or even the historical.)

Emerging here is the possibility of identifying the difference between the Baroque and modernity. Their presence demands resisting any conflation in which, as moments within historical time, they could come to be identified. Perhaps the best single moment announcing their difference is marked by the presence of the word *Erwachen* in Benjamin's writings. It figures in a number of entries in 'Konvolut N' of the *Passagen-Werk*.[15] Usually it is present as a final word, almost as though it had been added on. In order to indicate the necessity of this term, though equally the necessity of what this term designates in relation to the nature of historical time and thus in relation to thinking of the present – i.e. the epochal present – within Benjamin's own work, its movement – the necessity for and the process of 'awakening' – will be traced through parts of Benjamin's own analysis of fascism. This analysis bears on modernity because the analysis is made possible by modernity's own particularity, namely the effacing of dislocation as that which is generated by modernity's own self-grounding and thus founding dislocation. Fascism remains as what modernity's own founding particularity may continue to allow.

Why is there the need for an awakening? Any answer to this question must begin with the recognition that not only will there be a conception of awakening that is proper to modernity in the precise sense that it will be linked to that experience yielding modernity's own propriety, but that there will be another type of awakening which will efface modernity's particularity because it will be situated within the flow of continuity and will thus be explicable in terms of the temporality of historicism. It must be remembered that this second occurrence is not antithetical to modernity. In other words, it is not anti-modern. Rather, it is precisely that effacing movement generated by modernity itself. The necessity to distinguish between forms of shock opens up a path that, in the end, will demand recourse to the language of authenticity.

TIME AND TRAGEDY: ANALYSING FASCISM

As should be clear from Benjamin's own writings, time is not an adjunct. The critique of progress – as indicated in 'Thesis' XIII of 'On the Concept of History' – involves a critique of time. Furthermore, the point of departure for his critique of the Social Democrats' own response to fascism was based on their acceptance of the time of progress as naturalised time (what he will call elsewhere the 'vulgar naturalism of historicism' [N 2, 6]; it is precisely this set up that is captured by Benjamin in 'Thesis' VIII). The language used displays an emphatic rhetorical force.

> One reason why fascism has a chance is that in the name of progress its opponents treat it as an historical norm. The current amazement [*Das Staunen*] that the things we are experiencing are 'still' possible ['*noch*' *möglich*] in the twentieth century is not philosophical. This amazement is not the beginning of knowledge – unless it is the representation of history [*die Vorstellung von Geschichte*] which gives rise to it that is untenable.

It is worth pausing here to identify the role philosophy is playing in this description. As a beginning, what is offered is a diagnosis of the way in which the opposition to fascism has been advanced. The expression of amazement is a disquiet at the way in which political life is progressing. It is as though the response expresses amazement at the fact that what is out of line with a progressive improvement in civilised life is actually taking place within that very form of gradual development. The aberrant nature of fascism is defined – and thus muted – by its incorporation into the temporality of progress. After having made this claim, Benjamin suggests that being amazed in this way is 'not philosophical' (*kein philosophisches*).

Here, it as though Benjamin is alluding to Aristotle, and in so doing, allowing for a repositioning of the philosophical in response to fascism. In the *Metaphysics*, there is the famous linking of amazement to the advent of philosophical thinking:

> For it is owing to their wonder that men now and at first began to philosophise.
>
> διὰ γὰρ τὸ θαυμάζειν οἱ ἄνθρωποι καὶ νῦν καὶ τὸ πρῶτον ἤπζαντο φιλοσοφεῖν
>
> (982b, 8–12)

There is a tradition of translating the Greek to θαυμαζειν by the German *Staunen/Erstaunen*. Benjamin's position is that, in contradistinction to the Aristotelian heritage, the shock generated by finding fascism at odds with progress does not generate a form of knowledge providing the basis of philosophical thinking – the exception being, of course, that move in which philosophical thinking (here 'knowledge') was directed at showing the untenable nature of that conception of historical time which, in turn, had generated this non-philosophical state of being astonished. What is revealed by these lines is twofold. On the one hand, it opens up a place for the philosophical in determining how the response to fascism is to be thought. The demand concerns time. On the other hand, it indicates that, despite any surface similarity, there will be a thoroughgoing distinction between this conception of 'amazement' and the process that is presented by this positioning of the word *Erwachen* ('awakening') at the end of a number of the entries in 'Konvolut N'. In the latter there resounds the terminology of both Marx and Proust, while the former expresses no more than petit bourgeois apprehensions. What is involved in both the passages is *Erkenntnis* ('knowledge'). It is worth recalling the formulation of this knowledge in the first entry of 'Konvolut N'.

> In the fields with which we are concerned knowledge [*Erkenntnis*] exists
> only in lightning flashes. The text is the thunder rolling long afterward.
>
> (N 1, 1)

Furthermore, it is possible to go a stage further and rescue shock from that set up in which it has been rendered banal. Shock cannot be an intentional misgiving, no matter how genuine it may be. Shock – more accurately, perhaps, what could be designated the structure of shock – demands a necessarily different formulation. The structure of shock defers intentionality by its inherent connection to experience. As a structure, it demands the presence of a revealing dislocation. It is thus that a link can be drawn between shock and the dialectical image insofar as the latter will be linked to a form of transformative experience. Not only will it involve a transformation or dislocation, but it will reveal that the temporality of continuity, and thus of the always the same, is a naturalisation of time occurring within and thus as an integral part of modernity.

> It is the unique property of dialectical experience to dissipate the
> appearance of things always being the same. Real political experience is
> absolutely free from this appearance.
>
> (N 9, 5)

The interconnection between real political experience and the dislocation founding modernity is deployed in the analysis of fascism.

Later in the same text, Benjamin broaches the question of what he describes as 'revolutionary historical consciousness':

> A phrase which Baudelaire coins to describe the temporal consciousness
> of someone intoxicated by hashish can also be applied to the definition
> of revolutionary consciousness; he speaks of an evening in which he is
> absorbed by the effects of hashish: However long it appeared to
> me . . . it nevertheless seemed that it had only lasted several seconds, or
> in fact that it has not taken place in eternity.
>
> (N 15, 1)

What is immediately striking about this passage is the relationship that it establishes between consciousness (though equally experience) and time. Baudelaire's description of time is of a moment that has been wrested from time. The time from which it has been taken is, of course, the time that is measured by the movement of clocks. In contrast, the expanse – the distance that is measured – can be contracted into the moment. This set up is described elsewhere in 'Konvolut N' as 'thinking reaching a standstill'. At this particular point, what appears is 'the image'. This image will be described, finally, as the 'caesura in the movement of thought' (N 10a, 3). It is vital to note that what is being described in this latter passage is the 'movement of thought'. The caesura is irreducibility linked to the process of awakening. It will be as though the same sundering sounds in each. This movement has its own temporal description. Describing it would involve a reiteration of the above formulation pertaining to consciousness, since what 'revolutionary historical conscious-ness' occasions is that particular break or dislocation identified as the caesura. Indeed, it is possible to go further and suggest that what is at work here is the possibility of delimiting a politics of the caesura. The subsequent development of this argument establishes a connection between this form of politics and experience or consciousness. In other words, a politics of the caesura takes experience as the point of intervention. In order to indicate why such a poli-tics is not straightforwardly voluntaristic, reference will need to be made to the particular moment at which Benjamin begins to identify the task of the writer or historian. Both need to be understood as commentaries on the famous closing line from 'Thesis' VII that the historical materialist 'regards it as his task to brush history against the grain'.

Such a task is a possibility that is given with the famous and often cited passage from 'The Work of Art in the Age of its Mechanical Reproducibility' concerning the effect of 'theses' on the development of art under what is described as the 'present conditions of production'. The emphasis on the present is not a simple reiteration of the indispensability of the conjunctural but, more exactly, the way in which an insistence on the present can effect an opening up of time by denying the naturalisation of time or by exposing conti-nuity as the result of a process of naturalisation. The passage in question is the following. It begins by indicating the possible role played by such 'theses'.

They brush aside a number of outmoded concepts, such as creativity and genius, eternal value and mystery – concepts whose uncontrolled (and at present [*augenblicklich*] uncontrollable) application would lead to a processing of data in the fascist sense. The concepts that are introduced into the theory of art in what follows differ from the more familiar terms in that they are completely useless for the purposes of fascism. They are, on the other hand, useful for the formulation of revolutionary demands in the politics of art.[16]

Leaving aside the success (or otherwise) of a strategy that intends to allow for this conception of the dysfunctional to emerge, what is significant here, given the particularity of the function, is that Benjamin's intervention into the present is not utopian. He has already dismissed conjectures concerning the art of a yet to be realised society. Rather, what predominates is the refusal to allow for the incorporation or reincorporation of a specific moment of thinking. The timelessness (albeit the putative timelessness) of 'creativity', 'genius' and 'eternal values' reveals them to be concepts which are 'outmoded' once attention is paid to the concepts and categories demanded by the advent of film. It should be added that while film can always be re-absorbed into a dominant aesthetic tradition, and furthermore that if attention were paid merely to content, then the specificity of film would come to be denied. Nonetheless, the particularity of film – what film demands in order that the particularity of its being film is maintained and not elided under the general heading of either the visual or cultural sign – holds it apart from the repetition of, and that is to say the operation of, the dominant tradition.

What is at work here is the connection between fascism and tradition. Understood temporally, tradition has allowed fascism to arise unchecked insofar as these 'outmoded' concepts have been utilised by its own project. It is worthwhile recalling here that Benjamin's own analysis of fascism outlined in his review of Jünger's *Krieg und Krieger* identifies the interconnection of the eternal and the present, a connection importantly mediated by war, as being fundamental to fascism.[17] This particular set up can be pursued in greater detail by taking up the concerns exemplified in a description from another section from 'Konvolut N'. While containing no reference to fascism as such, it is a description which can, nonetheless, be understood as presenting a distinction between conventional historicism (which is, simply put, the inexorable movement of time, incorporating and holding what are taken to be historical events, for example, Ranke's real events of history) and a more complex construal that brings with it the motifs, both temporal and historical, already identified as part of fascism's project:

> It is inevitable that the concept of progress should run up against the critical theory of history, the moment that progress was no longer presented as a measure of specific historical changes, but rather as a

measure separating a legendary beginning from a legendary end of history.

(N 13, 1)

While the contrast will be only momentarily dramatic, it is instructive, nonetheless, to contrast this claim with the following extract from a speech made by Hitler in the summer of 1937. The speech was given at the inauguration of *The Great Exhibition of German Art*. This particular exhibition took place at the same time as the *Degenerate Art* exhibition. The intention of the former exhibition, the occasion for Hitler's speech, was to demonstrate the inherent greatness of German art. (The juxtaposition of the two exhibitions was itself intended to be instructive. Retrospectively, it was far more instructive than could ever have been intended.) Benjamin and Hitler, then, were writing almost contemporaneously. Perhaps this occurrence, plus the nature of the contrast, indicates a complexity within time, a complexity that makes it always more than the passage of moments in the calendar.

> Until the moment National Socialism took power, there existed in Germany so-called 'modern art', that is, to be sure, almost every year another one, as the very meaning of this word indicates. National Socialist Germany, however, wants again a German art, and this art shall and will be of eternal value, as are all truly creative values of people. . . . We National Socialists know only one morality, and that is the morality of the people itself. Its causes are known to us. As long as people exist, however, it is the fixed pole in the flight of fleeting appearances. It is the being and the lasting permanence. And for this reason art as expression of the essence of the being, is an eternal moment.[18]

Hitler's speech invokes what can be called the 'language of legends' and thus maintains a necessarily mythic dimension. The importance of both legends and myths is that they allow for another description of the positing of a unified totality, one in which the totality is yet to be given a voice and, as a consequence, is yet to find a form of expression. The critique of the here and now at work within fascism – i.e. fascism's own reason for demanding a dislocation in which the present, fascism's own formulation of the epochal present, is identified as needing to be differentiated from itself – is structured around a construal of the present as a site of betrayal and abdication. The present is construed as being marked by an insistent loss and by the sustained denial of that particular responsibility which is demanded by the 'eternal'. (Precisely because this sense of loss has yet to determine the precise nature of the lost object – here the yet to be instantiated 'eternal' – there will be an important link between melancholia and fascism.) Fascism needs to be understood not

93

simply as a critique of the present, but as the other possibility within modernity. It becomes the possibility of realising a dislocation dictated by a posited externality, the realisation of which is still to come. To this extent, fascism is to be understood as futural.

Within fascist thinking, therefore, the 'eternal' becomes the structuring force of destiny. The precise nature of this eternality is complex. The most direct formulation that can be given to it involves two elements. The first is a sustained myth of origin that will necessitate the interconnection of soil and blood, i.e. the relationship between geography and race. What is mythic is an eternal presence. This opens up the second element insofar as eternality is linked, again necessarily, to the yet to be realised. As such this eternality sets the conditions for the future. It is perhaps possible to go further and suggest that the 'eternal' and the approach to it are essentially futural. The 'eternal' is effectively present. Not only is the eternal a key component in the way fascist thinking construes the present, but it also shows in what way time and politics are always interarticulated within any thinking of the epochal present. As such, of course, time and task are fundamental to the operation of fascism. Not only is there a political commitment; that commitment is justified by a particular stance taken within the philosophy of history. Fascism does not posit a 'golden age' that has somehow been lost. What it posits is the existence of that which has yet to be realised (or had yet to have been realised). Holding to the centrality of this 'yet to be . . . ' can be identified in the passage from Hitler's speech both in terms of its internal particularity as well as in regard to its externality. In the first case, it is the greatness of the 'people', while in the second, it is the greatness of the 'race'. Given that centrality has to be given to time and to the work of the present, comparing this formulation to Benjamin's own conception of that which arises at the present becomes central.

In 'On the Concept of History', a specific project is outlined. Within it not only does the interarticulation of time and task delineate the project of the present, but their connection reinforces the fact that it takes place at the present.

> In every epoch the attempt must be made anew to wrest tradition away
> from a conformism that is about to overpower it.[19]

An important question arises with this passage. In what way is the project identified here different from the Hitlerian and perhaps, therefore, from the fascist project? The initial point of intersection involves the relationship to the present. For Hitler, permanence – the 'fixed pole in the flight of fleeting appearances' – is the 'morality of the people'. The people can only be defined in racial terms. Their own purity – its realisation – is a historic possibility that the people themselves can take over. In taking it over, they then identify themselves as a people. This is, of course, the inherent populism within fascism. The appeal is to the people. It is an appeal that takes place in the name of the people. What the name names, however, is the eternal and yet to be realised dimension which correct naming will come to instantiate. In this instance, naming is the enacted presence of myth. The opening up and transformation of the present is essentially mythic. In specific terms, this occurs precisely because the projected transformation of the present depends upon a founding myth of origin. Once again, dislocation takes place in order to realise a potential continuity that had hitherto never been realised. Benjamin's position is, fundamentally, a demythologisation which does not take place in the name of another myth. The cessation of the work of myth, therefore, becomes the intrusion of the political into philosophy.

The attempt described by Benjamin 'to wrest tradition away' signals the necessity of that act which will disrupt continuity. 'Conformism' is another way of identifying naturalised time. The question that must be asked is the following: In whose name is wresting away being undertaken? Again it is a question of the name, and yet here, rather than having to delimit naming in relation to the eternal, the name will identify particularity precisely because there will have been no unity in whose name this activity could be undertaken. This is the move countering the mythic. Rather than attributing a unifying quality to race, nation, people, etc., they will have to be taken as names without an essence and hence as marked by an ineliminable irreducibility. The absence of the essence means that what is involved is a unity that will only ever be – precisely because, on one level at least, it always was – the belonging together of the different. It is not just that what is involved here is the complex relationship between class and nation. More exactly, it is the attempt to counter the possibility of an undifferentiated mass as being the agent of dislocation. Wresting away pertains, in the first instance, to the proletariat. Even if a more nuanced conception of conflict than the one provided by Benjamin will, in the end, have become necessary, it remains the case that the conflict marked by the presence of antagonistic class relations will have supremacy over the 'people'. With the people there will be the utilisation of the eternal present in the form of a founding myth of origin. Awakening and shock become, therefore, interventions within the terrain of myth. They are present as forms of demythologisation that work through experience. Moreover, rather than occurring within the bed of continuity such that they reveal an essential homelessness pointing to a futural being-at-home, they check that opposition between home and homelessness by yielding not just the specificity of dislocation that founds modernity, but modernity's own incorporation of a disequilibrium of power relations.

Giorgio Agamben provides a more than apposite formulation of what is being staged by Benjamin's conception of 'awakening'. Not only is it a position that rearticulates Benjamin's own undertaking, it brings with it a form of necessity. As will become clear, this necessity has a twofold force. In the first place, it is there on the level of content: changing the world. In the second, it is at work within the process of change itself. What this latter point means is that accompanying change is its own disruption of the place where it is articulated.

> Every conception of history is invariably accompanied by a certain experience of time which is implicit in it, conditions it, and thereby has to be elucidated. Similarly, every culture is first and foremost a particular experience of time, and no new culture is possible without an alteration in this experience. The original task of a genuine revolution, therefore, is never merely to change the world but also and above all to 'change time'.[20]

With considerable force, Agamben underscores the link between time and history that comes to be filtered through a thinking of the present. And yet what is also at work here is the recognition that even though there may be an authentic conception of time and thus an authentic conception of history, there is a necessary and enduring gulf between the authentic and the actual. As such, there is a return to that thinking conditioned by the ruin. The actual is neither a moment nor a part nor a particular instance of the work of the universal. The relationship between history thought authentically and the actual will not have been given in terms of the universal–particular relation, nor, moreover, will a conception of the All of history – the varying forms of the history of the absolute – condition and determine the nature of the particular. There will be a different sense of the particular. It is this point that has to be pursued if the role of the caesura is to be understood. It is a role that incorporates necessary particularity while also retaining that which has general force. It will be in terms of this formulation of the relationship between the general and the particular that it will be possible to reintroduce the problematic term 'universal history'. It is, after all, this term that is evoked by Benjamin in the *Passagen-Werk* in the following terms:

> The authentic concept of universal history is a messianic one [*Der echte Begriff der Universalgeschichte ist ein messianicher*]. Universal history as it is understood today, is the business of obscurantists [*Dunkelmänner*].
>
> (N 18, 3)

As this passage suggests, history – and here it is history as proper (*echte*) rather than authentic (*eigentliche*) and thus as not linked to the project of thinking the essence – is of necessity connected to a particular thinking of time. It is thus that there cannot be an easy evocation of history, as though there were history *tout court*. Universal history is linked to the messianic not in the sense of the finality of completing, but in the generalisability of thinking the interruption of the present. Interruption will become that act by which the nature of the dislocated will come to be revealed and the necessity of continuity to hold the present open will have emerged. Holding the present open is to work with the necessity of allowing and endeavouring to make occurrences and moments of the 'past' a concern for the present. As open, as held open, the present endures as inherently incomplete.

Holding to the demand of the present, i.e. Benjamin's conception of the epochal present, involves allowing for what has already been called the politics of the caesura. Here, this opening will not be a poetic form – a formal hiatus – but the counter-measure to myth. Moreover, this is not just a strategic moment; it is the opening – the effaced opening – that marks modernity. Working with the caesura entails holding to the necessary presence of the incomplete in the precise sense that a politics of the caesura allows for the reality of the present, while occasioning a more generalised philosophical response to that insistence in terms of maintaining an ontology and temporality of the incomplete. As has already been argued, repetition is the other term that is central to the realisation of this possibility. Holding open means allowing for another thinking of repetition. Iterative reworking will defer the hold of myth while refusing tradition the complacency of its own self-articulation as a repetition of the Same. The caesura allows for – is, perhaps – the otherness of the Same because it names the anoriginal otherness *within* the Same. Hence, for the Same to be the same as itself, it will always have to have been irreducible to itself. In being more, already more than one, it becomes the affirmed presence of the plural event.[21]

ABSOLUTE TRAGEDY: PRESENT IMPOSSIBILITY

Writing of absolute tragedy, Steiner concedes in the opening line that its instances are 'rare'. It will be essential to return to this word. Not because it will be necessary to equivocate over Steiner's examples of absolute tragedy – the accuracy or not of various examples is not the point – but because of the implicit conception of history that such a word brings with it. What will it mean for examples to have been 'rare'?

As has already been intimated, Steiner's sense of absolute tragedy is inherently connected to that which has already been identified as the 'crime' of having existed; and yet this is a very specific type of existence, one which Steiner works through with considerable care. Once they are given, examples lead, in the course of their being analysed, to the theological and thence to the possibility of salvation. However, while salvation may appear to be an option, such a possibility is found to be wanting. Absolute tragedy ends up in a position which Steiner describes as heretical and yet, whilst being almost inescapable, and thereby defining the age, it also works to define, by delimiting, the task of art. Once art is located at such a juncture, this also generates the conditions in terms of which he is able to judge. Steiner's conception of the age – namely the interplay of time, task and thus the epochal present – yields the site of judgement. This will, of course, be true despite the evocation within his writings of a certain thematics of universality.

The 'heretical' position identified by Steiner as a response to the presence of absolute tragedy, is the following:

> Absolute tragedy makes implicit or explicit the intuition that there can be, neither through a messianic nor a Christological coming, any reparation. There is no *felix culpa*, only the eternity of the fault and the cursed but eminent dignity of man's refusal either to forgive himself or to forgive the pain visited upon him.[22]

For Steiner, this position, as he succinctly argues, is not just heretical; more dramatically it 'sins against the Holy Ghost of hope'. And yet, even if this 'sin' is linked to the heretical, what would its opposite be like? In other words, against what is this position a heresy? It is in his response to this question that Steiner's deliberations take on their greatest urgency. In their absolute refusal of any easy compromise, his own unremitting questions open up what, within his conception of the present, will be that present's own unrelenting insistence. After having identified what he calls the 'tragic absolute' as that which 'can address or metaphorize a receding, an exhausted, a lamed deity', he then goes on to raise the question of the 'counter-measure'. In his terms, what this means is identifying the place of a form of questioning, part of whose force would lie in the need for it to have been posed 'today':

> Can the conventions of the raw material and the mythical which are axiomatic to tragedy be *quickened into life* where the problem, the question of God, is either that of his absence – whatever that may signify – or is a non-question, an atavism, a ghost of unreason?[23]

Once again, this can be read as part of an argument for a return to the conditions of tragedy. It would be a return that had walked through the world of despair. On one level, this is almost precisely the motif that has already been deployed in terms of the question of repetition. Within it, responding to the Shoah demands the question not of an end, but of how to go on. However, Steiner's argument is not concerned with repetition as continuing but with repetition almost as a type of reactivation. This position is formulated in terms of the concerns of tragedy being 'quickened into life'; to quicken would be to cause to be repeated. The question, therefore, will be the nature of the repetition. Expressed in terms of being 'quickened into life' obviates the question of how to continue by its articulating an opposition between mere continuing or having to dwell in the aporia of not being able to continue. The possibility of another repetition – that conception which arises from allowing for the opening yielded by having to continue without there being a already determined from within which continuity is possible – will distance the hold of the quick and the dead.

Responding to Steiner's formulation need not involve questioning either the viability or the applicability of what he identifies as absolute tragedy. Steiner's initial expression of absolute tragedy, namely in terms of having committed the 'crime of being', touches on one of the unavoidable questions within any attempt to understand both the Shoah and what has already been identified as 'mass death'. And yet there could be a point of differentiation since there need not be the necessity of having to locate this set up in between the absence of God on the one hand, and differing forms of nihilism on the other. Part of the argument to come concerning the poetry of Paul Celan – in particular the poem *Es ist alles anders* – and Daniel Libeskind's Jewish Museum in Berlin, are attempts to present these other possibilities. At this stage, the key issue concerns the more general question of what happens to tragedy once it is no longer assumed to be given within the in-between of theism and atheism. Answering this question will demand paying much closer attention to Steiner's formula 'quickened into life'. Addressed by this expression, precisely because of its emphasising survival and therefore of a form of repetition, is a possibility that could be harboured by any conception of history once there has been a departure from the twofold grasp of Ranke's 'facts' and historicism's temporality. Yet at the same time there would seem to be a complicating factor. It is this complication that must now be pursued.

For the most part, what is implicated in formulations of tragedy as given by the relationship between humans and the divine serves as an adequate description of the canonical moments of Attic Tragedy at least. Moreover, suggesting that myth forms an indispensable if not axiomatic element within tragedy is once again a claim that is for the most part viable. The difficulty emerges once it is thought to be possible to reposition these elements – to cause them, or to envisage them as having been caused to be given again, for example to allow for the animation of myth. (While it is not central at this stage, it nonetheless needs to be noted that such a possibility would, of necessity, leave the structure and content of myth unexamined.) What matters here is neither the viability of this possibility – myth's endurance – nor the potential pathos that would be occasioned by its failure. What remains central is the question of time. What is the conception of historical time through which, and thus also in terms of which, this giving has to take place?

This movement – giving as returning – almost has to presuppose that such return is possible, for if it were not then all that would remain is a world darkened by despair. However, this is not the central problem, since underlying this twofold possibility is the necessity that the very structure, temporality and ontology that has had to incorporate absolute tragedy will itself allow for this return. The necessity, in other words, that the return – the quickening – its possibility – is neither implicated nor plays any significant role in the causes of absolute tragedy, and that consequently there is no impediment to the successful operation or effectuation of this form of return. Not only must the tradition (complete, as it will have to be, with its own figures and mythology) not be implicated in absolute tragedy; whatever it was that marks out this form of tragedy could not figure in any way that would cast doubt upon the conception of repetition – a repetition of the Same – in which what was involved was the quickening into life of that which a certain version of modernity had made moribund.

Within the framework of this argument, secularisation has been positioned, as that which enacted the demise of tragedy. And yet, for Steiner, responding to the presence of absolute tragedy – its imperative – involves either overcoming the secular or plunging once again into the place of absolute despair. That this is not the choice is an argument that derives a significant part of its force from the fact that both poles of this position depend upon the capacity to separate the conditions for absolute tragedy from what enables its presence to be lived through. However, once it is argued that what would be needed in order to respond to this position is a resurgence of theology and mythology, then not only are they divorced from the conditions of absolute tragedy, but their return will have to be staged across a certain conception of historical time. They will be 'quickened into life' through time. The time in question will have to be an empty medium, untouched by the conditions generating absolute tragedy. Once again, it is essential to allow for the failure of this resurgence. The negative pole must also be given credence. Nonetheless, even allowing for the failure of such a resurgence, that failure would itself still be situated within a conception of historical time marked by a necessary neutrality. With failure there will still be the endless repetition of what there is. The return of the conditions for tragedy – the gift of theology and mythology – will only work as counters, as providing the 'counter-measure', if their realisation will have been untroubled by the work of time as well as by that which works time.

When Steiner identifies examples of absolute tragedy, describing these instances as 'rare', the concentration is on the examples, not on their setting. Citing works by Sophocles, Euripides, Marlowe, Shakespeare, Racine, Shelley, Büchner and Beckett, there is the evidence of a certain theme, its repetition providing whatever generic hold absolute tragedy has. Holding hard against the provision of hope, these literary moments will stage an enduring universal theme. It is its very universality, however, that will, in the end, efface the urgency that came to be given to the initial formulation of the absolutely tragic. While, in the period of the Shoah, the Jew and the Gypsy may have 'committed the crime of being', and while the site had some particularity, the crime had been committed before, such that they were only acting out an already present generic possibility. (This does not obviate the crime; rather, it removes the possibility of its having provided the point of intersection between a thinking of the present and modernity.) Consequently, the real particularity of the occurrence that is their setting – the Shoah – is incorporated within the hold of genre and thus articulated within the temporality of genre's own untroubled repetition, namely the repetition of the Same. What this means is that, within the formulation of absolute tragedy, there is the systematic failure to allow for the possibility that the Shoah could have had a determining effect on how its own presence within thinking is to have taken place.

Once the determining ground of time is allowed to be central, once this is mediated by the hold of particularity, then the force of absolute tragedy as formulated by Steiner begins to fold. Eschewing the problematic presence of time and the insistence of the particular, all that remains is a resurgent universality. It is, of course, precisely this universality that will have been checked by the presence of the Shoah: the Holocaust within thinking.

CODA

It is not as though it would ever have been possible to escape the concerns of tragedy. The word harbours the present. Also harboured by it, however, is the structure of historical time that will have to be resisted if the particularity of the present, the locality given by the interrelationship between modernity and the present, is to hold sway. Benjamin's insistence on the specific has a twofold exemplarity. First, because it demands that what is specific be presented outside of the hold of a universal–particular relation; second, because the setting of modernity – the founding dislocation present in its being effaced – demands the excision of the universal if its own determinations are to be taken over. Tragedy is left, therefore, as marking the enduring presence not just of a generic universality, but of the temporal neutrality within which the genre would have to be repeated. Escaping the concerns of tragedy would mean escaping the hold of the universal. And yet it is, of course, its presence that is the mark of modernity, because recourse to tragedy is an integral part of the movement effacing dislocation. Holding tragedy to one side is to allow for – precisely because it will have to be – an instance of the awakening or the shock yielding the particularity of modernity itself. Holding tragedy in this way is to allow for the 'lightning flashes'. Writing after their presence is the still distant thunder: a redolent silence voicing the present.

5

THE ARCHITECTURE OF HOPE
Daniel Libeskind's Jewish Museum

The question of remembrance works to bring historical concerns into the present. Understood as part of the project of building, commemoration works to make the presence of the historical in the present an actual problem by occasioning an architecture of remembrance. Formulated in this way, it becomes a problem of the present and thus one with necessary concrete determinations. While this formulation brings with it a certain accuracy, and while it allows for a distinction to be drawn between general concerns and specific places and practices, it leaves unaddressed the way in which remembrance, the historical and the present may be interrelated in such a way that they bear on each other. Here the concerns are specific. The Shoah resulted in the death of six million Jews. As part of what occurred, swathes of Europe — countrysides and towns — were stripped of their Jewish population. Throughout Europe little was done by other inhabitants to stem the attempt — a German attempt aided actively or passively by local populations — to make Europe 'free' of Jews.[1] How then within a European city, within a German city, within Berlin, is it possible today to acknowledge the now predominantly absent Jewish population? [2] How is it possible today to acknowledge their contribution while acknowledging in Berlin a certain local complicity with that annihilation on the part of its non-Jewish residents? How are Jews commemorated? This final question is in part an architectural one; after all, it is architecture that conserves.

When taken in conjunction with all the other questions, what arises is the need to think the relation between an architecture of commemoration and remembrance and the inevitable occurrence of that architecture as being a concern for today. What is the thinking appropriate to this day, once the day and thus the present are allowed a resonance that is no longer given by the simple interplay of dates and genres but has to allow for complexity? In what way has the Shoah delivered a call upon thinking that determines the nature of thinking today, of thinking this day, today, the present? It is thus that there can be no such thing as mere memory or simple remembrance. James Young has captured the detail of memory and signals its ineliminable link to the present in the suggestion that, with the Shoah,

> [w]e should also ask to what ends have we remembered. That is, how do we respond to the current moment in light of our remembered past? This is to recognise that the shape of memory cannot be divorced from the actions taken on its behalf, and that memory without consequences contains the seeds of its own destruction.[3]

With any consideration of remembrance in its connection to Jews, it is not necessary to begin with absence. It is not as though Christian Europe has not acknowledged its Jewish residents. And here it is by no means essential to allude either to ghettos or to places of expulsion and pogroms; the urban geography of, for example, Venice and York are not in this instance the issue.[4] Christian Europe has inscribed its Jews within sculptured forms and philosophical and literary presentations. Emphasis, however, must be given to the possessive – its Jews – since what is involved is Europe's Jews and not a concern with the Judaism that may be proper to Jews. There are different registers of concern. It may be, therefore, that the concern to commemorate – the project of remembrance – will have to involve a radically different thinking, plus a fundamentally different conception of the architectural, than that which is already linked to the project of annihilation. This will be true even in those cases where the link may appear tenuous and not marked by logical necessity. After all, how could a sculpture be connected to let alone be part of what occasioned the programme of annihilation? Could a sculpture entail the Shoah? What is initially striking about these questions is their apparent absurdity. Sculpture could not have been implicated in annihilation. And yet, despite the difficulties it generates, the question retains a hold. Part of that hold resides in the fact that it remains as a possible question. Any attempt to understand that possibility will involve a return to the present because the question's purchase opens up more than can be accounted for by a return to history understood as the passage of occurrences. Allowing this question its possibility – even if only because it marks an ineliminable suspicion – will necessitate confronting the problem of what it is that plays a determining role in the present; a problem whose acuity resides in the fact that the question of understanding cannot be withdrawn from the present itself. Philosophy, in other words, is already implicated in the activity that it seeks to describe.

As a way into the issues raised here, two figures will be taken. The first will be the allegorical figure of the Jew that stands on Strasbourg Cathedral. The second is the project to build an extension – a Jewish extension – to the Berlin Museum. The extension is the work of architect Daniel Libeskind. The project and thus the building is known officially as the *Extension to the Berlin Museum with the Jewish Museum Department*. The import of its being an 'extension' (*Erweiterung*) will need to be pursued. Nonetheless, as both these works can be attributed the status of figures, it is possible to begin with the work of each figure. And yet *figure* has neither a single nor a simple determination. Rather than taking the figure as given unproblematically to interpretation, emphasis will be given to the figure's work and thus to the question of what it figures. What figures, therefore, is action rather than substance, the actative in lieu of the substantive.

THE CATHEDRAL

On the cathedral in Strasbourg, there is a statue usually described as the allegorical figure of the synagogue. To understand the figure, to understand its position as a figure, will be to grasp the twofold determination that provides the image of the Jew within Europe; the allegory, or rather its stone enactment, figures Christian Europe's Jews. There are many ways of tracing the work of this positioning. It would be equally as possible to start with Sartre's laudable though in the end problematic presentation of the pitiable Jew in *Réflexions sur la question Juive*, as it would to start with Hegel's argument in the long note to §270 of the *Philosophy of Right* in which it is argued that it would be wrong to exclude the Jews from civil society. For not only would that 'confirm the isolation of which they have been reproached', it would, and perhaps more interestingly, deny the fact that in Hegel's terms the Jew is a 'person with rights' (*rechtliche Person*).[5] The first of these formulations positions the Jew as victim. It would be almost as though the Jew were in essence a victim. Sartre addresses the 'authentic Jew'. However, the second is able to overcome the position of victim as Jews are in Hegel's formulation 'above all men' (*sie zuallererst Menschen sind*). Hegel's formulation is of great interest. He argues against the position that being a Man is an abstract quality on the basis that to be a Man is to be someone who feels themselves to have rights. The capacity for feeling is, of course, universal, and as such what it does is efface the particularity of Jew in favour of a more fundamental and perhaps primordial position. Jewish being is replaced by *Selbstgefühl*.

In his *Réflexions*, Sartre is concerned to delimit the specificity of being a Jew, the identity of that being. This position is articulated in terms of authenticity. 'Jewish authenticity consists in choosing oneself as Jew, that is to say, in realising one's Jewish condition' (166). This condition is the one in which the

Jew is positioned as 'segregated, untouchable, shamed and proscribed'. For Sartre, the Jew knows the inevitability of being positioned in this way and 'as such he asserts himself' (*c'est comme tel qu'il se revendique*) (166). As authenticity and the assertion of identity are constrained as well as defined by this position, for Sartre the Jew will reject universality in order to live out particularity.[6] While Sartre's Jew rejects universality in order to remain a Jew, Hegel's has to give up the particularity of Jewish being in order to attain citizenship in order then, perhaps, to reclaim another Jewish identity. This time, of course, it would be a secondary identity, the identity of being a Jew. Indeed, both Sartre and Hegel can be taken as addressing the identity of being a Jew. It will be in relation to this attribution of identity – a relation that must involve an acknowledgement of, but at the same time a profound divergence from, this set up – that it will become possible to take up the question of Jewish being.

These two positions, here no more than tersely sketched, position the Jew around universality. It is the nature of this universality that must itself be questioned. Questioning it will necessitate that the statue – the allegorical figure of the synagogue – be brought into play. Initially, the statue needs to be situated within debates concerning iconoclasm. In its response to the imperatives against images and idols in *Exodus*, Judaism had not created its own image. It was the Word that came to be represented, represented as word. Nonetheless, due to the problematic presence of Judaism, for Christianity, this situation – the absence of icon – needed to be overcome. Michael Camille describes this diagnosis and its subsequent overcoming in the following terms.

> If Judaism had no image, the Christian Church would create one, in order to enact its destruction. This is Synagogue, constructed as an anti-image, a pseudo-idol specifically for the purpose of being toppled at the moment of crucifixion.[7]

While the overall accuracy of this formulation is considerable, what will need to be formulated in a more nuanced way is the status of destruction. While there are different ways of treating the band that covers her eyes, the subsequent blindness needs to be situated in relation to the role played by sight – both real and symbolic – in the Christian Bible. Sight is not simply linked to revelation; it also demands a correlative blindness. Here, blindness is equally real as symbolic. In both instances it demands refusal, an emphatic not-seeing. Blindness and sight were not part of a simple opposition. It is precisely this complex set of relations that is captured by, amongst others, Pascal in the *Pensées*. There the Jew's sustained lack of in-sight – sustained despite the fact that what was there to be seen is '*si clair*' – has a specific role. For Pascal, 'it is their refusal which is the foundation of our belief'.[8] The blinded Synagogue is linked to the Jew's blindness and refusal as portrayed in Pascal. It repeats, moreover, the reciprocity between blindness – symbolic blindness – and the viewed recognition of revelation as portrayed, for example, in the Fourth Gospel.[9] Sight demands that the blind remain as blind. Thus, the Jew is positioned by Christian thought *not* as the other, as though there were a simple opposition between same and other, but as involved in a relation of dependency that holds the Jew outside. It is the nature of this dependency which will mean that the destruction of the Jews – the continual actualisation of the project of annihilation – will involve that move in which the dependent object will have become abject. It is this relation that can be formulated in terms of what will be called the logic of the synagogue.[10]

What characterises this logic is that the Jew is acknowledged as providing the basis of the truth of Christianity, by providing what, for Christianity, became the Old Testament – the repository of prophecy – while at the same time affirming revelation by remaining blind to it. The Jew – the figure of the Jew, the Jew of Christianity since what is not being addressed is Jewish being – thus brings a certain necessity into play. In both instances, what is maintained is the Jew's particularity. First, Jews are particular in their having provided the possibility of Christianity; second, their particularity is maintained by their having affirmed that possibility by failing to see. It is because of this failure that the Jew is maintained as blind. It is their affirmation that, in being turned back on the Jews, positions them as outside of Christianity, while sustaining them as Christianity's outside, its other. They become the other within a relation of dependency. Again, this introduces a necessary disequilibrium of power into the self–other relation, reiterating, thereby, the fact that otherness will always have been more complex than the positing of the self–other relation usually assumes.

The presence of the relation of dependency coupled to this disequilibrium of power has significant consequences. Once dependency is recognised – be this recognition conscious or unconscious – it demands the expulsion of the dependent. In sum, the dependent has to be excluded. Expulsion and exclusion will necessitate a violence that can only be sanctioned to the extent that the object becomes, or has become, abject. What is abject demands, by its very nature, to be expelled. Consequently, in order to overcome dependency there will be the need for that final expulsion that would rid Christianity of its relation of necessity to the blind Jew. This move is actualised in the politicisation and related secularisation of the nature of this subject–object relation. Given the continual move from object to expulsion, a move that is necessarily mediated by the object becoming abject, it becomes possible to rewrite the place of the Jew within Christian Europe as the continuity of the becoming-abject. (Universality, and the move to integration, which is an elimination of particularity, become the other moves within the becoming-abject.) In sum, therefore, it is possible to read the development of Christian–Jewish relations in these terms. Again, it should be emphasised that these are not relations positioned from within Judaism but from within Christianity's hold on Judaism. The point that needs to be underlined is that the Judaism it yields is one in which the Jews were positioned – as Jews – within the process of becoming-abject. Even though this is an obviously abstract claim it will allow the particular and the specific greater force than that which would arise from treating each instance in terms of an apparent lack of humanity, a lack whose overcoming would be the inevitable work of progress. There is more, therefore, to the becoming-abject of the Jew than the denial of autonomy which yields, as its counter-measure, the need to espouse greater autonomy. The logic of the synagogues operates in a completely different way. Abjection is necessitated by a relation of dependency.

And yet abjection cannot be taken to exist *tout court*. Hence the reference to becoming. The passage to abjection is mediated by universality. On the one hand, there is the refusal of universality. But such a move does no more than normalise the universal and rid it of its posited relation of dependence on the other. On the other hand, there is the acceptance of universality. Again, this leaves the nature of the universal unquestioned. Moreover, it will allow for particularity only in the most fragile of ways. In *The Merchant of Venice*, Portia's final revenge was, after all, the insistence that Shylock give up his Jewish identity: the identity that would allow for, and which was also the consequence of, Jewish being. The law that allowed him, despite particularity, equality before the law – the most elementary form of universality – was also that which had the power to strip him of that particularity, rendering him merely the same. If universality were thought to have provided the possibility of escape from the continual work of the becoming-abject, its failure will be all the more profound since it emerges, as was suggested above, from the recognition that such an appeal was already incorporated into the process of abjection.

The allegorical figure of the Synagogue is a work of sculpture. As a work of art, even as a figure, it is neither anti-semitic nor merely neutral. Such terms have little force when what is in play is understanding the way in which a particular figure works. The band on the figure's eyes which marks her stubborn blindness cannot be suddenly lifted. It is not as though the Jew can, *qua* Jew, come to see. Moreover that band – the banderol as figure – must endure in order that the function allocated to and demanded of the blindness be maintained. Jews cannot come to see. They have no sight. This is what figures.

Pursuing the logic of the synagogue, and in pursuing it allowing that logic to mediate the question of universality, can be taken a step further by taking up the question of Jewish identity. Identity here is the identity of being a Jew, not the identity proper to Jewish being. The nature of the difference between these two modes of existence resides in the particularity of those for whom the question of identity is a question. Once the ascription of identity comes in the form of a gift – a gift whose defining scope allows neither for a simple refusal nor complete destruction – it limits the Jew by its bringing with it the intention that Jews, in order to be Jews, would then have to live out the expectations and possibilities that have been created. In other words, it would only be by living out the identity that was given that it would be possible for the Jew to remain a Jew. (The fact that this is not the case and that there remains a continual struggle between the affirmation of identity and the necessity of having to encounter the identity that is given, attests first to the viability of the distinction between the identity of being a Jew and Jewish being, and second to the need to work through the mediation of this distinction.)

In forming both sides of the opposition within which universality works, Sartre's 'authentic Jew' and Hegel's 'citizen first Jew second', have the question of identity closed off to them. The question of identity can no longer be asked because the question has already been answered. Once the question is answered – and here it must be remembered that the question is answered from outside and, in being answered, placed the Jew within the logic of the synagogue – the structure of the question, a structure with its own inherent temporality, is necessarily eliminated. The becoming-abject will always pertain to the identity of the Jew, where that identity is taken as bearing no real relation to Jewish being. (Parenthetically this may also be the site of Jewish self-hatred.) The point of intersection between these two ways of posing the question of identity resides in the fact that taking up the question of Jewish being will entail having to allow the logic of the synagogue a place within it, in the precise sense that part of the question of Jewish being will be its relation to the ineliminable historical presence of that logic's work. This becomes an even more emphatic necessity when what is at stake is the attempt to think the relation between the Shoah and the question of Jewish being. It is both the necessity of that thinking coupled to that in terms of which it is to take place which may signal the inescapable possibility of a post-halachic Judaism. In other words a Judaism that maintains the question of Jewish being as a question. As will be suggested, it is the role of the question – the temporality and ontology of the question – that will play a central part in distinguishing between these two figures; the statue of the synagogue on the cathedral in Strasbourg and the Extension to the Berlin Museum.

In a more general philosophical sense what is involved here is the way in which specific concrete architectural forms can – in their effectuation, in their coming to presence, and thus in their actual structuration – involve the differential, though nonetheless interarticulated presence of what can be identified as the ontologico-temporal.[11] Here, since, as was suggested, the work's work is positioned in relation to the temporality of the question – in relation, that is, to different temporalities of the question – accounting for that difference can no longer take place in terms of signification. It has now to take place in terms of the ontology and temporality of the question. What this signals is that the centrality of work will admit, from the beginning, fundamental distinctions that will preclude the essentialising of work. It will be vital to return to this point.

THE MUSEUM

What then of the Extension? The Berlin Museum – a museum incorporating and thus dealing with the history of the city of Berlin – needed an extension to incorporate its Jewish past. The position of the Extension is close to the intersection of Wilhelmstrasse, Friedrichstrasse and Lindenstrasse. It is, therefore, close to an area once populated by an important part of Berlin's Jews. The area around Lindenstrasse, perhaps the one that was most populated by Jewish residents, is of course still populated. It is not as though there is an absence, and yet there is clearly an absence. In the place of Berlin's Jews there is an other presence; others are present. Absence and presence cannot be exchanged as though they were counters in an elaborate game. Loss, and the addition that replaces the lost, cannot form part of a simple calculation involving numbers. Loss has to be represented. Its nature and cause delimit representation. They delimit it by raising the question of its limits. The difficulty – and it is a difficulty that exists as much for philosophy as it does for architecture – is how this representation is to be understood. The inescapable question concerns representation in the era of mass death.

Mass death brings with it determinations that cannot be incorporated by a simple adaptation of thought. Moreover, the place of mass death gives a specific turn to the question of remembrance. However, it should not be thought that memory is an unproblematic term in itself. There is a problem with memory. Part of what yields the problem is the impossible possibility of classical theories and conceptions of memory. Their limit emerges because of their inability to engage with the present. Even though, by its very nature, the museum always articulates a commitment to a particular determination within the philosophy of time – in general historicism articulated in terms of the inescapable and hence normalised presence of chronology – what has to be confronted with the Shoah is the presence of a unique determination. This occurrence, the Shoah (allowing the term a necessary and enduring resonance), needs to be situated in relation to the distinction between universal and particular. Particulars instantiate the universal; they are part of the universal; they maintain a connection such that with the particular the universal either can be found or assumed. Here the question that must be answered in relation to the Shoah concerns the possibility of its connection to an already given universal. Of what universal is the Shoah a particular? The absence of an immediate answer to this question will entail that, were it to be thought, thinking the Shoah must begin with particularity and thus with the unique.

As has been argued on several occasions, if it is possible to argue that the Shoah is unique, uniqueness must pertain not just to what took place, but equally to the relationship between occurrence and thinking. The challenge for the present, which is at the same time a challenge in the present and is thus part of the present's own proper concerns, is one of taking up the question of particularity. Taking it up yields a specific conception of the epochal present. Within the framework of the overall argument being developed here, what this means is responding to the demands of modernity. The question of memory will need to be situated with these concerns. Consequently, the analysis of memory as it is present in the texts comprising the history of philosophy will need to be rethought in relation to the effective presence of either their implicit or explicit conception of historical time. In such a thinking, the present will insist. Part of that insistence will be the detail of mass death. Detail emerges at the moment where numbers, despite the cumulative addition, the logic of addition, with each addition begin to add nothing. This is not simply the end of quantity; it is equally the stage in which the move away from quantity is necessitated. Yet the question of how that movement is to be understood, let alone precipitated, endures as a problem

The detail, with its absolutely necessary and inescapable presence (which is often taken to be the material of memory), causes the process of remembering to fall apart once that detail comes to be given centrality. Libeskind refers to the fact that it is possible to acquire a two-volume work – *Gedenkbuch* – from the German government. This book lists the names of all those who were deported from Berlin. It lists their name, their place of birth and the probable place and date of their death. Halfway through the first volume, the procession of names begins to lose meaning; the names have almost lost their power to name, let alone to represent. In grouping and holding the dispersal of Berlin's Jews, the volume names them. They are grouped in a way in which they would never have been grouped. Neither Synagogue congregation lists nor burial lists nor even a list of professions would have held them all. Berlin's Jews were, for a significant part, secular and assimilated. Their Judaism lay in what are usually described as cultural ties and affinities. Even a census that would have demanded the registration of religion could not have incorporated them all. Urban life is, in general, too varied and too cosmopolitan. Some would have married out, others would have disavowed their Judaism, still others may not have even known – or for that matter would not have cared to know – that they were Jews. It would have needed a special occurrence to bring all Berlin's Jews together and to allow them all – for the most part all – to be named. They came to be named in a book that marks their mass death. They can all be named insofar as the *all* who were named are dead. Naming may have here reached the point at which it no longer names. And yet these names do name. The search for a family name may reveal a name. What will emerge is the stark recognition that what is named is a loss. A life that was once incorporated into the book hovers at the site of an encroaching anonymity. Name upon name, name after name, one date of birth compared with another, will indicate that in certain instances no-one may have been left to mourn; an entire family, across the generations, all could have been deported, all may have died. It is the copresence of the nature of the loss and the name's gradual though inexorably diminishing power that forces architecture and philosophy to respond. The insistent presence of the Shoah must be taken as insisting at the present, and, in insisting there, as demanding a response at the present. Both allowing for this insistence and recognising the force of responding – of having to respond – work to strip the present of its feigned neutrality, since that insistent presence and its enjoined response will have become an integral part of the constitution of the present.

Questions will no longer have a simple generality. With the gradual diminution of the name's power to name, another aspect of naming will have come into play. An essential part of what the process of naming now names is this loss of power. It is not a loss that can be overcome by attempting to supplement what can no longer take place. The loss means that another form of remembrance will be necessary insofar as the inscription of names is inevitably caught up in the name's own vanishing power. It is thus that the inevitable question here concerns the limits of representation once it is linked to the concrete practice of remembrance and commemoration. What power does representation have in the era of mass death? How is commemoration to take place today? What here will remembrance have to be now? It goes without saying that these questions are as much philosophical as they are architectural.[12] While they take on different forms, the same questions keep returning. Once questioning begins to hold sway, the place of the question – the here and now of the question – will have to be given a determining role in any attempt to take up what is being asked.

Within these questions, there is what appears to be a level of generality that would need to be overcome before the specific practice of a single museum might be taken up. The specificity of the museum needs to be linked to the purpose of remembrance. (More pointedly, it can always be asked whether memory and the complex politics of remembrance may be used for another and thus a different end or purpose. It is this possibility that haunts what are known as Holocaust memorials.) Leaving to one side the delicate and difficult question of the rearticulation of remembrance beyond its own original concerns, it remains the case that the question of remembrance, of what remembrance will be at the present, still endures. It is possible to repeat the question: What, here, will remembrance have to be now? In its being repeated, it demands clarification. Two words within the question work, at the same time, to locate it and give it its obvious contemporary force. It is a question posed 'here'; equally it is a question posed 'now'. 'Here' will be Berlin. 'Now' will be the present, today. How is the 'here', and with it this 'now', to be understood? Their interarticulation is already presupposed.

Answering the question of the interarticulated presence of the 'here' and 'now' can be undertaken by working through one of Libeskind's own descriptions of the Extension. Writing in *Between the Lines* – an essay containing some of the theoretical aspects of the project – he describes the project as seeking

> to reconnect the trace of history to Berlin and Berlin to its own eradicated memory which should not be camouflaged, disowned or forgotten. I sought to reopen the meaning which seems to be only implicit, and to make it visible. In terms of the city the idea is to give a new value to the existing context, the historical context, by transforming the urban field into an open and hope-oriented matrix.[13]

Prior to taking up these transformations it is worth noting that part of the transvaluation of the context resides in the fact that the Extension is not just a simple extension. It is not an element that is merely added on. Its relation is neither that of addition nor supplement. It does not work, therefore, to complement loss. Rather, the Extension enacts its relation to the whole in virtue of its mode of entry and its complex internal formation. A relation is being traced out rather than being that which is given; for the visitor, it is a relation that will have to be worked out and thus worked through. Consistent with what will be argued at a later stage, it works as an extension only to the extent that as the Extension it questions what an extension could possibly entail 'here' and 'now'. What is the link between extension and absence? Equally, what is the link between the Extension and annihilation? It was, after all, only the annihilation and the destruction of synagogues that yielded part of what will come to be displayed in the Museum.

Already present within the formulation of the here and now, and within the Extension, is the unpredictable architecture of the question. The structure of the open, where the open is taken to be a condition of the present – the caesura as already present – is repeated within this formulation and thus, as shall be argued in greater detail, within the Extension. Here, openness does not harbour the sham of a liberal architecture – the architecture of universality, albeit a putative universality. As with freedom, openness demands the complexity of relation. What marks out the specificity of the question is its temporality, the time that will be present in the structuration of the building. Within this argument, therefore, time will be taken as comprising an essential part of the building's work. Rather than its being an adjunct, the articulation of time will be central to the work of the Extension: not historical time – though that will have a determining effect – but built time. Built time is the temporality proper to the building's self-realisation: i.e. its work as a building.[14]

The transformations – to employ the word used by Libeskind – that are intended to be made (and it should be added they are transformations that pertain to the eventual – though now actual – structuration of the building) are linked, in his own formulation, to hope. Given Libeskind's use of the term 'hope', it is vital to acknowledge the presence of the counter-argument. Once again, would it not seem to be the case that hope is a condition of the future? And, therefore, would there have to be something for which hope was held? Linking hope to the future will demand a particular form of architecture. It would need to be an architectural practice that remained indifferent to the determinations of the present. Indifference would not give rise to only one form. Nonetheless, regardless of the formal considerations, the architectural programme would have to maintain spatial neutrality. Here, however, what is essential is the present. Consequently, another form of questioning will need to take place. Given that what is at stake is architecture, the questioning will turn on the possibility of an architecture of hope occurring within the present. While it may appear to be no more than a nuanced change, a distinction can always be drawn between openness to something such that openness is linked to a coming occurrence and thus to something that could take place in the future, and an already present openness in which the state of being open is not linked to a futural and thus hoped-for occurrence but is at work necessarily in and at the present. (As what is being reworked here is the present it will follow that the future can no longer maintain its own already given place.

The future will demand another thinking.) With this latter determination of the present, the condition of the future is already located in the present. Within architecture, what is hope at the present?

The answer to this particular take on the question of hope – what is hope at the present? – needs to be situated within this distinction. What is at work here is the structuring and, therefore, effective presence of time. While it may begin in an apparently simple manner – the temporality at work in the move from to be built, to being built, then finally to having been built – the time of building in fact admits of a far greater complexity. A building is not just built. Even in having been built it may always be yet to be completed. The 'yet to be . . .' must pertain at the same time as the 'having been'. The time of this at the same time is the site of the insistent presence of the complexity at work within the present. The question yields what, in more general terms, could be thought of as an architecture of the incomplete. It is thus that built time will have importantly different permutations.

And yet, of course, a building would seem to be complete once it is finished. From this position, in having been built the building is. In other words, in its having been built, it is in its being completed. The usual description of this state of affairs would be in terms of that which had been finished. In having been finished it is able to be used. Use and the varying possibilities open to the building once the building is understood as built and thus understood as finished, would themselves have already been delimited by the building as built. Quite literally, they would already have been built in. A change in the nature of the building and a related reallocation of function would demand a rebuilding, a transformation on the level of building. The finality that pertains here is linked to the interarticulated presence of *finished*, *end* and *function*. What has been built must function in a specific way. The building ends once the possibility of its end is realised. However, despite the language of ends, what has marked both the tentative presentation of Libeskind's undertaking thus far as well as the possibility of representation and remembrance in the era of mass death, is the question.

The temporality of the question eschews the interarticulation of end and function; even though the activity of building may have been finished, the question will endure. It has to endure for once it is closed off – once the answer to the question is constructed – then the question *qua* question will no longer insist. Here, it may be that what has been built is a question. With built time, the temporality in question is the temporality of the question. What this would mean is that which would be at work here is a building that guards the question of representation, refusing it finality and thus necessitating its retention as a problem to be investigated, while allowing at the same time for presentations; a building that questions display while allowing for display; a building that, in its effectuation as building, holds open the question of remembrance as question, enjoining humility while providing – because of the question – the necessity for a vigilance that can be identified as present remembrance. With this project there is the interarticulation of presentation, display and remembrance held within the question. Thus, both in terms of its actual specificity and its inherent temporality, the question works to maintain the present as incomplete. It is incomplete while being complete. The present is absolute only to the extent that it is yet to be resolved. The present cannot be complete unto itself because there is no 'itself' which will allow for that finality. This state of affairs – a caesura which is the norm rather than the project – is the structure of hope. Once it is allowed this structuring force, hope becomes part of the constitution of the present. It loses its mystical attachment to the future by its being held by the temporality of the question. There will always be answers, but not the answer that close off the question. It may be that the building – the Extension – has what Libeskind describes as a 'hope-oriented' matrix because it is an architecture of the question. What holds hope and the question together is on the one hand time, and on the other the present. Time and the present need to be worked through the building. Part of this work will be the already present mediation by the Shoah. Discounting or trivialising this mediation is the present form of nihilism in which forgetting always involves refusing the task that is given by the present. What will need to be done at this stage, therefore, is to return to the actual building. It will only be in relation to the building and thus to its architecture that it will become possible to take up the architecture of hope. Central to this return must be a description of the way in which its structure works around and includes a productive void, a void space that is always charged with absence. It will be here that the work of mourning will itself be transformed. The transformation will pertain to what happens to the structure of mourning once it is imbued with the present quality of vigilance.

Libeskind describes the relationship between the extension and the void in terms that will demand that the role of the negative be taken up.

> The new extension is conceived as an emblem where the not-visible has made itself apparent as a void, an invisible. The idea is very simple: to build a museum around a void that runs through it, a void that is to be experienced by the public. Physically, very little remains of the Jewish presence in Berlin. I thought therefore that this 'void' which runs centrally through the contemporary culture of Berlin should be made visible, accessible.

(67)

With the inscribed and insisting void – a void space that is always being encountered and which is inscribed into the structure, as part of the structure, as being part of the building's structuring force – its presence will insist, giving rise to the necessity that each exhibition, if not the policy of exhibition itself, will have to negotiate with it. On the one hand, the negotiation will take place between the visitors to the Museum and the building itself. Each visitor will have to confront the void – the place that holds the presence of absence – in viewing either the permanent or temporary exhibitions. On the other hand, curators will have to negotiate with the void in constructing and planning exhibitions. The void becomes, therefore, a productive absence. Encountering loss will occasion the possibility, here, in this instance, of a transformative experience. Neither the building nor the policy of exhibition therefore could ever be taken as a *fait accompli*.[15] The policy of exhibition – and with it the related politics of display – will always have to work in relation to the given. However, the given will be the negotiated space, the space to be negotiated. What this entails is that, by the very nature of its presence, the building cannot work to close off the question of display. The void that is to be encountered as an essential part of the building's work will work in relation to what will have to be displayed. The utopian and the futural as gesturing towards a museum to come – a museum of forgiveness and reconciliation – are ruled out by the structure of the building and by what the building will demand. Its demand is its work. One of the consequences of this demand is that the structure of mourning comes to be transformed by its having been incorporated into the present's determination, the determination that it presents. While explicating further the workings of the Museum – describing the gardens and the towers – remains an essential activity, it is still the case that each aspect of the Museum will combine in such a way as to hold the question in place while giving and presenting. Their combination will define the ambit of curatorial practice. Holding must here be allowed the dual determination of holding to – holding to the question – and holding back. The latter will reiterate the presence of the incomplete. The void, the workings of the building's own dynamic, effect a state of completion that holds back from completion.

Finally, at work here are two figures: the allegorical figure of the synagogue and the Museum. Their importance lies in the way in which they work, in what they allow to figure. In this instance, the question of what figures need to be taken in relation to the distinction – albeit a difficult and problematic distinction – between Jewish being and the identity of being a Jew. The point of such a return is that it will allow the question of identity to be refigured in terms of a question. It is as though it will take on the quality of a question. In the case of the synagogue, the question of Jewish identity had been answered and thus the structure of the question no longer pertained. Responding to the position cannot just involve the simple claim that, for example, there is no necessary link between Judaism and blindness, or even that Jews are not blind. There are two reasons for resisting such a move. The first is that within the history of anti-semitism there is such a link. It must be acknowledged. The second is that the response to the link cannot be a simple countering, a form of counter-positing. Attempting to counter the link by denying it is to accept that such a set up provides the frame of reference in which the question of identity is to be posed. It is not that the history of anti-semitism is not to be allowed to play a role in the question of Jewish identity. Rather, it is that this identity cannot be established as the consequence of the negation of the way in which Jewish identity is given within that history. As has been intimated, this is the basis of the distinction between the identity of being a Jew and Jewish being. With the latter, there is another way of taking up the question of identity. The way in question lies in the question.

Here, with the question, there is the possibility of drawing out the distinction between the two figures. The first closes off the question. On the other hand, in being an architecture of the question, the Museum allows identity to endure as a question; this is a way of interpreting what Libeskind may have meant by hope. What endures as a question is the nature of the Museum: the question of remembrance, the act of commemoration. While enduring as questions, there is still a museum: there is still remembrance, there will still be acts of commemoration. What endures, what still remains, the acts in question, takes place in the present. This is the possibility of the Museum in the present once the reality of the Shoah is acknowledged as part of the present. Moreover, it is the only possibility – a singular possibility that has no single predictable concrete form – for a Jewish museum. At work within these possibilities is the question of Jewish identity after the Shoah. It is at work within them because what is held in place is the reality and actuality of Judaism at the present. Whether or not those visiting the Museum are Jewish is irrelevant. What is of relevance is that the architecture can be situated within the concern of Jewish being insofar as what it holds in place is the link between being and questioning. Only by holding to the centrality of ontology, therefore, can the politics of the present – here, they are given the particular form of the question of identity and its connection to the practice of memory – have any real hold.

6

CONTINUING WITH POETRY
Celan and Jabès

THE PRESENCE OF HOPE

Hope is not awaited. On the contrary. Hope awaits. What gives this move its force is not the distinction between negation and assertion. Nor, moreover, is it to be located in the projected realisation of an end. Rather, it is that hope is taking place. It is continuous with the present. Hope awaits. It is the simplicity of this location that causes both site and sited to be denied. Hope pertains, pertaining at the present. What this means is that, within any attempt to take up hope, hope itself must figure in the enterprise that its name maintains. It is as though it could never lose sight of itself. Its site persists. Even its being taken up — when it is allocated a place within literature, philosophy, art, even when it is taken as founding an architecture — hope must always be more than that for which hope is held. In a sense, it will always be more because of the ineliminable insistence of hope's site. Thus, while always being incorporated into that which is to be hoped for — i.e. hope's end — hope will be more than an envisaged occurrence. This always more will involve the incomplete nature of the present which, in turn, is to be thought beyond the hold given by the interplay of plenitude and loss. Being already open, a present opening, will take the form of a plural event.

To reiterate this point of departure: with hope something else is enacted, something other than what is being hoped for. The question to be answered concerns how this other quality — that which is more, the insistent — is to be thought. This question involves the place of hope, its location. However, allocating centrality to the place of hope is not to promulgate the necessity for a type of conceptual geography. In this setting, place is linked to time. The inter-articulation of place and time resides in the formulation 'hope awaits'. In enacting this complex site, hope becomes another possible site in which time — time at the present — can come to be played out. Here, the time in question pertains to poetry. With poetry, time inheres in openings, in the complex presence and relation of words, in repetition and, therefore, in versification as

119

well. The identification of such a site restricts the force of having to concede to the presence of an already mis-stated – mis-stated because stated – presence within the poem. Here there is another opening, another holding apart. The poems will work in a way that defeats the mournful absence of the aporetic by defending absence as the mark of an insistent, productive, already present opening. Here, absence will come to be refigured.

Hope opens up the problem of poetry's time. Thus, the question of whether or not there is time for poetry comes to be posed emphatically. And yet, despite the acuity of questions of this nature, their all-too-apparent generality demands the context of a specific poetry. Here that context is provided by the names Paul Celan and Edmond Jabès. However rather than names, what will be taken up are the specific enactments of hope. It is not as though the relationship between Jabès and Celan has not been offered before. It is not as if it has not been suggested and thus become the subject of an inquiry, subject to an inquiry all the more rigorous for its preoccupation with the poetic and with it – it, that name for the yet to be named – with language. In Jabès' own final written encounter with Celan, the relationship is presented as involving complex determinations:

> Skirting at the border between shadow and light before finally crossing over at a certain hour of the day, Paul Celan's word [*la parole de Paul Celan*], like us, at the edges of two languages of similar proportions – that of renunciation and that of hope [*celle du renoncement et celle de l'espérance*] – advances and asserts itself [*s'affirme*].[1]

In his treatment of Celan, Jabès locates a similarity of poetic enactment in the presence of a twofold structure involving the copresence of 'hope' and 'renunciation'. And yet, with hope there is the possibility of its positing a future in which the present would lose its place to the future. However, the presence of an opening onto the future is, as will be suggested, mediated by the presence of repetition and thus of the present; an already present opening within the present.[2] Located in the move and practice of versification – whether that practice involves simple rhyme or the more complex paronomasia – repetition will work to delimit the present, turning it into a site of intensity. Though it will have to emerge from the detail to come, what will be essential here is to try to trace the working of this structuring effect: hope's opening. Rather than assuming the generalisable presence of this opening, what must be allowed to emerge is the anoriginal presence of a productive caesura which, within the context of the work of poetry, will take the form of a founding *auseinandergeschrieben*.[3]

DENN ALLES FLEISCH ES IST WIE GRAS

The word *auseinandergeschrieben* figures twice in Celan's *Engführung*. Of the many elements that figure within this poem – and it must be added that there is a terrible quality to this work, terrible in the precise sense that there is an enduring feeling of menace or of an inevitable threatening arrival, the nature of which remains both unnamed and unstated – perhaps two of the most complex are the reiteration both of sundering and of the mark of endurance. Taking up this word *auseinandergeschrieben* is already to raise the question of the status of the word. Here there is a twofold opening. In the first place, the first four lines of the poem form, in a different form, the last four lines. The sense of between is dramatised both by this set up as well as by the poem's content. One opening signalled by the word is given by the poem; it is formally enacted by it. The second sense of opening is more complex. Presenting it involves taking the thematic content of the poetry – content that cannot be readily or easily distinguished from its being enacted – as having a precise determination. On one level, that determination can be stated very simply: things go on, *malgré tout*. Of course, they do not just go on. And yet they do go on. It is essential to underline the horror at work in the poem. References to gas, to ash, perhaps even to a place of execution, all insist in the poem. All mediate and are mediated by an impoverishment of expression, not an impoverishment within the poem, but a loss of knowledge and experience. Continuity is marked by uncertainty.

The word *auseinandergeschrieben* is linked to grass.[4] Initially, it is grass that is 'written asunder'. References to both the Hebrew and Christian Bibles abound; equally, the haunting use of *The Gospel of St Peter* by Brahms in *Ein Deutsches Requiem* is just as demanding. Whether it is grass that is thus written, or whether writing and grass are simply juxtaposed, depends in the first instance upon how the comma is read, and in the second upon the spacing of lines. Despite the possibility of an ambiguity concerning the word's placing, the presence of *Gras* forces a link between writing and human mortality upon any interpretation. It may be that the specificity of human mortality reiterated throughout this poem is what determines the particularity of writing, demanding that it be sundering writing. However, in order to take this point a step further, the lines introducing the strain of continuity need to be noted. They have their own setting. They are set between two formulations of the Psalmist's plea to be saved: *Hosianna* (Psalm 118). The first formulation, *Ho, ho– / sianna* almost evokes the bitterness that such demands will have after the Shoah. There is perhaps a dark laughter sounding within it. In the second, the word is split over two lines, though without repetition: *Ho– / sianna*. Even if the first spurns the psalmist, the second does not, or at least does not do so straightforwardly. Between them the following lines occur:

> Also
> stehen noch Tempel. Ein
> Stern
> hat wohl noch Licht.
> Nichts,
> nichts ist verloren.

> So
> there are temples yet. A
> star
> probably still has light.
> Nothing,
> nothing is lost.

Here, the key is not necessarily in the allusion to the destruction of the Second Temple, or the day marking its destruction – as well as much other destruction – namely Tisha b'Av. Nor is the key at work in star's opening up a link to redemption and thus to a form of eternality via Rosenzweig.[5] (This is only to begin the varying references announced by the linkage of star and light.) These references are not unimportant. If there is a key, however, it is there in the *noch*. (As will be shown, this word will also play a major role in *Es ist alles anders*.) While it is possible to suggest that the interplay between *also* and *noch* in the first instance, and the juxtaposition of *wohl* and *noch* in the second, can be taken as introducing a bitter irony, it remains the case that there is a sense of continuity. Something endures. Given that this is the case, the question concerns how this endurance is to be understood. How is the *noch* to be understood? Here, more dramatically, the question is how it – both *noch* and its still being present – is to be written.

The poem continues: *Nichts, / nichts ist verloren.* But why does the poem not announce that all is lost? In this context – be that context biographical (Celan's life) or historical (the Shoah) – the all has gone. Again, there is the possibility that the doubling of *nichts* does, in fact, announce that all is lost. The problem, however, is that insofar as such a proposition is true, it is equally not true. Arguing that all is lost is to argue that, in the loss of the all, what is retained is that which marks this loss, notes this loss, registers this loss, writes in the wake of this loss, remembers this loss. If all is lost then nothing is lost. With loss, endurance figures. What the lines actually announce, therefore, is the complex, difficult, perhaps even harrowing, problem of continuing. After which comes the second *Hosianna*. It is now a question of what this plea means. The nowness of the plea – the nowness given by the impossible work of the *Nichts, / nichts* – returns to the problem of writing. Here, writing will be the province in which that plea is being voiced.

It is at this point that it becomes possible to reintroduce the figure of *auseinandergeschrieben*. Writing will have a twofold determination. On the one hand, it is what brings language and whatever sense of propriety language will have into play. On the other hand, in the context of this poem, writing stages an act of recovery, as long as this is understood as claiming, first that language can never recover what is lost, and second, that language will have had to have recovered from what has been lost. Part of what will be involved in its capacity to recover from, will be the recognition that it cannot recover what was lost. This second sense of writing is *auseinandergeschrieben*. The difficulty lies in linking this sense to the question of language itself.

Once it is thought that language has an essence or a mode of being that continues to show itself in the place of poetic activity, then independently of the complex problematic of recovery, there must be, at the very least, a gesturing towards the work or the presence of the essential. The problem of continuing could not be posed within such a set up. What is essential – in that determination of the essential – would continue. If the figure of the *auseinandergeschrieben* is to be linked to the question of that which is proper to language, then, what has to be addressed must concern how the essential is to be thought such that it occasioned the problematic of recovery to be enacted within language's own work. Working through the demands of this possibility will have to allow for the eventuality that language's own work will have always resisted the possibility of closure and completion. (This is, of course, an ontological and not a semantic claim.) This will be the operation of language thought essentially. Within such a formulation, finitude – the actual presences of language at work – while absolute, only occurs in conjunction with the infinite. In sum, what this means is that the impossible possibility of recovery detailed above in fact registers the essential quality of language. Language's continuity, what it allows to live on, is such that language can never be made, or make itself, absolutely identical with what it occasions. Its impossibility, which is its possibility, is the sign not of a loss but rather of that which is incomplete *ab initio*. This is the founding *auseinandergeschrieben*; its presence as a figure, figuring language's work. Consequently, it is only because of this founding sense of the incomplete that language is able to stage that which marks the interconnection of modernity and the present. It can stage its harrowing presence whilst allowing the question of how to continue to be one that is not banished to the domain of a mute yet brutal pathos, but is the question that is allowed to make writing work because it will have become, by holding back completion, the work of poetry itself.

The opening and the conflict will inhere in the practice and activity of writing – the work of poetry as work – thereby showing, in the place of a problematic of loss, that language's work will always hold itself open. Openness is not loss. Thus, rather than the poem being ensnared by lack and thus having to work as a site of remembrance, remembrance will work within the poem rather than being the poem's topic. It may itself come to affirm this anoriginal opening. In the case of Celan, this will come to be connected to that moment given by the complex interrelationship between modernity and the present marked by the Shoah. Again, with Celan's poetry the question, as always, concerns how to continue.

OPENING CELAN'S HOPE

Of course, there is a place for 'a hope' in the poetry of Celan. Hope is allowed a place and named as such. Here, however, 'a hope' is the translation of *einer Hoffnung* in the poem *Todtnauberg*. In the context of this poem, it is given a definite location, a site that brings with it the present, *heute*; *einer Hoffnung, heute*, Celan writes. The line is not simply specific – though as a line, it must already enjoin a certain specificity. It is linked to an occurrence, an envisaged occurrence. What is at stake, therefore, is the possibility of an occurrence that has yet to occur and thus one the likelihood of which exists as 'a hope', a contemporary 'hope' ineliminably linked to a future. The specificity of the future is tied to the present that has produced it. Again, contextually, what is involved concerns a line inscribed in a visitor's book which, while sustaining an ambiguity pertaining as much to origin as to time, nonetheless takes up hope by announcing it. With it, any gesturing to an occurrence to come opens up a type of future.

> die in dies Buch
> geschriebene Zeile von
> einer Hoffnung, heute,
> auf eines Denkenden
> kommendes
> Wort
> im Herzen.

> in that book
> a line inscribed about
> a hope, today,

of a thinking man's
coming
word
in the heart.

(2/255, 293)

The heart, as heartfelt and thus as hopeful, delivers a present, presented and marked out for its own delivery, to be delivered of or from itself. In other words, what is involved and what determines the specific nature of the task at hand, is a present that is structured by a form of lack, one which enjoins the move from a given absence to its having been overcome. Moving from the present – this construal of the present – to the future that it both generates and sustains, will involve a particular strategy. This strategy will emerge from the present understood as a place lacking the finality that gives rise to the need – a need which will then be taken as instructional – for it to be completed in the future. The future becomes the place of completion, a place made possible by the action of having completed. The move to it, the answered need, is the delivery of hope. Its having been delivered occurs in and as the future and thus inevitably as hope's end. Its finality will demand a specific politics of time, a policy and practice of accomplishment, a finitude existing in the infinite. Here, hope (and again it should be remembered that what is being worked out on this occasion is 'hope' as an immediate translation given by an already determined present, namely the translation of a given within the poem) is, within the terms set by its being given, its context and role within the poem, necessarily linked to finitude and thus to its own eventual overcoming. There will have been a realisation.

There are two aspects of this construal of 'hope' which are important. The first is the present that it entails, whilst the second is the specific presentation of that hope. In the case of poetry, these two aspects are clearly interarticulated. Allusion has already been made to the present entailed by – and thus presented in – the complex time of writing. Taken generally, the present is the complex time of writing. Again, what this involves is not the present as a simple temporal location, a contemporary moment in the passage of time. On the contrary. Here, in its differentiation from passing time, the time of dates where dating is taken as an absolute determinant – though it is an absolute determination that will emerge as existing in name only – the present is the time given within the construal of the task at hand; in other words, as regards what has already been identified as the interarticulated presence of time and task. The presentation of a task brings with it its own reciprocal relation to the site of its enactment, a site that provides the task with its own self-designated inscription of contemporary force. Of course, in this instance, generality must give way to the particular. Celan is continually concerned with the singularity of the poem. And yet, this awareness is marked by the recognition that the singular is never just singular. It is that and more; it was, of course, always more. This accounts for why singularity is impossible, taken either as a point of departure, or as an absolute.

In 'The Meridian', this set up has a specific formulation. The poem as 'conversation' will always involve otherness, The identification of the other brings its alterity into play, the alterity already determined by the 'self' of the poem. (It will be a self that inscribes within it itself that which is already other; the other within the same.) The 'you' is worked on such that it 'brings its otherness into the present [*Gegenwart*]'. In 'The Meridian', this complex reflection continues by working away from the possibility of a founding singularity. The question will be the place of the otherness.

> Even in the here and now of the poem – and the poem has only this one unique momentary present – even in this immediacy and nearness, the otherness gives voice to what is most its own: its time.
>
> Whenever we speak with things in this way we also dwell on the question of their where-from and where-to [*ihrem Woher und Wohin*], an 'open' question 'without resolution' [*zu keinem Ende kommenden*], a question which points towards an open, empty, free space – we have ventured far out.
>
> The poem also searches for this place.
>
> (3/198, 50)

The search is an integral part of the poem's self-activity. As such, therefore, it is a fundamental aspect of its being as poem; in sum, it is the work's work. It will be essential to return to this formulation once the work of 'hope' in *Todtnauberg* has been traced.

In the context of this poem, present 'hope' – *einer Hoffnung, heute* – is located within and generated by a present that is marked out and thus sustained by the possibility of – though in the end the necessity for – its own overcoming. This present is to be overcome because of lack. What should have been said will have been said. The moment's having been completed, reconciliation will establish propriety by having overcome again the given impropriety of the present which exists 'today'. This hope, 'a hope', is not simply strategic and thus limited to the moment of its being announced. As will emerge, it is not hope at all; rather, it is hope to be ended, the cessation of hope. Announcing the self-restriction of an end, hope announces the end of its being maintained. There is, therefore, here, now, *heute*, no hope. Which means that despite the presence of the word, hope itself as a mode of thinking – as a time that maintains time and thus as a productive presence having an ontology that needs to be thought beyond the confines of lack and negation – is not being enacted here. It should immediately be added that the presence of 'a hope' – the words *einer Hoffnung* in the poem – will allow for the possibility of their being reworked; in the process of reworking there will be hope for 'hope', but only in overcoming, overcoming while retaining the place and force of the founding inscription *einer Hoffnung, heute*. There are significant intimations of this possibility – this complex move which is neither negation nor inversion – within a question broached in *Todtnauberg*, in the 'same' poem. It is almost as though the poem enacts the division within the word hope: on the one hand hope as mere name, and, on the other hope as a structure.[6] It is not simply that the presence of this other possibility within the poem must not go unnoticed. It is its presence within a question – a presence that brings the temporality of the question with it – that is central. The poem will never have been the same as itself.

There is another moment in *Todtnauberg* in which even though the temporality of hope – this other hope, the structure of hope – is checked, insofar as hope is still linked to the realisation of a future occurrence, there is a gesturing towards the possibility of temporal complexity. In this instance it is not harboured in the temporality of the question, but, more specifically, in what the question demands. It will be possible to link this movement to the description of poetry's original complexity in 'The Meridian'.

Prior to the poetic inscription of 'a hope' in the visitor's book, the poem announces:

> die in das Buch
> – wessen Namen nahms auf
> vor dem meinen? –,
> die in dies Buch
> geschriebene Zeile von
> einer Hoffnung, heute,
>
> the line
> – whose name did the book
> register before mine– ?,
> the line inscribed
> in that book about
> a hope, today,

> (2/255, 293)

127

Between the two references to the book, there is a question. This questioning is deliberate. Who was there in the hut before this writer? What name, what inscription had been left? The force of these questions is not simply epistemological. Certainly there is the question of knowledge, of knowing who it was that preceded the current visitor and whether or not there was any message left in the book. But here, knowledge pales once time is introduced. The question asks: of what continuity will the inscription about to be placed in the visitor's book form a part? If it is the continuity of disavowal and complicity, then hope, even the hope asked for, will wreck that continuity. The hoped, the end asked by Celan, will sunder that continuity. Even the wish, the hope, for Heidegger to speak, to allow for the possibility that Auschwitz could be thought philosophically from within the thinking of being, would sunder the philosophical silence. Moreover, and as part of overcoming the enforced silence, an overcoming in which language emerged as 'enriched',[7] there could have been the possibility that the currently identified abyss within language had more to do with contemporary history than with the history of being. In such a case, the relationship between language – taken in general – and its inevitable articulation within and through history would be that which gave the present its form. It would be a form from which there could have been no escape – except via the nihilism of intentional forgetting. Nor, moreover, could there have been that strategy that involved holding back the force of history's unfolding in order to allow what would be taken as that which most properly pertains to language to show itself.[8]

As a consequence, the foundational nature of the abyss will have been shown to have been more complex. The visitor's book could have recorded names and comments of those for whom this mode of questioning had neither actuality nor possibility. The inscription of hope has already introduced an unmanageable moment. The necessary interplay of time and hope coupled to their inevitable plurality means that silence cannot be taken as existing *tout court*. (Indeed, there could no be such a thing as mere silence.) Rather, silence itself will always be placed within a specific conception of historical time. Differences within hope will generate different conceptions of silence. In sum, silence will always depend on that which gives it its presence; it will present it; it will have been presented by it. Finally, therefore, while there will have been an allusion to the structure of hope by the more formal attempt to subdue or check the flow of continuity, it remains the case that this is a continuity that is itself enacted by the denial of hope's structural presence. Despite the presence of the unmanageable, there is an-other hope.

What, then, of this other hope – a hope whose affirmed presence brings time, hope's time, into play? Hope's time will become the opening – an intense present – holding the present as always opening, as always being the irreconciled. This is a state of affairs that has to be understood in terms of the ontology and the temporality of the incomplete. Maintaining that site of irreconcilability and hence the continuity of present discontinuity, enjoins a different propriety. It is this propriety which is hope.

POETIC DIGRESSION

Holding to hope as marking the continuity of the present's opening – the discontinuity within continuity – demands a representation of the poetic. Rather than following a path that oscillates between terms such as 'possible' and 'impossible', the 'known' and the 'unknown', central to any digression on poetry is the twofold possibility in which poetry will be able to differentiate itself from the totality of that which it is taken to name, while at the same time affirming an already present conception of work. With regard to the latter, work will identify the inextricable presence – here, the effective copresence – of language and ontology. What is involved is authenticity. And yet this word brings with it a reversion to, on the one hand, a type of moralism, and the eschewing of history on the other. As such, there is the inevitable question: what would it mean, today, to invoke any form of authenticity? Part of the discussion of Celan's poem *Es ist alles anders* needs to be understood as an attempt to answer that question. At this stage, the authentic is used to open up the question of work. Rather than concentrating on meaning and thereby on problems of interpretation that stem from attempting to differentiate between an object's potentially different meanings, work becomes a description of the object such that the object can be said to be in its being at work. Despite appearances to the contrary, this formulation is not cumbersome. It is meant to reinforce the claim that an integral part of the object is not its work, as though that work were an element that could be predicated of the object. Work, the continuity of work, *is* the object insofar as the object can be taken as that which is always at work with the process and thus the movement of its own self-effectuation or self-realisation. What this entails is not just a division between those objects which affirm the workful nature of work and those which seek continuity. It also allows for the recognition that work will be precisely what the object is. It thus becomes possible to identify authenticity. In other words, authenticity is linked in the first instance to the ineliminability of work. There is, however, a complicating factor.

Even in allowing for the presence of work (emphasis being given to the actative rather than the substantive), what is at work with the process of self-realisation is language, and thus language's own work. With poetry it is as though it is essential to return to the question of language. When, in the *Posterior Analysis*, Aristotle argues (97b 35) first for clarity in definition and thereby for an avoidance of the problem posed by equivocation or homonymy, and then warns against advancing argument in terms of metaphor, even though this does not address poetry itself, it rehearses the distinctions in terms of which poetry will be understood. Once more, caution is necessary. Not only is there the temptation to respond to this set up in terms of charting its demanding course through the history of philosophy. Equally, there is the temptation to subdue it beneath particularity, waves of examples which, in the movement of their being presented, would in the end erode what is substantial here. With poetry, there is the possibility that it hides the true nature and potential of language because it draws attention away from language's inherent and thus primordial literality, the literal as that which always precedes the figural. Language's capacity for definite descriptions would be denied if poetry were thought to be close to the nature of language itself. And yet there is another strategy in which language is also betrayed by poetry. It would be here that language comes closest to poetry precisely because of a founding lack. What emerges, therefore, are differing sites of investigation. As has already been intimated, poetry brings with it the differing possibilities for language. Equally, poetry will also put into play the relationship – whatever it may be – between what is proper to language, recognising that there will be different and hence incompatible senses of propriety, and the movement of historical time (itself marked by its own ineliminable plurality). The opening given by Aristotle's argument will provide the setting within which the question of poetry is repeatedly staged.

And yet, if there is a poetics in Celan, it is one in which the propriety of language is given in relation to a particular conception of historical time. Celan's 'realism' positions him as no longer held by the twin possibilities opened by Aristotle, though, equally, as distanced from the sense of 'mystery' guiding Heidegger's interpretation of Stefan George's poem *Das Wort*. With Celan, poetry comes closest to figuring the nature of language, the twofold possibility that has already been identified as at work within the process of sundering writing: *auseinandergeschrieben*. This occurs *beyond*, on the one hand, the hold of lack, and on the other, *beyond* the remembrance dictated by the work of language rather than the work of history.

Having traced George's own relationship to the word occurring in the poem *Das Wort*, allowing for a relinquishing announced almost unmistakably in the famous last line *Kein ding sei wo das wort gebricht* ('Where words break off no thing may be'), Heidegger argues that with this line,

The poet must relinquish the claim to the assurance that he will on demand be supplied with the name for that which he has posited as what truly is. This positing and that claim he must now deny himself. The poet must renounce having words under his control as the portraying names for what is posited. As self-denial, renunciation is a Saying which says to itself:

Where words break off no thing may be.[9]

While Heidegger's claim forms part of an analysis of George, it has a greater extension. The importance both of denial and of Heidegger's own work on 'renunciation' is that they open up the site of mystery in which poetry will figure. In virtue of this location, poetry will become closer to the truth of things. This truth is recognised within poetry, for even in poetry 'there is no Saying which could bring the being of language to language'. Poetry becomes the work of remembrance, perhaps even the work of a particular form of melancholia (melancholia as opposed to mourning, because the lost object is a 'mystery' and must remain a 'mystery'). For Heidegger, the 'treasure', the locus of the poet's search, is 'the word for the presencing of language'. Loss will figure here at its most emphatic.

His renunciation [*Verzicht*] having pledged itself to the word's mystery [*dem Geheimnis des Wortes*], the poet retains the treasure in remembrance by renunciation [*durch den Verzicht im Andenken*]. In this way, the treasure becomes that which the poet – he who says – prefers above all else and reveres above everything else. The treasure becomes what is truly worthy of the poet's thought. For what could be more worthy of thought for the saying one than the word's being veiling itself, than the fading word for the word [*das sich verschleiernde Wesen des Wortes, das entscheinende Wort für das Wort*]?

(236–7, 154–5)

The details of these differing formulations needs to be noted. Not only is 'remembrance' positioned as what gives the poet that recognition of a place in relation to the 'treasure'. The place of a founding lack is given by the formulation of 'veiling' and the 'fading word for the word'. Remembrance, veiling and fading position. They position not just poetry, but what has been described above as poetry's work. Allowing for the centrality of ontology and signification opens up the series of interconnections created by these terms. What conception of the ontological is at work here? Moreover, what conception of the word is held by the formulation 'the word's being veiling itself'?

Heidegger's engagement with George's *Das Wort* is positioned around a particular problematic of loss. The central line of the poem, the line guiding his interpretation, announces this loss: 'The treasure never graced my land' (*Und nie mein land den schatz gewann*). The question concerns the nature of this 'treasure'. Its position will yield the way in which 'veiling' and 'fading' are to be understood. As a point of departure, it could be noted that the initial way of construing the contrast to veiling/fading would be in terms of full presence. Presentness would have delimited that which stood opposed to 'veiling' and 'fading'. And yet, rather than taking this as a determining opposition, what is being played out here is importantly different. What is present, what presents itself, moreover, is 'the word's being veiling itself' and thus 'the fading word for the word'. There can be no contrast to presence since what is present is precisely what could itself be described as the movement of absenting. (Hence the earlier allusion to melancholia rather than to mourning.) Heidegger formulates this presence, the way in which the 'treasure' commits itself to this form of presence, in the following terms:

> The treasure which never graced the poet's land is the word for the being of language [*ist das Wort für das Wesen der Sprache*]. The word's rule and sojourn, abruptly caught sight of, its presencing [*sein Wesendes*], would like to enter into its own word. But the word for the being of the word is not granted.

> (236, 154)

Here the problematic of loss is straightforward. The words for 'the being of the word' mark what cannot be in the poet's land. What is there is a remembrance. There is also the sign of mourning, though, perhaps more accurately, the sign of a type of melancholia since the object of loss is itself a mystery, the 'word's mystery'. What pervades is a sense of loss. Loss is again underwritten in the last line quoted above: 'the word for the being of the word is not granted'. While there will have been an absence, while loss has been recorded, while there may be a marker, a form of remembrance, there is no question as to what it is that has not been 'granted'. Again, what is absent is the 'word for the being of the word'. But what is this word? It is, Heidegger writes, that which is 'worthy of thought'. The continuity of thinking, the response to the call to think, is sustained by the 'mystery of the word'.

What, then, of this mystery? Here, that which is mysterious must be distanced, and yet as Heidegger indicates, in its being experienced it is also near. For this mystery the word is lacking. It cannot be named. But why? Why is it that the last line of George's poem is taken to announce the word's truth? It is not just that the 'word makes the thing into a thing' (232, 151), thereby establishing a productive element within the word. There is an addition. What is there in addition is paramount. To the extent that 'we are thinking with poetry' (*denken wir dem Dichten nach*), not just about poetry but with it, in the wake of it, 'we' adopt the same stance in relation to thinking, in the sense that poetry and thinking are in being together. There is a mutual calling. This calling is what thinking and poetry are. It is what it means for them to be. Having made this claim, Heidegger then draws this into the larger project.

> What first looks like the title of a thesis – making poetry and thinking – turns out to be the inscription in which our destined human existence [*unser geschickliches Dasein*] has ever [*von altersher*] been inscribed. This inscription records that poetry and thinking belong together. Their coming together has come about a long time ago. As we think back [*zurückdenken*], we come face to face with what is primevally worthy of thought, and which we can never ponder sufficiently.
>
> (237, 155)

What is of immediate concern in this passage as well as from the description of thinking poetry, is Heidegger's use of personal pronouns. These pronouns will have to be set against the temporal marker *von altersher* and its linkage to destiny.

Who are 'we'? Positioned in relation to poetry and thinking the 'we' repeats the position held by the 'our' (*unser*) united in its having the same 'destined human existence'.[10] Whatever the answer to the question, our destiny has always been positioned by the always already interconnected presence of poetry and thinking. Therefore, the mystery of the word demands on the one hand the singular subject position identified by the 'we', whilst on the other, it has to hold to the uninterrupted passage of history in which there is the continuity of responding to veiling and fading and thus to the impossibility of the existence of a word for 'the being of a word'. This abyssal position, this founding absence – an absence already marked by its own presence thus there as a form of remembrance – will have always been older than any occurrence. It will therefore always have been the same despite any occurrence. 'We' will also have been the same – occupying the same position – again positioned by the interrelationship of poetry and thinking, despite any occurrence and in spite of any necessity to take the 'we' as the mark of an already present plurality. 'We' are only in being the same as ourselves. In this way, 'we' will continue to be positioned. Coming to recognise the primordiality of this positioning will amount to taking over the destiny that is proper to us. In addition, our taking it over is the only proper destiny that 'we' have.

Moreover, the use of the term '*zurückdenken*' (thinking back) is here doubly informative. In Heidegger's use of this term there is the possibility of thinking back not only to that which is far older but to that which has always endured;

the destiny that has always been ours. In addition, this formulation also reiterates the point that emerged earlier and in which Heidegger used a similar verbal form. In *An Introduction to Metaphysics*, the 'task' was given in relation to asking the question of being with sufficient radicality such that the power at work in the distinctions – Being/Becoming, Being/Appearing, Being/Thinking and Being/Ought – might be restored. Heidegger's precise formulation is 'restore [*zurückbringen*] them to their truth'. The verbs are not the same. Nonetheless, what is at work in both is a type of movement, a similarity sustained by the form *zurück–*. In both cases there is a moving back. That through which this movement takes place is not just unaffected by the activity of movement; it is also the case that the movement of thinking and restoring remains untouched by their own self-defined activities. Finally, the movement both backward and forward – thinking and restoring – works to define the nature of the philosophical task. As such, therefore, they generate and thus circumscribe a particular conception of the epochal present. It will be one in which the question of the temporality of the passage remains unexamined, perhaps necessarily so.

Emerging here are the central points of contrast. As has already been indicated, the question of the extent to which this is a correct description of poetry's work, the subject position demanded by it and the implicit conception of historical occurrence and temporal movement, is not central. What is central is just how applicable such a formulation will be in relation to Celan and to Jabès. Finally, in order to end the digression, and as will become clear in what follows, the ontology and temporality of viewing and fading are precisely those which are inappropriate for Celan's poetics. This lack of propriety is neither ethical nor hermeneutic. Here, propriety is linked to the ontologico-temporal.

'ES IST ALLES ANDERS'

As a beginning – though here what will be involved is just a beginning – the poem *Es ist alles anders* (1/284–6, 216–21) will be taken as providing that opening in which the all (*alles*) comes to be rehearsed and thus repeated in its difference such that the presence of its difference cannot be taken either as the inscription of an original lack nor read as the promulgation of singular hope. In the end, that singularity – as a form of enclosing and encapsulating – allows a turning back upon itself such that it can no longer be completed by the 'coming word' (*kommendes / Wort*). In contradistinction to this putative completing, the singular will be marked by that which announces its possibility whilst at the same time locating that possibility within the complex structure of repetition, a structure in which the copresence of the finite and the infinite comes to be played out. Indeed, the 'word' to come that envisaged a form of completion can be contrasted – a contrast that would demand recourse to their different effectuating logics – to the 'word' in *Engführung*, the 'word' that 'came through the night' (*kam durch die Nacht*). It may be that this coming word will have to take on another quality in order that it be present as a word.

If that which is being taken as central is repetition, then the question of how entry is to be effected must arise. If, rather than its being effaced by completion, it is allowed to continue, then the question of what breakage is demanded by entry must also occur. Put another way, what stemming of repetition's structuring work occurs with the intrusion? In other words, here with this poem *Es ist alles anders* – though this in the end will perhaps be true of all poems – is there an opening within it that allows a way in? Does the poem itself – whatever this 'itself' may be – open of its own accord, providing thereby a way towards it, and into it, that in some sense accords with the poem? This apparent prevarication on the edge simply attests to the difficulty of conceiving of that into which entry has to be made. The problem of conception here refers to the site: the place of poetry, the poem. It is perhaps easier to make this claim in relation to a poem such as *Todesfuge* which, with its fugal structure, already presents itself as the site of an enacted repetition such that the citation of any line not only stills the force of repetition, but also brings with it the more immediate problem of determining which moment within repetition has been excised and then repeated within and as the citation. Again, the problem of the citation also endures within *Engführung*, whose title announces the place of repetition even though the self-evident problem of citation does not exist with nearly the same force as before. Nonetheless, the clue that is provided by this formalised presence of repetition is to take each opening as itself already mediated by its content, denied and affirmed. An opening which is given within the text and which is also withdrawn, allows the poem to work against the hold of completion, while at the same time locating that activity outside of the hold and determination of loss. Loss will come to figure in another way within the poem's work.

The theme of writing – writing as the inescapable figure of *auseinan-dergeschrieben* – this other writing, being other writing, sundering writing, enacts neither negation nor mystery, but maintains the opening, an opening intense because present; not hermetic, therefore, but complex. The figure of *auseinandergeschrieben*, and it is essential that it be retained as a figure that yields, in addition, the question of citation, announces the originating place of language by bringing this place with it, a place that figures essentially in the

135

practice of poetry. And yet, the question of language's original work cannot be posed outside of the possibility of future determining considerations, since the question, the ineliminable question that insists here, concerns the relationship between historical sundering and loss on the one hand, and this original state of writing's work on the other. This work, the place of poetry, will need to be understood as a writing that involves neither lack nor negation nor loss. All such terms only figure as a feigned nostalgia that, having lost the innocence of the feint, have become naturalised and thus reapplied. In other words, they generate a specific interpretative practice, an essential part of which is that they mourn the possibility of the complete. Completion, plenitude and the desire for coextensivity have, however, always been marked by a necessary impossibility. Rather than taking this necessarily impossible site as the condition or aspiration for language, once the necessity of the impossibility vanishes, what will emerge in the place of mourning is the anoriginal presence of the caesura that will have already the condition of writing/language. (*Auseinandergeschrieben* as figure, then.) Poetry may enact this state of affairs; it may be its insistent presence. As such, poetry would allow for a thinking that works within the opening allowed by the abeyance of the oscillation between projected completion and its emergent impossibility.

While it is always problematic to refer to 'The Meridian' to try and support Celan's poetry in an unequivocal way, it nonetheless may be the case that this complex set up is captured in the following formulation:

> The poem makes for an other [*zu einem Anderen*], it needs this other, it needs an opposite. It seeks it out, it articulates itself to it [*Es sucht es auf, es spricht sich ihm zu*].

> (3/198, 49)

This other is in its being within. It is not an either/or. The poem incorporates alterity. The alterity is not, however, one more thing that can be predicated of the poem as though the poem were able to keep itself, essentially, apart from this inscription. Nor, moreover, does it mean, as one recent commentator has argued, that the 'poem posits itself as a lack and only is, then, insofar as it does not fulfil itself'.[11] On the contrary. Lack will have been transformed within the poem's work. The transformation will not have been the negation of negation. It is, rather, that the all-encompassing hold of negativity will have been put to one side: negation's abeyance. The difference hinges on the word 'fulfil'. It is not that the poetry fails to fulfil, or even that it aspires to fulfil. Rather, it is that poetry does not work within a productive space created by the oscillation between the desire for fulfilment and its consequent impossibility. Moreover, aspects of the work can be read as affirming this other possibility, perhaps even another place of poeticising. What is maintained and thus what is effectively present within such works, is the structure of hope. Moving from the negative – the description that hinges on the 'not' – will involve complexity. The reason is straightforward. What is of concern here is not poetry as such, nor even the activity of the poet. What pertains is the present, i.e. the way time and task articulate themselves within and as the poetry's work.

This is the dramatic point within Celan's poeticising. It is, moreover, the point which makes the confrontation with the Shoah – a confrontation drama-tised for poetry by the pronouncements of Adorno and Szondi – all the more insistent.[12] The difficulty is that in the confrontation language may have emerged, perhaps re-emerged, as 'enriched' because of the explicit nature of the confrontation itself; because, that is, of its having been undertaken. Celan alludes to precisely this possibility in his Bremen speech. The speech sites unreachable goals on the poet's itinerary, all of them identifiable places: Vienna, Bremen itself. What can be reached has an altogether different status:

> Only one thing remained reachable, close and secure amid all loses: language. Yes language. In spite of everything, it remained secure against loss. But it had to go through its own lack of answers, through terrifying silence, through the thousand darknesses of terrifying speech. It went through. It gave me no words for what was happening, but went through it. Went through and could resurface 'enriched' by it all.
>
> (3/186, 34)

What is to be understood by 'enriched' will here need the setting of the work of language within the poem. This will account for why, though only operating on a level of generality that will in the end have to give in to the necessity of the specific – a specificity given by what has already been identified as authen-ticity – that it is possible to suggest that being 'enriched' brings language's original form into history by affirming the ineliminable presence of history. History is, in this instance, the province of the present.

It is the interplay of language's founding caesura and the structure of hope – an interplay in which both parts may be one and the same – that provides a way of giving an account of the opening of *Est ist alles anders*. It will be an account that opens the poem.

> Est ist alles anders, als du es dir denkst, als ich es mir denke,
> die Fahne weht noch,
> die kleinen Geheimnisse sind noch bei sich,
> sie werfen noch Schatten, davon
> lebst du, leb ich, leben wir.

> Everything's different from how you conceive it, I conceive it,
> the flag still flutters,
> the little secrets are still there,
> they still cast shadows, by that,
> you live, I live, we live.

(1/284, 217)

The alterity, the otherness given by the first line, introduces a complex split between subject and object; a split more complex than that signalled by its simple existence. The first person (*ich*) and the second person (*du*), their thoughts or conception of what there is, are conceptions opened, sundered, by the 'all', the totality, being other than those conceptions of it. With this split there arises the possibility of a joining up, a bringing together.

However, it is within the space opened by that split that the *noch* comes to be repeated. Already the site of repetition – this specific repetition – is a gulf that holds and disperses this specificity. Within the opening, at play in the grounding gulf, a continuity is inserted that is itself realised through repetition. What is asserted here, present as continuous, is that which can be taken as the presentation of symbols and thus as further sites of interpretation. The flag endures as the symbol of that which it names or designates but is not. In symbolising, it holds to an opening, holds open a space in which there will always be, if only potentially, more than is given by the simple relation, be it semantic or ontological, of the one-to-one, itself another formulation of coextensivity and completion. There is another site of meaning, and with it another possibility of meaning, for – and thus as – its place.

With this opening, the 'little secrets' (*die kleinen Geheimnisse*) endure and find a home. However, with that endurance what has been given a home is the perduring casting of shadows. While already the site of a potential obscurity, the shadows are nonetheless also to be taken as being another site of memory. The shadow marks out a possibility tracing its mark, and with that move demands the necessity of its retention. Even more the shadow has to be attributed a role that recasts the question of truth – of truth in poetry. Recall *Sprich auch du*, in which the interrelation of truth and light and thus truth as that which is illuminated for the eye is dispensed with in favour of the shadow: 'He speaks truly who speaks the shade' (*Wahr spricht, wer Schatten spricht*) (1/135, 98). Truth speaks in the afterwards of light, an already present afterwards. But of what are these shadows? What was there? A preliminary answer would be that it is an already present dispersal that finds form. Again, what insists here is the question of the site, the place, though now it is a question of the complex of these sites. It is in relation to them that its possible permutations are developed; *lebst du, leb ich, leben wir*. The temptation here is to insist upon the presence of life, a presence linked to its actualisation through person, through the verb, as itself the affirmation of continuity. However, this would only be possible to the extent that the setting was itself not taken into consideration. The repetition of the *noch* brings endurance with it. What it is that endures is to be located in the gulf opened by the split between subject and object. The repetition of the *noch*, enacting a continuity that would take place independently of the subject–object relation and operate in generating the reality of what was given outside of the relation, if it were not for the fact that what are given are bearers of meaning disassociated from a self-evident relation to the ground of meaning; hence the gulf. That which is torn down, broken up, can only ever be brought together fleetingly. In this way, its coming together is also its coming apart. It is not that this is the structure of restoration and finality; what is at stake here is neither self-evidently apocalyptic nor messianic.

Within what is given as itself continually opening, located within a movement enacted by repetition, both combining to produce the poem's work, there emerges the presence of proper names. Such names should designate without equivocation. And yet, of course, though it is now a common place, the designation is absolute only on the condition that it is always other than absolute. It is this paradox that not only opens up the proper name, thereby ridding it of any putative singularity, but compounds the problem of the site by both deepening it while forcing out, forging another approach to the place of meaning, naming, calling, knowing. While different, they brush against each other – almost in the mouth – with the repetition of sound patterns. Within the poem's complex work, therefore, another place is announced:

> wie heisst es, dein Land,
> hinterm Berg, hinterm Jahr?
> Ich weiss, wie es heisst.

> what is it called, your country
> behind the mountain, behind the year?
> I know what it is called.

(1/285, 219)

But to the question of the name, to that which is otherly placed *hinter*, there comes a response. There is an answer. And yet, rather than giving the question an essential finitude by its having been closed, the answer resists being placed (though, as will be suggested, it is a resistance that also places, thus moving the interplay of question–answer beyond purely epistemological concerns; and this despite the *Ich weiss, wie es heisst*). What it is that answers the question of naming 'wanders off everywhere like language' (*wandert überallhin, wie die Sprache*), after which come the lines:

> wirf sie weg, wirf sie weg,
> dann hast du sie wieder, wie ihn.

> throw it away, throw it away,
> then you will have it again, like that other thing.

$$(1/285, 219)$$

The displacement from the 'way' (*weg*), its being a casting forth that necessarily reorients the search for the name, repeats a point that has already been made. Has it not already been announced in the Bremen speech that 'poems are en route [*unterwegs*]: they are headed toward something [*sie halten auf etwas zu*]' (3/186, 34)? In necessitating its being thrown away, the dispersal of the name, the response to the question *wie heisst es* also sanctions a retaining. In a sense, retention is not the problem. The difficulty resides in what it is that is retained. Within the poem's unfolding the 'thing' is like a pebble – perhaps becomes the pebble – which was carried over to Prague and then placed on a grave. The placing of stones on the grave is, of course, a fundamental part of Jewish ritual concerning the remembering and honouring of the dead; significantly, however, it is a remembrance that works to rework the present. There are moreover magical and Kabbalistic elements attached to this process in which the present comes to be redeemed – saved – by the carrying out of ritual. Part of that redemption is linked to a conception of *tikkun* in which the act of restoration brought with it necessary eschatological implications.[13]

The redemptive nature of ritual is evoked earlier in the poem. Again, it concerns a remembrance that causes the present to be reworked. With the emphatic 'Tekiah', the passage has the potential to be charged with redemptive time. The passage continues:

> am Heck kein Warum, am Bug kein Wohin, ein Widderhornhebt dich
> – Tekiah! –

> on the stern no why, on the bow no whither, a ram's hornlifts you
> – Tekiah! –

$$(1/284–5, 217)$$

The passage continues with the incursion of the 'trumpet blast' 'over nights into day' (*über die Nächte hinweg in den Tag*). Leaving aside the obvious translation questions raised by the 'word' Tekiah, its presence announces something else. With Tekiah breath enters. With breath the name endures recalling the double question concerning a possible arrival in *Hüttenfenster*:

— ein Atem? ein Name? —

— a breath? a name? —

(1/278, 213)

Here, the breath is maintained with and within repetition. Tekiah is a glissando which begins with low swells and moves to higher ones. At both Rosh Hashanah and Yom Kippur, a Tekiah begins and ends the blowing of the shofar. The last Tekiah, known as the Tekiah Gedolah, is held, prolonged until the breath runs out. The blowing of the shofar announces renewal; it is not a simple rebirth but an overcoming that works within continuing, i.e. it involves repetition thought beyond the confines of the same, an-other repetition. Rather than ritual being central, what needs to be thought is the possibility of reworking the temporality of ritual. Ritual may be able to be taken up such that it could allow for a thinking of anoriginal complexity. Part of such an argument would involve locating the present's repetition in the present and not in a putative deliverance of or from the present. It would mean, moreover, casting the present in terms of the continuity of a transformative potential. It will be essential to locate breath — perhaps what could be described as the work of breath — in the context of the poem *Es ist alles anders*.

In his commentary on this line, Stéphane Moses attributes an important and disruptive quality to the sound of the shofar within the actual ritual itself. At Rosh Hashanah, prayer is interrupted by the blowing of the shofar. He goes on to suggest, invoking the *Zeitloch* (time hole) of *Die Posaunenstelle*, that:

> this caesura of speech (in the ongoing process of liturgy) is itself the reflection or the representation of a more general caesura of time, of a breakthrough which a radical otherness can manifest itself. Here the 'time hole' would indicate the suspension of profane time for the sake of another experience, that of the festival ritual.[14]

It is essential to stay with the closing points of Moses' argument before returning to the question of time. While his ostensible concern is with the poem *Die Posaunenstelle*, what is significant is the general setting of his conclusion. Via an intertextual and syllabic analysis, he argues that the poem 'actualises the process by which the physical breath is transformed into a human voice' (222). The intertextual references (namely, to Revelation and prayer) are to a site in which Revelation and prayer have lost their hold. Taken together, both of these elements — the intertextual and the syllabic — allow the

sound of the shofar to be reworked in terms of a metonym of 'poetic revelation'. As such, he concludes, 'the breath of inspiration is transformed into a
sequence of words exhaled through the poet's mouth' (223). What is significant is that the overall setting of this part of his interpretation is a particular
construal of the present: a growing postenlightenment secularism. Once
more, its significance is to be found in the reciprocity between the nature of
the time and the poetic and interpretative task it generates.

> Through this ongoing process of secularisation the fundamental religious
> categories transmitted by the Judaeo-Christian tradition (such as
> Creation, Revelation, and Redemption) have become meaningless. But
> their very absence has opened a void which constitutes, in some way, the
> space where modernity works.
>
> (223)

Within this context, Celan becomes the exemplary poet of 'modernity',
thereby having the reciprocal effect of rendering a great deal of contemporary
poetry premodern. (This attests to the difficulty of these categories if they are
taken to mark out specific historical periods.) The empty state of ritual is
enacted with secular force in the work of poetry. Central to all of these issues
is time.

The emphatic 'Tekiah' is set within lines signalling renewal. Life will be
contrasted to death. Yet neither exist in a straightforward way. In the first
place, it is a matter of life not as lived but as that which comes to be relived,
to be re-enacted within a transformative repetition. Death, as has already been
suggested, is itself held within a ritual of remembrance in which, while dead,
the dead live on and in which the living, now dead, endure.

> die Auguren
> zerfleischen einander, der Mensch
> hat seinen Frieden, der Gott
> hat den seinen, die Liebe
> kehrt in die Betten zurück, das Haar
> der Frauen wächst wieder,
> die nach innen gestülpte
> Knospe an ihrer Brust
> tritt wieder zutag, lebens—
>
> the augurs
> devour one another, man
> has his peace, God
> has his, love

> returns to beds, the hair
> of women grows again,
> the retracted
> buds on their breasts
> emerge again, life –

(1/285, 219)

While recognising the difficulty of excising isolated passages, what is immediately striking about these lines is the repetition of the word *wieder* ('again'). The question concerns the nature of this repetition. Involved here are considerations that have already figured in the repetition of *noch*. This question of this repetition needs to be set against another, namely the extent to which the 'Tekiah' of *Es ist alles anders* repeats the use and function of this term within liturgy. There is a repetition. The question is one of how it is to be understood. Once more, time and repetition bear on each other without either being essentially one and the same. These questions are difficult because they demand the presence of the present. Liturgical and secular time – to utilise the distinction advanced by Moses and implicit in some of the above formulations – are already caught in an identity giving an either/or. And yet even from within it, the nature of time in liturgy is far from settled. While there is the repetition within the liturgical calendar, this repetition is already the transformation of the natural into the historical. It is a transformation that has important consequences for how liturgy and the reality of liturgy are to be understood. Liturgical time is already incorporated into a series of distinctions and transformations that come to define it.

In the lines cited above there is renewal. The hair that had been shorn grows back. The general context insists. Within the context of Celan's poetry, hair must recall Shulamith's 'ashen hair'. This hair – the hair of Germany's Jew – was condemned: *Dein aschenes Haar Sulamith wir schaufeln ein Grab* (your ashen hair Shulamith we dig a grave) (1/41, 61). There will have been a return from the grave. However, it will not be a return to the same. It will be a return in which the same is present within difference, both one and the other. Once again, breasts may sustain life, and while life will be the same it will, at the same time, be importantly different. Life could not have remained the same. The dilemma with using the structure of liturgical time is that the demands which it makes are for a renewal in which there is a return to a sense of propriety. In this sense liturgical time may in fact invoke a certain timelessness. Indeed, following Rosenzweig, it could be argued that timelessness is the time prior to the messianic interruption.[15] The repetition within liturgy – the repetition that marks out its time – is a continual return of the human to God. As such, therefore, to intervene within liturgical time – even that intervention

143

that causes liturgy to take on another form – cannot be thought in terms of its traditional temporal demarcation. The reworking of liturgical time – perhaps, to be more accurate, its *attempted* reworking – will cause it to be necessarily other than how it was conceived. It may form, therefore, an instance of the more general claim that *Es ist alles anders, als du es dir denkst, als ich es mir denke.* The apocalyptic nature of this claim, as has been suggested, is from the start mediated by what comes to be repeated in the repetition of *noch.* Alterity will need to be thought in relation to the primordial insistence of that which is 'still' there, and, equally, in terms of that which occurs 'again'. Here there is little mystery. Moreover, it may be that Celan has already addressed this quality in terms of the *Immer-noch* of the poem. While the tendency to subjectivity would need to be examined in considerable detail, this quality is formulated in 'The Meridian' in such a way that it returns poetry to the present, a return that was already present in terms of its being made possible and necessary by poetry's point of departure:

> This 'still-here' of the poem [*Dieses Immer-noch des Gedichts*] can only be found in the work of poets who do not forget that they speak from an angle of reflection which is their own existence, their own physical nature. This shows the poem yet more clearly as one person's language become shape and, essentially, a presence in the present [*und seinem innersten Wesen nach Gegenwart und Präsenz*].
>
> (3/197–8, 49)

Provisionally, therefore, the triumphant 'Tekiah' raises neither the question of the purely liturgical nor invokes an emptiness given by withdrawal of theological sites of meaning. Neither religious experience nor secular emptiness are allowed centrality. The 'Tekiah' plays in the place of the *noch* and the *wieder.* It signals the possibility of another beginning that is neither nostalgic nor melancholic on the one hand, nor caught within the hold of the dominance of the Same on the other. Articulating the structure of hope, 'Tekiah' announces a renewal that allows for remembering. It is thought in relation to liturgical time because it is initially given within that time.

Finally, therefore, there is a prevailing return working within the poem *Es ist alles anders*, providing it with its work. This is a return which opens up the poem's already present self-inscription of the continuity of its giving out, a continuity named in terms of the anoriginally present caesura and, therefore, as the work of the structure of hope. It is present with the 'it' of language. Initially, however, the sense of return within this poem takes a distinct and initially divergent form occurring both with the evocation of the 'windmills' and then with the more apparently comfortable proposition that 'what was severed joins up again' (*was abriss, wächst wieder zusammen*). The windmill spins. The continuity of a movement takes place within the always the Same. And yet, as the poem's opening demonstrates, the surety and the security of this continuity is broken. What is broken up shows the original rift. Here, the rift is not prior to the advent of time, nor is it time's precondition; the rift works with time, the time of complex repetition. The important point here is that this disruptive, though inevitable 'again' in which language works to show the movement of enriching – hence the *noch* – is itself given within a conception of language which will already have worked against the possibility of closure and completion. While there has to be a pragmatic moment – the point of communication and even translation – language is anoriginally there within a giving and breaking up, a movement thought within the inevitable determinations of repetition and history.

Having been 'enriched', language has a setting. The possibility of bleak humour remains in the double movement in which 'enriched', moving through the impossible translation of 'en-reiched' (*angereichert*), would move to the truth that language had been impoverished. Again, what seems to be at work here is the curious logic of the *Nichts, / nichts* in *Engführung*. In this instance it is not as straightforward. Here, it is essential to begin with the recognition that what is being stated by Celan in the speech has neither a directly moral nor ethical dimension. In other words, the continuity of language is inevitable, real; moreover, there is no choice. Indeed, rather than being positive, the continuity of language could be the opposite. For Celan, what may have been most harrowing is the fact that language did not let go, that language remained demanding to be used. Having to write, therefore, the inability not to write, might well have been the cruellest consequence not just of what language endured, but of what language forces onto the writing subject. Whether the allusions to metallurgy are retained in the attempt to translate *angereichert*, whether the already present inverted commas are taken to be the mark of irony, whether 'en-reiched' is deployed as the translation that captures the work of history, what remains is the fact that language will not let go. As such, what continues to return is the question of continuity. Rather than the despair of silence and impossibility – in the end an evocation that will obfuscate the presence of history by denying its particularity – there will emerge the more demanding, though perhaps equally as despairing, question of how to continue.

JABÈS' HOPE

At the end of *Le Retour au Livre*, at the book's closure, the end is marked out by the presentation of finality in terms that turn it away from that particular summation and termination which would seek to set out the final enclosure:

> L'homme n'existe pas. Dieu n'existe pas. Seul existe le monde à travers Dieu et l'homme dans le livre ouvert.

> Man does not exist. God does not exist. The world alone exists through God and man in the open book.[16]

An opening always resisting closure: such is the book in which man and God come to take their place. This opening without end is not to be understood as the simple but inexorable mark of a time trapped by and thus reduced to that constraining presentation occurring within the ends of teleology. Here, and despite the constraint of sense, the work having meaning, perhaps even having moral force, something else is at stake. The necessary presence of distance works to position the book and the Jew. What emerges from Jabès' own work is the recognition that the question of identity, be it of either the book or the Jew, is one without end. The question of identity remains a question. The force of this point pertains neither to semantic ambiguity nor the openness of inter-pretation, but to the nature of naming once it is understood in terms of an anoriginal ontological plurality.

The immediate difficulty is not just the question: To what does this opening refer? but the more complex one of just how this opening is to be thought. The question involves complexity since the opening is staged both by the physical presence of the words – their materiality – as well as within the content of these words. It is thus that the language of traditional ontology will come to be displaced by the process of having to think through this opening. Stasis will yield to becoming insofar as closure gives way to opening. While the detail cannot be explored here, it needs to be understood that the movement in question is not the simple and inherently nihilistic oscillations set within the frame of a binary opposition.

The opening refers, referring within the world of its multitude of possible referents, first to the Torah, to its very structure as book and thereby to the temporality of that structure: the copresence of repetition and renewal. Second, reference is made to the recurrent possibility of the enactment of the famous revelatory – if not redemptive – component of Lurianic Kabbalah, the component in which it is suggested that the 'white fire' which is the absent presence of writing will finally – even though it is a finality eschewing finality – burn through the 'black fire' or printed page to reveal itself as the true writing. In both cases, the end of revelation is a revelation without end. The movement or process signalled by these formulations, their evocation of flight, is not intended to re-tell (even if it were only as a recalled figure) the story of Ahasuerus, the wandering Jew.

Jabès' concern with movement needs to be situated in terms of his frequent evocation of *la brisure des Tables*. The fragmentation of the word of God does not introduce an element of nostalgia into his work, one which would work in terms of a deliverance towards – a work still turned by a type of hope – a return to the unity of man and God. The futural project of nostalgia is not involved. Rather, it is that Jabès rejects the desire for what would amount to a pre-Babelian paradise, and in so doing comes to rework both time and hope. The question to which this gives rise is the following: What is at play in this reworking? In spite of its apparent simplicity, the enormity of this question must be appreciated since, for Jabès, Judaism does not demand distance and exile. Rather, it itself *is* distance and exile itself. Even if exile were to be overcome, the Jew would remain as exiled from exile. The position of the exile is thereby compounded. In *Le Parcours*, Jabès voices this dangerous position for himself both as writer and as Jew.

> Je me suis senti l'exilé de l'exilé, le jour où je me suis reconnu juif.

> I felt myself to be an exile from exile the day I recognised myself to be Jewish.[17]

The doubling in this passage is both striking and disturbing. It introduces the paradox of identity which emerges both for the writer as well as for that which is considered in the writing when it is a matter of articulating the relationship between Judaism and writing. In *Dans la Double Dépendance du Dit*, the doubling of distance, the movement that effaces distance by maintaining it, is once again pronounced.

> Le rapport à la judéïcité, à l'écriture est rapport à l'étrangeté – dans son sens primitif et dans celui qu'il a acquis depuis. Il peut faire de nous, au plus fort de notre incondition, l'étranger de l'étranger.

> The relation to Jewishness, to writing is a relation to foreignness – both in its original meaning and in the one that it has acquired since. It can turn us, at the pinnacle of our non-condition, into the foreigner of the foreign.[18]

In *Le Livre des Questions*, the interplay of Judaism and writing is also charted in a way such that, in the end, and thereby also from the start, they are positioned as inextricably linked, a simultaneous identity and difference. While it is a continual and significant moment within Jabès' own writings, this link is succinctly presented in a line that has almost become a *sine qua non* within commentaries on Jabès. Despite the line's familiarity, it remains problematic and thus still engenders questions pertaining to the identity of that which has come to be linked. (It should already be clear that what will count as delimiting identity is itself already a complex issue.)

> Le judaïsme et l'écriture ne sont qu'une même attente, un même espoir, une même usure.

> Judaism and writing are only the same awaiting, the same hope, the same wearing away.[19]

Again what is central is 'hope' (*espoir*). Later in the same text, hope is presented anew – though this new presentation resists novelty in being a form of repetition – in terms of the book. *L'espoir est à la page prochaine* (Hope is on the next page). The introduction of 'the next page' reintroduces time and the book. (It will be essential to return to the temporality of the 'next'.) This connection is also present in *Le Petit Livre de la Subversion hors de Soupçon* where, in response to the question *Quelle est ton espérance?* (What is your hope?), comes the reply: *Celle de mon livre* (That of my book).[20] The response of the book to the question of hope needs to be given the larger context of writing itself. How can the question of hope be addressed, let alone answered, by the book? The response to this question will stem, in part, from what is signified in the opening, from, in other words, what is marked out by the book as open.

A further part of the answer is provided by Jabès' own description, given in response to a question from Marcel Cohen in *Du Désert au Livre*, of the necessary role of questioning, in establishing identity:

> Je crois que c'est par l'interrogation que nous créons notre identité. Être juif signifierait donc le devenir peu à peu. Nous ne serions, chaque fois, que sur le point d'être juif.

> I believe that it is through questioning that we create our identity. Being Jewish would mean, then, to become it, little by little. At each moment we would only be on the point of being Jewish.[21]

Later in the same passage, he goes on to suggest that to do no more than remain with the simple affirmation of Jewish identity articulated in the phrase 'I am a Jew' is to encourage complacency. While Jabès does not suggest it as such, this would have the further consequence of reopening the trap of a traditional ontology. This would occur because identity, and thus identity statements, would have a singular referent. Moreover, that to which reference was made would have a singular designation. Once identity is linked to questioning, and thus once it is maintained within the process and continuity of questioning, the contrary will be the case. Identity will inevitably have to endure as a quest always marked the temporality of the incomplete.

The formulation of *être juif* (a term whose very specificity resists any straightforward, let alone automatic, translation: 'being Jewish', 'Jewish being') takes place in terms of the process of a becoming that only yields identity via a continual opening. It is this opening that is staged by the writing. (As well as this staged opening, it would be possible to explicate both the temporality inherent in the interplay of identity and the ceaseless continuity of questioning in terms of the sundering writing – the figure of *auseinandergeschrieben* – which emerges from Celan's poetic practice.) What is deferred is the finality demanded by a traditional philosophical conception of identity. Therefore the question of Jewish identity comes to be posed – perhaps as a continual reposing – within the temporal structure that positions 'hope' in relation to 'the next page'. However, the distancing of completion should not be understood as failure, as something still undone. It is not as though identity has yet to be achieved or finality to be attained. Identity is not presented as the incomplete moving toward an inevitable completion. Any such movement would entail a devalued present, marked by loss and failure and where hope would be no more than the desire to efface the present. Thus construed, the present would only attain value in its having attained the future. However, as the question of identity is no longer posed within an ontology of stasis, the strategy of overcoming the incomplete in order to establish identity is no longer apposite. The question opens and there is no pregiven answer that can be given. Jabès' work should be read, therefore, as enacting a dramatic shift within the practice of questioning. The reposing of this question – its mode of being in having been reposed – works on hope. Rather than designating a future which, in being gestured at, causes the present to have become empty and the site of reconciliation's lack, hope will be the continuity of the process of questioning itself. Hope is the continuation of that process. The 'next page' is the book as continually read. The book is, henceforth, the book of questions and hence there is the Book that is always to be questioned.

It is this continuation which means that hope is not to be relegated to the future. Hope informs the present by yielding a present that is continually charged with hope, hope taking place in and as the now. Expectation is always to be lived out *now*. This is the opening. The future is not dismissed; it is present. The contemporary presence of the future means that it exists as an always present possibility. However, its being at the present has the result that were the future to be achieved, hope would have been abandoned. The book would have been finished, at last. The question would have been answered, finally. Standing apart from this finality – though part of it in terms of its inherently critical dimension – is the temporality of the 'next page'. It is not just that the hope may lie on the 'next page' and therefore be only ever futural. It is more profoundly at work in the always present possibility of there being the 'next page'. This generates a present whose complexity is marked and maintained by the copresence of an irreducible ontological and temporal difference. Hope is at the present in being 'on the next page'. There is the book. This is Jabès' hope. It is precisely the structure of hope that is also at work in Jabès' description of what could be described as anoriginary insistence. As he writes elsewhere: *Faire progresser l'origine, telle est la vocation de toute origine.*[22]

ANORIGINARY INSISTENCE

In a remarkable passage from *Le Soupçon, le Désert*, Jabès addresses the question of the origin.[23] However, it will be an origin that needs to be situated within a particular space. Blanchot writes of this particular setting in relation to the Jew.

> The Jew is the man of origins, who relates to the origin, not by dwelling, but by distancing himself, in this way saying that the truth of beginning is in separation.[24]

While for Blanchot there is a restriction of this position to the Jew, Jabès will have already extended it to cover and thus to incorporate the question of writing. As has been shown, the structure of hope is linked to both. Here in Blanchot's description, separating – and thus a distancing that is itself originary – not only introduces a certain nomadism, but at the same time separates distancing from loss, where loss is understood both as the source of melancholia as well as its sign. Distancing and separation become original conditions. Thus Jabès writes:

> 'Ecrire, signifierait-il assumer l'ultime lecture, d'abord mentale puis, à travers nos propres vocables, d'un livre dont la nécessité se confondrait avec notre raison d'être?
>
> 'En ce cas, le premier vocable serait l'annonciateur espéré, attendu de tous les livres. Il se marquerait comme point de ralliement et l'unique chance des innombrables mots qui, à sa suite, deviendraient visibles, lisibles.
>
> 'A cause de lui, la page jamais n'aurait été blanche.
>
> 'C'est pourquoi, d'emblée, il éveille nos soupçons – soupçon d'un

livre déjà écrit dans le livre à écrire et que sa brusque apparition trahit,
où régnait le silence, l'innocence,' disait-il.

(19)

'Would to write mean to undertake an ultimate reading, mentally first
of all, then through our own articulation, of a book whose necessity
would merge with our own reason for being?

'In this case, the first vocable would be the hoped for and awaited
harbinger of every book. It would show up as the rallying point and the
only chance of countless words which, after it, would become visible,
readable.

'Because of it, the page would never have been blank.

'This is why, immediately, it arouses our suspicion – the suspicion of
a book already written within the book to be written and the suspicion
that its sudden appearance betrays innocence where silence once
reigned,' he said.

(12–13)

Commenting on the passage has to begin with a recognition of its position
within the text. It is present as reported speech. What is said occurs as a
response. The lines preceding take neither the form of a direct question nor a
reported question. Nonetheless, they illicit this as a response. The lines in
question are the following:

Tu commentes le livre qui n'est pas celui offert à ta lecture, mais le livre
que tu t'appropries; le livre donc qui ressemble au livre que tu as lu.

(18–19)

You comment on the book which is not the one you read, but the one
you appropriate; the book that thus resembles the book you have read.

(21)

What is awaited? For what does every book hope? On one level, the answer must
be that the book awaits the opening inscription that enables it to be a book: from
the empty space of an unproductive nothing to a space filled within the differing
resonances of meaning. Such a conception of the book's effectuation is absent
from Jabès' demanding formulation. There is a word prior to the word. Its
presence means that the page *n'aurait été blanche*. But what is the force of this
claim?

An initial distancing works to hold the book. Holding it open means that
it has already begun. How, then, does a book or even a poem by Jabès, come
to be read? To ask this question is to ask about the place of meaning. While
the place of meaning will be the book, what is being opened up here is the

possibility that such an answer, the book *in simpliciter*, will simply not do. What would have to be taken into consideration is the status of the book and thus the nature of its being written. What the refusal of an original emptiness to the page entails is that if the work is already doubled – a word prior to the word – then the site of meaning is going to be a terrain that works to stage this doubling. An attentive reading of Jabès' work would show that the very structure of the page, the location of blocks of print within it, the use of different voices creating a narrative while defying any insertion into a narrative of untroubled continuity, all form part of an undertaking to enact precisely that founding set up. What is at work, therefore, is an attempt for the page to stage what was called above anoriginary insistence. With any opening there is always a risk; affirmation has to be understood as allowing for an opening that will always bring with it the risk of closure. Despite its insistence, the structure of hope has no necessary guarantee. It is this risk – captured by the doubling of *pas* – that announces the risk at the heart of opening:

> Il ne peut y avoir de lieu pour le commencement qui ne soit commencement d'un lieu infixable toujours à atteindre, à éteindre.
>
> Ainsi le pas n'est jamais que l'espérance – le risque, la blessure – du pas suivant.
>
> (29)

> There can be no place for beginning but the beginning of an unfixable place always to be attained, to be subdued.
>
> Thus the step is only ever the hope – the risk, the wound – of the next step.
>
> (21)

At work here is the recognition that the complete and the incomplete, the reality of a sundering writing, are not simply open possibilities. Effacing remains as a marked possibility. Yet the opening, marked by its anoriginal insistence, will sustain the structure of hope. The risk brings hope with it.

Jabès' drawing-together of the Jew and writing is not only revealing about the nature of writing and Judaism, but also makes a demand on thinking. What is demanded – for example, the need to allow for the possibility that opening and the incomplete provide the original possibility – is a thinking that is appropriate to such a set up. Part of what is demanded is that which allows hope – the structure of hope at work in these texts – to repeat the presence of a present that is always incomplete. It is this hope itself that structures his work and thus precisely this that his work enacts.

It is not a matter of Celan and Jabès being philosophical poets. Rather, the work that characterises their work – the work's work – becomes the affirmation of a founding and productive opening which, when it comes to be written – and perhaps their writing can best be named sundering writing, writing that is written asunder, *auseinandergeschrieben* – forces the *via negativa* aside and holds the intertwining of loss and nostalgia in abeyance by working with and thus allowing for the work of hope.

7

CONCLUSION
The renewal of hope

Hope endures. Hope is not a projection into the future. Such a projection would abandon the present, refusing to grant it any quality except the demand that it be effaced. Thinking the present, allowing for the present to insist, is not to remain complacent. The present exists as a complex set up which, whilst always allowing for forms of complacency, nonetheless provides the very setting in which complacency can be challenged. The difficult problem is one of explicating the present's own complexity. A way into understanding why such a difficulty may be at hand has to do with what has already been identified as characterising modernity. Once it becomes possible to allow for anoriginal complexity – i.e. a complexity that is there at the origin defying the reduction either to the axiomatic or the self-identical – then the counter-assertion of simplicity, the incorporation into the flow of continuity, the evocation of explanatory myths, all come into play. The affirmation of complexity and thus of irreducibility will always be met by moves attempting to establish forms of Sameness. The constant interplay between these two possibilities is the mark of modernity. Recognising the centrality of dislocation – the dislocation generating this interplay – demands an experiential interruption; a transformative experience. Dislocation entails a specific subject position. It is a position that is antithetical to the ones entailed by the varying forms of incorporation, continuity and myth. Opening up the subject will allow for a way into the problematic presence of hope at the present. It will also occasion the possibility of concluding.

THE SUBJECT OF HOPE

The subject, once understood as the self, is positioned in relation to the other. The self–other relationship can be taken as providing, in different ways, the place of the subject; the subject *is* in its already present relation to the other.[1] It is the subject's positioning that provides the locus of the ethical. While there may be necessary ethical reason to allow the otherness of the other to be, there could be no such thing as absolute alterity. The absolutely other would be simply unrecognisable. For the presence of the other to function as that which demands an ethical response, the other must be both same and other; the other must have this position at one and the same time. The copresence of sameness and otherness depends upon some type of recognition. The simultaneity of time is what allows for the introduction of this form of complexity. At any one time the sameness of the other must endure along with its otherness. The force of this description pertains once it becomes important to take up the particular determinations of human existence. Within such determinations the self is defined as both self and other. The self can recognise its own being as an other in the claims for its autonomy. Autonomy becomes the assertion by the self not of its selfhood per se, but of its alterity. The possibility that such an assertion could be given any credence relies, at the most minimal level, on an enduring and shared conception of self. And yet the situation is more demanding than it seems. There are two additional factors that need to be sketched prior to any conclusions being drawn. The first pertains to the recognition of alterity and the second to that which delimits the place and positioning of the autonomous subject. These two positions are obviously interrelated. Addressing them, therefore, will demand that consideration be given to their necessary connection.

Recognising alterity may mean recognising a physical difference: 'I am not that person'. Equally, it may mean recognising that difference involves a form of dependency: 'I am myself to the extent that I am not that person'. Both forms of recognition start with the coherence of the self. The 'I am' is identical with the consciousness announcing that it is. Here, there is an important form of identity. It is not the traditional I=I (and in this instance whether it is Fichte or Hegel is unimportant) but the identity between the 'I' asserting its existence, and the existence of that which asserts the 'I'. On one level, it cannot be disputed that there is an identity between consciousness and the assertion of the 'I am'. Any 'I am' would be conscious of its existence. The difficulty emerges when the claim is that one is absolutely identical with the other. Absolute identity would amount to the assertion that 'I am the same as my self: thus I am self-identical'. It will be in suggesting why this formulation fails to grasp both the complexity of the self and the complex levels of subject positioning, that the subject itself will open up, thereby allowing what pertains to the subject of hope to be addressed.

There are two ways of addressing the presence of complexity. What is involved in each are differing processes yielding and positioning subjects. The first would be via the distinction established by Freud between the 'coherent ego and the repressed'.[2] Arguments claiming absolute self-identity tend to conflate the two halves of this distinction. Furthermore, it is a distinction that can be taken a step further once it is recognised that not only are there conscious responses between individuals but that the unconscious – and therefore unconscious responses and reception – are also at work. Therefore, not only is the self no longer strictly self-identical, but the relationship between individuals cannot be construed in terms of a conception of intersubjectivity based on purely self-identical agents.

The second way in which it is possible to address complexity has to do with the assertion of autonomy. While the individual can refer to him or herself using a proper name, while the proper name may be that through which the particularity of an individual's autonomy is advanced, and while the proper name will always identify a given individual, the control, use, indeed the actual construction of the network that is the proper name's field of activity, can only allude or refer to the individual bearing that name to the extent that the complete mastery of its field of operations eludes the particular individual. The proper name must be both. In other words, it must refer, even though its operation will always involve more than that which is given by pure reference. What constructs the operation of the proper name is its capacity to operate within a particular field. The name is deployed within the field which marks the presence of the individual, even though it can never be made identical with the individual's presence. While there will always be a referential relation, there will always be more than that which is identified by this relation. This 'always more' is not adduced; it occurs at the same time. It would be in these terms that it would be possible to rewrite the history of the proper name.

The dispersal of the name, however, is not absolute. It still names and identifies, and is thus that through which autonomy is asserted. In the end, the limits to arguments concerning autonomy are to be located at this point. Once it is allowed that there cannot be a pure reduction to the individual, then the assertion of autonomy becomes a claim to finitude. It is, however, never just finitude, since finitude is that which will always have a determination. In a sense this is almost the definition of finitude. Autonomy is asserted in the name of a given individual. However, that name will always incorporate more than it designates at a particular moment. Arguing for this position cannot be a simple exercise in the semantics of the proper name. Any argument would need to deploy the necessary relation between naming and ontology. Once a claim is made about the self, the subject, the individual, in sum that which will bear, in arguments to do with autonomy, a proper name, then what is being advanced is a claim about identity.

Disagreements concerning naming and the self will, in fact, be disputes staged within the philosophy of identity. The dispersal of the name which, while occurring, still demands identification, as opposed to a conception of the proper name as that which refers in a direct manner to what is necessarily individual in nature, is an opposition between a conception of complexity allowing for individuation on the one hand, and the restriction of reference to what is originally simple on the other. With regard to the latter, it will be possible to universalise on the basis that the uniqueness of each individual is, quite literally, there in name alone. As for the former, universalising will involve a more difficult argument.

Universalising beyond the name – the name as direct referent – is possible precisely because the proper name will allow for a process of individuation within the Same. Arguments for the sanctity of the individual which link individuality to that which bears a proper name, will only reiterate the impossible opposition between the individual and the group. What will have been left out of any consideration will be the possibility that being a self or subject means already being in relation to the other. Not, however, as an individual in relation to an already determined other – the other individual – but as part of a field involving conscious and unconscious determinations within which the individual is continuously constructed and maintained. In other words, the opposition here is not between two different conceptions of the individual. The opposition can only be understood once it is recognised that the opposition in question concerns two different conceptions of identity; the difference, in sum, is ontological. Moreover, while ontology maintains the opposition, there is a necessarily temporal dimension. It will be in terms of the ontologico-temporal that it will be possible to open the two different conceptions of universality and in so doing to return to the subject position demanded by dislocation.

Positing the centrality of the individual brings with it a conception of universality that takes the Same as its overriding determinant. While this may seem a merely abstract claim, what it indicates is that the individual will be linked to differing conceptions of universality all of which hold to the centrality of the Same. What will have to be specified is how the Same is to be understood. It could entail the universality of the subject of right, it could be universal human nature. It could even be more specific and refer to a nation, to a continent (e.g. Europe) or to a potentially mythic construct (e.g. the West). Nonetheless, each time the Same is invoked it brings with it its complex opposition to the individual. The Same may be opposed to the individual such that the individual comes to be incorporated; or it is opposed such that the individual resists or is refused incorporation. In either case what is at work is the opposition between the individual and the differing forms of the universality of the Same.

Countering the dominance of the Same is, in fact, to counter that which continues to work against the insistence of dislocation. However, such a move should not be understood as a simple counter-positing, as though all that were being claimed is that in any opposition to the Same there is dislocation. Indeed, this can be taken as reworking the claim concerning the primacy of the individual. It is not as though in opposition to the centrality of the individual there is pure dispersion. It is, rather, that the individual is given in relation to the differing conceptions of universality. Countering that relationship will be a conception of the individual understood as the constant presence of individuated finitude across a field of activity that cannot be controlled by the individual – this would be the fantasy of the ego – but which itself positions, holds and determines the individual. The constant counter of one conception of identity with the other, stakes out the domain of modernity. Constituted by the nature of modernity, the reiteration of the Same is, nonetheless, that which seeks to efface its presence. Without exploring their detail, it is still possible to suggest that the Same brings with it differing modalities of completion. Incorporation into the universal is, after all, a form of finality. Interrupting, or holding back the activity of completion – the work of the Same – demands that the incomplete be linked to a form of finitude rather than being a mere counter-measure to the complete. Finitude without end – without project – can be contrasted to finality. Finality would be the refusal of hope. Finitude without end would be its affirmation. Finality allows for the future because it projects the completion of the present as the task of the future. Finitude is that which is given by the discontinuous continuity that marks the complex repetition within the present. The relationship between the incomplete and repetition is not just the reintroduction of the importance of time; it is the reiteration of the centrality of the ontologico-temporal. Rather than deferring the future, the future is occasioned by a repetition that is no longer the simple reiteration of the Same. This possibility for repetition could itself only be realised because of the continual presence of the incomplete. The subject position of dislocation is given by the relationship between repetition and the incomplete, and given in the transformative experience occasioned by the effective presence of that relationship.

REPETITION, RENEWAL

One of the predominating themes throughout the preceding has been renewal, understood as the inability not to continue. Celan, Jabès, Libeskind, can all be interpreted as working with a tripartite necessity. The first part is the necessity to go on. The second part is the necessity not to go on if all that is involved is a repetition of the Same. The third is the necessity that arises for formal innovation. What provides the moment of division, the opening up of necessity, splitting it into three elements which when taken together introduce important and productive difficulties, is the Shoah. The Shoah, as has been argued, brings the present and modernity into conjunction.

Again, it is worth pausing in order to ask how the despair of the Shoah could be linked to renewal. Renewal is not a letting go. Nor is it mere survival. It numbs to read poets writing of, or after the Shoah. Exemplary in this respect is Nelly Sachs' *Ein totes Kind spricht (A Dead Child Speaks)*[3] in which the dead child locates in its death the reality of already having been parted from its mother. Rather than death as a release, in the final moments there is the harrowing reiteration of already having been parted, of its mother having been struck down by 'the knife of parting'. Her poem doubles the horror. Having read the poem there is a temptation to argue that were it not for poetry then this doubled horror could not have been laid bare. There is neither comfort nor consolation to be found in the poem's work; not a moment within it attests to the universalising themes of the folly of war or the sometimes brutal nature of human existence. The poem ends with the following lines:

> Als man mich zum Tode führte,
> Fühlte ich im letzten Augenblick noch
> Das Herausziehen des großen Abschiedsmessers.

> A I was led to death,
> I still felt in the last moment
> The unsheathing of the great knife of parting.

As the title indicates, in this poem a dead child speaks. No attempt is made to describe the child. Here, the child is neither the object of description, nor does it have an actual autobiographical voice. The child is not speaking. The poem is a fiction. It is, of course, far from a fiction. There could not have been such a fiction. Outside of the deadening effect of reading the dead child's words, hearing its voice, listening to it speak, there would seem to be nothing. There is no attempt here to denigrate the poem or even to plot its limit. All that is being identified is its effect. While it may twist the language it is possible to suggest that it effects a nothing. There is no connective moment. The poem stands on its own. It is. While the poet may have wished to voice the dead child's words and may even have wished to have become closer to the victims, the reader will remain held and distanced.

After this poem there is nothing. Any possibility of admiring assonance will be stemmed by what is brought about by the juxtaposition of words. Here, nothing will be the mark of singularity. The poem is singular precisely because of the absence of a connecting link. Neither the human condition nor a generalised and therefore almost necessarily banalised conception of suffering are invoked. As was suggested, it is what it is; almost a monument to its own singularity. Each reader will be forced to encounter the chill of the singular. From within poetry, the determining effect of the Shoah is being registered. The response from within philosophy to the Shoah's insistent particularity has been addressed within the earlier chapters. What is important here is responding to the question that concerns how its unique nature bears on renewal.

The basis of any response to this question is the position of the reader as being both held and distanced. Being held is the moment of recognition – again, it attests to the impossibility of complete alterity – whilst being distanced. It marks both the singularity of what it is that occurred and the impossibility of its assimilation. Holding and distancing, therefore, provide the site of continuity in the precise sense that they mark out the place in which the already identified threefold necessity of continuity is to be enacted. Being held, once generalised, is to allow for the necessity of having to respond to the Shoah's insistence. Being distanced is the demand stemming from having to maintain as unique that which took place. Maintaining it as such involves differing undertakings. One will be the continual rehearsal of the categorical imperative identified by Adorno. Acting in a way that intends to preclude the repetition of the Shoah, thinking, writing in a form that does not repeat that which either accompanied it or was silent in the face of it, are inevitably forms of renewal. They are, however, forms of renewal that are given within the overall structure of repetition.

The philosophical task – the task announced by the interconnection of modernity and the present, this particular formulation of the epochal present – is given within repetition. There is, after all, the necessity to go on. And yet, here repetition cannot be a simple reiteration of the Same. In opening up the possibility of a repetition taking place again for the first time, it becomes possible to respond to Adorno's categorical imperative. Equally, it is to respect the structure of hope emerging from Celan's poetry. Both delineate the task of continuity as well as the complex nature of the continuity involved. Holding to the necessity of a discontinuous continuity is to reinscribe the centrality of the incomplete, to insist on the subject of dislocation and to maintain the effective presence of the structure of hope.

Their interarticulation is the site of present hope.

NOTES

CHAPTER 1

1 For a detailed engagement with Descartes and Hegel that takes the centrality of the incomplete – and thus the impossibility of absolute completion – as its point of departure, see Georges Bataille, *Oeuvres Complètes*, tome V, Paris: Gallimard, 1973, 123–30.

2 It is for this reason that this book continues the project of my earlier work, *The Plural Event*, London: Routledge, 1993.

3 I am taking this to be one of the defining motifs of Walter Benjamin's conception of modernity. However, rather than limiting dislocation to Benjamin's sense, it has been given far greater extension within the confines of this work.

4 Pursuing this 'moment' could take place in terms of tracing the nature of Freud's break with Breuer. I have attempted to describe this break in these terms in *Translation and the Nature of Philosophy*, London: Routledge, 1989, 110–26. For an argument showing that the nature of this split involved more than a mere redescription of the object, see Rachael Bowlby, 'A Happy Event', *Paragraph*, vol. 14, 1, 1991, 10–20.

5 There will always be a difficulty with this term. Whether the Holocaust is used, or whether Auschwitz is taken to name all places, a problem endures. What, after all, is being named? In part, this is the question that is being addressed in this chapter and, more specifically, in Chapter 3.

6 There is a considerable amount of important philosophical literature that has been written on this problem of continuity. See in particular Jean-François Lyotard, *Le Différend*, Paris: Editions de Minuit, 1983.

7 For philosophy, this question is perhaps at its most demanding in Adorno. The philosophical question would concern how to respond to what Adorno (in *Negative Dialectics*, trans. E. B. Ashton, London: Routledge, 1990, 365) identifies as a 'new categorical imperative':

> A new categorical imperative has been imposed by Hitler upon unfree mankind: to arrange their thoughts and actions so that Auschwitz will not repeat itself, so that nothing similar will happen.

8 Here, in *Present Hope*, the emphasis is on Benjamin and Heidegger. In *The Politics of*

Judgement: the Cosmopolitan Present, London: Routledge, forthcoming, emphasis will be given to Kant and Hegel.

9 Jacques Derrida, 'Canons and Metonymies', trans. R. Rand and A. Wygant, in R. Rand (ed.) *Logomachia: the Conflict of the Faculties*, Lincoln: University of Nebraska Press, 1992, 212.

10 Once again, this is to presuppose the argument of *The Plural Event*. I have tried, more recently, to argue this position in greater detail in 'Figuring Self-Identity: Blanchot's Bataille', in J. Steyn (ed.) *Other then Identity*, Manchester: Manchester University Press, 1997.

11 There are many examples of this staging. They will include Descartes' description in both the *Discours de la Méthode* and the *Méditations* that what is given in order to establish truth is no longer adequate. Philosophy at the present is wanting. Equally, Descartes' own autobiographical references introduce temporal concerns. Hegel, in the *Difference Essay*, and Kant, in 'Idea for a Universal History with a Cosmopolitan Purpose' (in H. Reiss (ed.) *Kant's Political Writings*, Cambridge: Cambridge University Press, 1992), refer to the determining presence of the age on their conception of philosophical activity. I have discussed Hegel's essay in *The Plural Event*. The important passage from Kant is the following:

> Although this political body exists for the present [*jetzt*] only in the roughest of outlines, it nonetheless seems as if a feeling [*ein Gefühl*] is beginning to stir all its members, each of which has an interest in maintaining the whole. And this encourages the hope [*Hoffnung*] that, after many revolutions, with all their transforming effects, the highest purpose of nature, a universal cosmopolitan existence, will at last be realised as the matrix within which all the original capacities of the human race may develop.
>
> (51)

12 I have retained the German title of Benjamin's text rather than the invented 'Theses on the Philosophy of History'. It is unclear that these fragments are theses in any conventional sense of the term. See Walter Benjamin, *Gesammelte Schriften*, vol. 1.2, Frankfurt: Suhrkamp, 1991, 696; trans. Harry Zohn in Walter Benjamin, *Illuminations*, London: Fontana, 1986, 257.

13 Martin Heidegger, *An Introduction to Metaphysics*, trans. Ralph Manheim, New Haven: Yale University Press, 1959, 95.

14 Martin Heidegger, *Nietzsche*, vol. 2, Pfullingen: Neske, 1961, 254; trans. F. Capuzzi as *Nietzsche*, vol. 4, San Francisco: Harper and Row, 1982, 195.

15 I have tried to argue this position in 'Present Remembrance: Anselm Kiefer's *Iconoclastic Controversy*' in my *Art, Mimesis and the Avant-Garde*, London: Routledge, 1991.

16 Theodor Adorno, *Prismen*, Frankfurt: Suhrkamp, 1976, 31; trans. S. and S. Weber as *Prisms*, Cambridge MA: MIT Press, 1984, 34.

17 Sigmund Freud, 'Mourning and Melancholia' in *The Standard Edition of the Complete Psychological Works of Sigmund Freud*, vol. XIV, London: Hogarth Press, 1975. All further page references will be given in the text.

18 For an important discussion of this theme, see Sarah Kofman, *Paroles Suffoquées*, Paris: Galiée, 1987, especially 15–17.

19 Here, I am making use of the formulation advanced by Edith Wyschogrod in *Spirit in*

Ashes: Hegel, Heidegger and Man-Made Mass Death, New Haven: Yale University Press, 1985.

20 This is why, for Fackenheim, the meaning of *tikkun olam* has a profoundly different force after the Shoah. See his *To Mend the World: Foundations of Post-Holocaust Thought*, New York: Schocken Books, 1989.

21 Maurice Blanchot, *L'Ecriture du désastre*, Paris: Gallimard, 1980, 131.

22 I have tried to develop the detail of this logic in my *Object Painting*, London: Academy Editions, 1994.

CHAPTER 2

1 The importance attributed here to writing is not intended to rehearse the issues involved in authorship. Nor, moreover, is it envisaged as raising generic problems: the relationship between philosophy and literature, for example. Here, writing attests to the necessarily textual nature of philosophy's presentation. Writing is, therefore, the site where the task – the philosophical task – is announced.

2 Here, 'Konvolut N' of Benjamin's *Das Passagen-Werk* and Heidegger's 'Time and Being' are, for reasons advanced at a later stage, attributed the status of forewords. See Walter Benjamin, 'N', in Benjamin, *Gesammelte Schriften*, vol. 1, Frankfurt: Suhrkamp, 1991; trans. L. Hafrey and R. Sieburth as 'N (Re the Theory of Knowledge, Theory of Progress)' in Gary Smith (ed.) *Benjamin: Philosophy, Aesthetics, History*, Berkeley: University of California Press, 1983. Martin Heidegger, *Zur Sache des Denkens*, Tübingen: Niemeyer, 1983; trans. Joan Stambaugh as *On Time and Being*, New York: Harper and Row, 1972. All further references will be given in the text, the German pagination preceding the English.

3 G. Scholem (ed.) *The Correspondence of Walter Benjamin and Gershom Scholem, 1932–40*, trans. G. Smith and A. Lefevre, New York: Schocken Books, 1989, 159.

4 Walter Benjamin, *Ursprung des Deutschen Trauerspiels*, in Benjamin, *Gesammelte Schriften*, vol. 1, 207; trans. J. Osbourne as *The Origin of German Tragic Drama*, London: Verso, 1977, 27.

5 Scholem, *Correspondence*, 159.

6 Walter Benjamin, 'Berliner Chronik', in Benjamin, *Gesammelte Schriften*, vol. 1, 486; trans. E. Jephcott and K. Shoeter as 'A Berlin Chronicle', in *One Way Street and Other Essays*, London: Verso, 1985, 314.

7 Part of the weight is the recognition that within these passages from 'Konvolut N' 'the present' even, whilst not made specific, nonetheless marks out and therefore incorporates the site of the task's enactment. Given that the project here involves thinking through the ontology of the present, the present itself has, in virtue of that project, a double burden.

8 In the end, what experience will demand is to be rethought in terms of the problem of agency. What this involves is a rethinking that arises out of the impossibility of singularity, even a complex singularity, of agency. While it is a problem of considerable intricacy, it is still possible to argue in general terms that another limit within the work of Benjamin and Heidegger concerns agency. With Heidegger, it is the retention of the necessary singularity of the agent, while for

Benjamin it will emerge as the inability to account in his terms for the agency of 'dialectical experience'.

9   Martin Heidegger, *Nietzsche*, vol. 2, Pfullingen: Neske, 1961; trans. Frank A. Capuzzi as *Nietzsche*, vol. 4, San Francisco: Harper and Row, 1982. All page references are given in the text, the German reference preceding the English.

10 I will return to this problematic of the 'we' in Chapter 6 of this volume.

11 Whilst it cannot be pursued here, it is nonetheless worth noting that Heidegger's emphasis on experience is presented most systematically in the opening of 'The Nature of Language'.

12 I have pursued in greater detail the interpretative problems opened up by this 'without' in *The Plural Event*, London: Routledge, 1993, 140–57.

13 While the projects are different, it should still be noted that the discussion of reconciliation presented here has been greatly influenced by Rebecca Comay's remarkable paper, 'Redeeming Revenge: Nietzsche, Benjamin, Heidegger and the Politics of Memory', in C. Koelb (ed.) *Nietzsche as Postmodernist*, New York: SUNY, 1990.

14 For a more sustained treatment of *Nachträglichkeit* within psychoanalysis, see the recent collection of papers by and about Jean Laplanche, edited by J. Fletcher and M. Stanton, *Jean Laplanche: Seduction, Translation, Drives*, London: ICA, 1992.

15 The reference here is to Walter Benjamin, Gesammelte Schriften, vol.2, 703; *Illuminations*, trans. Harry Zohn, London: Fontana, 1973, 264. While the passage warrants a detailed analysis, it is nonetheless essential to note the way in which the question of time – to be understood as the question of the present of historical time – is, within it, reposed away from a simple gesture toward the future:

> The soothsayers who found out from time what it has in store did not experience time as either homogeneous or empty. Anyone who keeps this in mind will perhaps get an idea of how past times were experienced in remembrance, namely, in just the same way. We know that the Jews were prohibited from investigating the future. The Torah and the prayers instruct them in remembrance, however. This stripped the future of its magic, to which all those succumb who turn to soothsayers for enlightenment. This does not imply, however, that for the Jews the future turned into homogeneous, empty time. For every second of time was the strait gate through which the Messiah might enter.

16 Tradition may seem to admit of a plurality, i.e. it may seem that there are many traditions. And yet, any such description misses the role of power within tradition. There is a dominant tradition. Its unfolding is construed as the site of continuity, the continuity of certain power relations. Blasting it apart, therefore, is more than the simple critique of a posited singularity.

17 See in particular H. D. Kittsteiner, 'Walter Benjamin's Historicism', *New German Critique*, 39, fall 1986.

18 References to Leibniz are to P. Janet (ed.) *Oeuvres Philosophiques de Leibniz*, vol. II, Paris, 1866. For the English edition of the *Monadology*, I have used that edited and translated by E. Latta as *Leibniz's Monadology*, Oxford: Oxford University Press, 1972.

19 Leibniz, *Oeuvres*, vol. II, 608.

20 The position under attack is brought out in Benjamin's quotation of Grillparzer:

To contrast the theory of history with Grillparzer's comment, translated by Edmond Jaloux in 'Journaux intimes' (Le Temps, 23 [Mai 1937]): 'To read into the future is difficult, but to see purely into the past is even more so; I say purely which is to say without mixing that retrospective gaze with everything that has happened in the meantime.' The 'purity' of the gaze is not so much difficult as impossible to attain

(N 7, 5)

The impossibility in question is not explicable in terms of the historian's failure. In other words, the point being made does not concern the ability or inability of the historian to complete a specific task. Furthermore, various historians and philosophers will always claim to have achieved the 'gaze' that Benjamin is describing here as impossible. The reason for this impossibility has, in part, to do with the ontology of the 'historical object' and, in part, with the way memory works both to inform and construct the present.

21 The substantive methodological point here is that any presentation of works – even if these were accompanied by written text – which oriented itself around the juxtaposition of images, drawings and photographs, in the belief that this illuminated Benjamin's project, would have taken the references to montage far too literally. As such, it would miss what is essential to montage, namely time.

CHAPTER 3

1 George Steiner, 'The Long Life of Metaphor: An Approach to the Shoah', *Encounter*, 68, 2, 1987.
2 Walter Benjamin, 'Einbahnstraße', in Benjamin, *Gesammelte Schriften*, vol. 4.1, Frankfurt: Suhrkamp, 1983, trans. E. Jephcott and K. Shorter as 'One Way Street', in Benjamin, *One Way Street and Other Writings*, London: Verso, 1979, 95.
3 Walter Benjamin, 'Schicksal und Charakter', in Benjamin, *Gesammelte Schriften*, vol. 2.1; translated as 'Fate and Character', in *One Way Street*. All subsequent references to the English translation will be given in the text.
4 *Gesammelte Schriften*, vol. 4.1, 398; *One Way Street*, 158.
5 T. Bhati makes a similar point, but pursues it in quite another direction. See T. Bhati, 'Theories of Knowledge: Fate and Forgetting in the Early Works of Walter Benjamin', in R. Nägele (ed.) *Benjamin's Ground*, Detroit: Wayne State University Press, 1988.
6 There is a similar formulation of the relation between tragedy and silence in Franz Rosenzweig's *The Star of Redemption*, trans. W. Hallo, London: Routledge, 1971, 77–8. For a detailed treatment of the relationship between the two thinkers, see S. Moses, 'Walter Benjamin and Franz Rosenzweig', *The Philosophical Forum*, XV, 1–2 (1983–4).
7 Rodolphe Gasché, 'Saturnine Vision and the Question of Difference: Reflections on Walter Benjamin's Theory of Language', in Nägele, *Benjamin's Ground*, 85.
8 Benjamin, *Illuminations*, trans. Harry Zohn, London: Fontana, 1982, 264.
9 This position is argued in much greater detail in Chapter 1 of this volume.
10 I have tried to develop this idea of present remembrance in the context of

interpretations of Anselm Kiefer's paintings. See my *Art, Mimesis and the Avant-Garde*, London: Routledge, 1991, Chapter 4; and my discussion of Kiefer in *Object Painting*, London: Academy Editions, 1994.

11 Similar questions have emerged within contemporary Judaism. For orthodoxy, as represented by Jonathan Sacks, see 'The Holocaust has not Changed the Meaning of Jewish Life', in *Tradition in an Untraditional Age*, London: Vallentine, 1990, 151. Within orthodox Judaism there is a continual preference to remember the Shoah within the structure of *Tisha B'av* (the fast day marking the destruction of the Second Temple), rather than allowing its remembrance a special day: *Yom HaShoah*. What is at issue here is the extent to which tradition already contains the resources to deal with any subsequent occurrence. In general terms, the question of how to remember involves a stand, one which defines the present, in relation to historical time.

12 See the more detailed discussion of this 'thesis' in Chapters 1 and 2 of this volume.

13 Theodor Adorno, 'What Does Coming to Terms with the Past Mean?', in G. Hartman (ed.) *Bitburg in Moral and Political Perspective*, Bloomington: Indiana University Press, 1990, 117.

CHAPTER 4

1 One of the real difficulties that confronts any attempt to be philosophical about the political is to give a philosophical description of fascism. Here, the approach that has been taken centres on time. In other words, what marks out the particularity of fascism is the way it positions historical time. The setting in which this positioning takes place is modernity. What makes fascism another possibility for modernity – another form of modernity – is that the demand to differentiate the present from itself takes place in the name of a yet to be realised possibility. What defines the 'yet to be realised' is not utopian, but draws upon the complex interplay of race and geography in order to locate an eternal impulse demanding realisation. For this precise reason, fascism is marked by an inherently futural dimension. The future will consist in an actualisation of the eternal; the present will be marked by the struggles to actualise it.

2 George Steiner, *No Passion Spent*, London: Faber and Faber, 1996, 129.

3 George Steiner, *Real Presences*, London: Faber and Faber, 1989, 140.

4 See George Steiner, *The Death of Tragedy*, London: Faber and Faber, 1961.

5 See Ruth Padel, 'George Steiner and the Greekness of Tragedy' in N. A. Scott and R. A. Sharpe (eds) *Reading George Steiner*, Baltimore: Johns Hopkins University Press, 1994.

6 See 'Building, Dwelling, Thinking', in Heidegger, *Basic Writings*, San Francisco: Harper and Row, 1984, 363. The question of the homelessness of man plays a fundamental role in a number of Heidegger's texts. Here it provides one of the key formulations of Heidegger's conception of the epochal present.

7 Heidegger, *An Introduction to Metaphysics*, trans. Ralph Manheim, New Haven: Yale University Press, 1959, 151.

8 Steiner, *No Passion Spent*, 137.

9 Gershom Scholem (ed.) *The Correspondence of Walter Benjamin and Gershom Scholem, 1932–1940*, trans. G. Smith and A. Lefevre, New York: Schocken Books, 1989, 159.

10 Walter Benjamin, *Ursprung des Deutschen Trauerspiels*, in *Gesammelte Schriften*, vol.

1.1, Frankfurt: Suhrkamp, 1983; trans. J. Osbourne as *The Origin of German Tragic Drama*, London: Verso, 1977. All further references will be cited in the text, English pagination following the German. The complex problem here is the meaning attributed by Benjamin to the terms allegory and symbol. For two important overviews of this problem, see S. Weber, 'Genealogy of Modernity: History, Myth and Allegory in Benjamin's *Origin of the German Mourning Play*', *MLN*, 106, April 1991, and M. Pensky, *Melancholy Dialectics: Walter Benjamin and the Play of Mourning*, Amherst: University of Massachusetts Press, 1993. The importance of these works is considerable. Nonetheless, the project undertaken here is not meant to provide an expository commentary on Benjamin, but to utilise aspects of his work. Holding onto elements – for example, retaining his insistence on dislocation – bending some back on themselves – for example, reading Baudelaire against Benjamin's own reading of the poet – while nonetheless still allowing the project of maintaining the particularity of modernity to be paramount.

11 There is an important tradition of interpretation that reads the history plays in terms of the crisis of legitimation. While assuming that tradition, I am trying to position two contrasting subject positions: one which can hold the world of disarray within a single vision, and another that will always see dislocation in terms of continuity and synthesis. The latter is uniquely modern. The former is Hal's vision. Only by maintaining their distinct determinations is it possible to establish a real distinction between the Baroque and modernity.

12 E. Bronfen, *Over Her Dead Body*, Manchester: Manchester University Press, 1992, 242.

13 José Antonio Marvall, *Culture of the Baroque*, trans. T. Cochan, Minneapolis: Minnesota University Press, 1986, 149.

14 Baudelaire, *Oeuvres Complètes*, Paris: Robert Laffont, 1986, 797.

15 See Walter Benjamin, 'N', in Benjamin, *Gesammelte Schriften*, vol. 5.1, Frankfurt: Suhrkamp, 1991; trans. L. Hafrey and R. Sieburth as 'N (Re the Theory of Knowledge, Theory of Progress)' in Gary Smith (ed.) *Benjamin: Philosophy, Aesthetics, History*, Berkeley: University of California Press, 1983. There are three central passages in which this formulation occurs. They are N 2a, 1; N 2a, 2; and N 2a, 3.

16 Benjamin, *Gesammelte Schriften*, vol. 1.2, 473; trans. Harry Zohn as 'Theses on the Philosophy of History' in Benjamin, *Illuminations*, London: Fontana, 1986, 220.

17 Benjamin, *Gesammelte Schriften*, vol. 3; translated as 'Theories of German Fascism', in *New German Critique*, 17, Spring 1979. Benjamin's analysis has exercised a considerable influence on the treatment of fascism in this chapter.

18 See M. Domarus (ed.) *Hitler. Reden und Proklamationen 1932–45*, vol. 1, Munich: Süddeutscher, 1965, 705–6.

19 In Benjamin, *Gesammelte Schriften*, vol. 1.2, 695; *Illuminations*, 257.

20 Giorgio Agamben, *Infancy and History*, London: Verso, 1993, 91.

21 Again, this formulation repeats a number of positions argued for in greater detail in my *The Plural Event*, London: Routledge, 1993.

22 Steiner, *No Passion Spent*, 139.

23 Steiner, *No Passion Spent*, 140; my emphasis.

CHAPTER 5

1 For an important analysis of the link between the question of German identity and

the inherent racism within totalitarianism which marked National Socialism, see Philippe Lacoue-Labarthe and Jean-Luc Nancy, *Le Mythe Nazi*, Paris: Editions de l'Aube, 1991. For a larger overview of the position and treatment of the Jew within German thought, see P. Rose, *German Question/Jewish Question: Revolutionary Anti-Semitism from Kant to Wagner*, Princeton: Princeton University Press, 1992.

2 This is not an abstract question. It introduces the issues that pertain not just to Holocaust memorial in Germany but, more particularly, the construction of the Jewish Museum in Berlin. The result of the work of the architect Daniel Libeskind, this museum is treated in a sustained manner in the second half of this chapter. While the context is different, it may be that Maurice Blanchot's description of Berlin as itself being 'the problem of division' could be of use in developing an understanding of the way in which absence and presence constitute a division at the centre and thus at the present. See Maurice Blanchot, 'Berlin', *Modern Language Notes*, 109, 1994.

3 James Young, *The Texture of Memory*, New Haven: Yale University Press, 1993, 15.

4 One of the most emphatic attempts to think the relation of Judaism and Christianity that situates itself outside of the synthesising project of Hegelianism – a project neces-sarily implicated in the overcoming, both philosophical and actual, of Judaism – is Jean-François Lyotard's *Un Trait d'Union*, Quebec: Editions le Griffon d'Argile, 1993.

5 References here are to Jean-Paul Sartre's *Réflexions sur la Question Juive*, Paris: Gallimard, 1954; and G. W. F. Hegel, *Grundlinien der Philosophie des Rechts*, Frankfurt: Suhrkamp, 1986; trans. T. Knox as *The Philosophy of Right*, Oxford: OUP, 1981. In the case of Sartre, the page number of *Réflexions* is given in the text. For a more detailed account of Hegel's writings on Judaism, see Rose, *German Question/Jewish Question*, 109–16. For a more sympathetic treatment, see E. L. Fackenheim, *The Religious Dimensions of Hegel's Thought*, Bloomington: Indiana University Press, 1967.

6 In commenting on this passage, Sander Gilman notes with succinct accuracy that:

> what Sartre – hardly a Christian thinker – incorporates into the
> model of the Jew is the model of particularist humility in the face
> of suffering. This does not permit Jews much range to create a
> discourse appropriate to themselves.

See Sander Gilman, *The Jew's Body*, New York: Routledge, 1991, 21–2. What Gilman refers to here as a discourse whose propriety is linked to Jews – recognising immediately the problem of universalising, even amongst 'Jews' – will be taken up here in terms of Jewish being. The importance of Gilman's observation demands that it be elaborated. For another critical account of this aspect of Sartre's work which attempts to place it within the larger context of his major philosophical writings, see S. Z. Charmé, 'Authenticity, Multiculturalism and the Jewish Question', *Journal of the British Society for Phenomenology*, vol. 25, 2, May 1994.

7 Michael Camille, *The Gothic Idol: Ideology and Image-Making in Gothic Art*, Cambridge: Cambridge University Press, 1991, 178. For an analysis that gives closer attention to the question of blindness, see B. Blumenkraz, *Le Juif Médiéval au Miroir de l'Art Chrétien*, Paris, 1972. In *Prodigal Son/Elder Brother: Interpretation and Alterity in Augustine, Petrarch, Kafka, Levinas*, Chicago: University of Chicago Press, 1991, Jill Robbins has traced the way the Jew is positioned as blind within

the writings of Augustine (especially 40–1). In developing the figure of this Judaism, she argues that

> Such a Judaism testifies to its own blindness (and to the Gospel's specular relationship to the Old Testament books) with a double blindness which is the radical self-opacity of the outside.

(7)

8 Pascal, *Pensées*, ed. Louis Lafuma, Paris: Seuil, 1962, 273, 745.

9 The structure of recognition forms an integral part of the structure of revelation in this Gospel. While it would demand a more lengthy analysis than can be undertaken here, what would need to be done is to read the structure of revelation that occurs in *John* IV:7–28 (in which the Samarian woman is brought to the position in which the 'man' who first gave her water is finally identified by the question 'Is not this the Christ?') in relation to the theme and structuring force of blindness at IX:5–8. The question to be asked concerns the nature of the relationship between sight (including recognition) and blindness (be it real or symbolic).

10 I have used the logic of the synagogue as part of an analysis of the paintings of Kitaj. See 'Kitaj and the Question of Jewish Identity' in my *Art, Mimesis and the Avant-Garde*, London: Routledge, 1991.

11 For an important defence of ontology within philosophy, though, more specifically, within any attempt to think philosophically about the political, see Jean-Luc Nancy, *Être Singulier Pluriel*, Paris: Galilée, 1996. Particular attention should be paid to the formulations which occur on page 67. I engage with Nancy's project in a more sustained manner in *The Politics of Judgement: The Cosmopolitan Present*, forthcoming.

12 I have attempted to take this problem further via an analysis of the work of Christian Boltanski in my *Object Painting*, London: Academy Editions, 1994, Chapter 4.

13 This text is available in the catalogue of the first exhibition of Libeskind's designs. The reference is to Daniel Libeskind, *Erweiterung des Berlin Museums mit Abteilung Jüdisches Museum. Extension to the Berlin Museum with Jewish Museum Department*, Berlin: Ernst & Sohn, 1992, 67. Future references to the work will be to the catalogue with page number and are given in the text. For reasons of space, a detailed description of the Museum cannot be given here. Considerable detail is provided in the catalogue. Furthermore, Mark Taylor's important analysis of the Museum also includes much descriptive detail. See Taylor, *Nots*, Chicago: University of Chicago Press, 1993, 122–66.

14 I have discussed the operation of 'built time' in greater detail in 'Not to Shed Complexity', *Fisuras*, 46–7, 1996.

15 Here, in terms of building and thus in terms of a specific structure of architectural practice, an important connection can be drawn between the work of Peter Eisenman and that of Libeskind. It is possible to argue that the actual structuration of Eisenman's Wexner Center at Columbus, Ohio, incorporates the structure and temporality of the question. In this instance, the question pertains to exhibition. Thus, what is maintained is the necessity for a continuity of negotiation between building – the architecture – and the need for display. I have tried to argue this point in more detail in 'Architecture et Contrainte', *Chimères*, 17, autumn 1992.

CHAPTER 6

1 Edmond Jabès, *La Mémoire des Mots*, Paris: Fourbis, 1990, 12; translated as 'The Memory of Words' in *The Tel Aviv Review*, 3, winter 1991, 141. Where these are available, references have been provided to English translations of Jabès' texts throughout. The texts have, however, been retranslated throughout.

2 There is a similar structure of argument in Stephan Moses' interpretation of the poem *Die Posaunenstelle*. It will be essential to return to the detail of this argument. See S. Moses, 'Patterns of Negativity in Paul Celan's "The Trumpet Place"', in S. Budick and W. Iser (eds) *Languages of the Unsayable*, New York: Columbia University Press, 1989.

3 The reference here is to the last line of *Engführung*. In fact it would be important to trace the movement of opening up throughout that particular poem. For a discussion of the importance of the 'word' *auseinandergeschrieben* in Celan, see H. Meschonnic, *Pour la Poétique*, Paris: Gallimard, 1973, 400. Rather than constructing a noun from Celan's 'word' – *auseinandergeschrieben*, for example – I have generally left it italicised so as to indicate that it is the figure of *auseinandergeschrieben* in Celan's poetry that is of concern here.

4 The first instance occurs in the fourth line of the poem:

> Gras, auseinandergeschrieben. Die Steine, weiss,
> mit den Schatten der Halme.

> Grass, written asunder. The stones, white,
> with shadows of grassblades.

The second makes up the last three lines of the poem:

> Gras
> Gras,
> auseinandergeschrieben.

> Grass.
> Grass,
> written asunder.

All further references to Celan will be given in the body of the text. References are to Paul Celan, *Gesammelte Werke*, Frankfurt: Suhrkamp, 1983. These are followed by references to the following English translations: for the poetry, *Paul Celan: Selected Poems*, trans. Michael Hamburger, London: Penguin, 1990; for the prose, *Paul Celan: Collected Prose*, trans. Rosemary Waldrop, Manchester: Carcanet, 1986.

5 Timelessness and its link to redemption is a complex problem in Rosenzweig. In part, this difficulty has to do with the particular position that he attributes to the Jews. In *The Star of Redemption*, trans. W. W. Hallo, London: University of Notre Dame Press, 1985, 339, he formulates the contrast between time and eternity in the following terms:

> It is the vitality of a life in the moment to be a life in time, to let
> itself be carried by the past, to summon up the future. Men and

nations live thus. God withdrew the Jew from this life by arching the bridge of his law high above the current time which henceforth and to all eternity rushes powerlessly along under its arches.

While the detail of Rosenzweig's argument has been pursued by various commentators, what has not been taken up in any detail is the connection between Celan's poetry and timelessness and redemption in Rosenzweig. There are, however, important intimations as to how this connection could be established in J. Felsteiner, *Paul Celan: Poet, Survivor, Jew*, New Haven: Yale University Press, 1995. See in particular 183–4. The connection between law, eternity and redemption in Rosenzweig has been treated with exemplary precision by S. Moses in *Système et Révélation: La Philosophie de Franz Rosenzweig*, Paris: Seuil, 1982. See in particular 291–9.

6 I have tried to provide the outline of an ontological description of the word in *Translation and the Nature of Philosophy*, London: Routledge, 1988.

7 The reference here is to one of Celan's most difficult and demanding formulations of the relationship between language and history advanced in the Bremen speech of 1958. It will be essential to return to the complex presence of this word *angereichert*. Part of its difficulty as a word lies in its possible, though nonetheless highly problematic translation as 'en-reiched'. For an importantly different interpretation of the word, see George Steiner, 'A Lacerated Destiny', *Times Literary Supplement*, 2 June 1995.

8 This is, of course, the point of divergence between Heidegger and Celan. The central work exploring this relationship is Philippe Lacoue-Labarthe's *La Poésie comme Expérience*, Paris: Christian Bourgeois, 1986. For a 'Heideggerian' interpretation of Celan, see Christopher Fynsk, 'The Realities at Stake in a Poem: Celan's Bremen and Darmstadt Addresses'; and D. Schmidt, 'Black Milk and Blue: Celan and Heidegger on Pain and Language', in A. Fioretos (ed.) *Word Traces: Reading Paul Celan*, Baltimore: Johns Hopkins University Press, 1994.

9 Martin Heidegger, *Unterwegs zur Sprache*, Neshe: Heske, 1990, 227–8; trans. Peter Hertz as *On the Way to Language*, San Francisco: Harper and Row, 1982, 146–7. All future references to this work will be given in the text, the German pagination preceding the English.

10 For a detailed analysis of the position of the 'we' in Heidegger, see Miguel de Beistegui, *Distopias: Heidegger in Place of Politics*, London: Routledge, 1997, Chapter 4.

11 A. Michael, 'Celan Signs', in *Paragraph*, 15, 2, July 1992, 176.

12 Peter Szondi, 'Durch die Enge geführt', in *Schriften*, vol. 2, Frankfurt: Suhrkamp, 1978.

13 As Scholem argues, 'a tikkun that is regarded as a restoration of unity from multiplicity is necessarily related in some way to redemption'. See Gershom Scholem, *On the Kabbalah and its Symbolism*, trans. Ralph Manheim, New York: Schocken Books, 1969.

14 Moses, 'Patterns of Negativity', 218. Further references are given in the text.

15 See the remarks in Note 5 above.

16 Edmond Jabès, *Le Retour au Livre*, Paris: Gallimard, 1965, 100; trans. Rosemary Waldrop as 'The Return to the Book', in *The Book of Questions*, I, New England: Wesleyan University Press, 1991, 402.

17 Jabès, *Le Parcours*, Paris: Gallimard, 1985, 93.

18 Jabès, *Dans la Double Dépendance du Dit*, Montpellier: Fata Morgana, 1984, 85; trans. Rosemary Waldrop as *Doubly Dependant Upon the Said*, in *The Book of Margins*, Chicago: University of Chicago Press, 1993, 176.

19 Jabès, *Le Livre des Questions*, Paris: Gallimard, 1963, 132; translated as 'The Book of Questions', in *The Book of Questions*, I, 176.

20 Jabès, *Le Petit Livre de la Subversion hors de Soupçon*, Paris: Gallimard, 1982, 27.

21 Jabès, *Du Désert au Livre*, Paris: Belfond, 1980, 99; trans. Pierre Jorris as *From the Desert to the Book*, Barrytown: Station Hill, 1990, 67.

22 Jabès, *Le Parcours*, 11.

23 Jabès, *Le Soupçon, le Désert*, Paris: Gallimard, 1978; trans. Rosemary Waldrop as *Intimations, the Desert*, New England: Wesleyan University Press, 1991. All subsequent references will be given in the text, the English pagination following the French.

24 Maurice Blanchot, *L'Entretien Infini*, Paris: Gallimard, 1969, 185; trans. Susan Hanson as *The Infinite Conversation*, Minneapolis: Minnesota University Press, 1992, 126.

CHAPTER 7

1 I have tried to develop some of the consequences of defining the subject in terms of this already present positioning in 'The Place of the Ethical', *Irish Philosophical Studies*, 5, 1988. See in particular 37–42.

2 See 'Beyond the Pleasure Principle', in *The Complete Psychological Works of Sigmund Freud*, vol. XVIII, 19.

3 Nelly Sachs, *Fahrt ins Staublose*, Frankfurt: Suhrkamp, 1988, 13. A translation of the poem can be found in D. Weissbort (ed.) *The Poetry of Survival*, London: Penguin, 1993, 57.

INDEX

abjection 107–8; becoming-abject 107–8, 109; as relation of dependency 108

absence ix, 17, 51, 110, 116, 120; founding 133; as 'void' space 116–17

absolute tragedy 76, 78, 97–8, 99, 100, 101; as crime of being 77; negative ontology of 76; *see also* Steiner

abstraction 64–5

Adorno, Theodor 4, 15, 20, 22, 71, 137

after (*nach*) 41, 42, 44, 59–60; after-life 41, 45–6

Agamben, Giorgio 96

allegory 29, 80, 83, 84, 86, 104, 105; ontology and temporality of 55; and the ruin 81–2, 84–5

alterity x–xi, 126, 136, 137, 144; complex 107

amazement (*Staunen*, θαυμαζειν) 89–90; *see also* shock

annihilation 104, 107, 114

anoriginal difference xi, 26, 97, 145, 146

anoriginal insistence 150, 152,

anti-Semitism 4, 118

apart/a part 23

apocatastasis 43, 51, 53

aporia 2, 120

architecture xi, 1, 2, 25, 110, 112; completion of 115; of hope 113, 114, 115; of the incomplete 115; of the question 114, 115–16, 118; of remembrance 103

Aristotle 89; *Posterior Analysis* 130

art 77, 91–3, 98

Auschwitz-Birkenau 6, 15, 23, 128

auseinandergeschrieben 121, 122, 130, 149, 153; as figure 135, 136; founding 120, 123; *see also* caesura, writing

awakening (*Erwachen*) 80, 88, 90–1, 96, 102

Baroque 76, 78, 81, 82, 84, 86, 88

Baudelaire, Charles 29, 86, 90–1

beauty 81, 82, 85, 86; beyond beauty 82, 84; Platonic delimitation of 85; and the ruin 82

Beckett, Samuel 101

being 11, 33–8 *passim*, 37, 128, 134; crime of 77, 98, 99, 101; history of 33 *see also* absolute tragedy; human 34, 38; propriety of 35, 38, 87; and questioning 118

Benjamin, Walter 1, 4, 5, 8, 12–13, 26–32, 35, 36, 39–45, 47, 48–55, 56–74 *passim*, 75, 76, 78, 79–82, 84–6, 88–97, 101–2; concept of awakening (*Erwachen*) 80, 88, 90, 102; concept of rescue (*Rettung*) 53, 82; epochal present 30, 39–41, 43–5, 51, 53, 70–1; and Heidegger 28, 30, 32, 37; 'A Berlin Chronicle' 30, 43; 'On the Concept of History' 11, 39, 66, 70, 88; 'The Destructive Character' 61; 'Fate and Character' 56, 57, 60–7, 70; 'Konvolut N' 31, 39–41, 48–55 *passim*, 80, 88, 90, 92; 'One Way Street' 60; *The Origin of German Tragic Drama* 29, 63, 79, 80–2; *Passagen-Werk* ('Arcades Project') 29, 30, 49, 72, 79, 80, 88, 96; 'The

character 60–2, 64, 66; and guilt 63,
64–5; and human being 63, 65; law of
62; and tragedy 63–4
figure 104; *see also* Jew: allegorical figure of
film 92
foreword 29, 30, 32, 36, 38–9, 48, 49,
51–4 *passim*
forgetting 21, 23, 39, 64, 67, 70, 71;
active 59–60, 68; intentional 128; *see
also* memory
fortune teller 66, 67
fragment, fragmentary, the ix, 3, 78;
fragmentation of the word of God 147
Freud, Sigmund 3, 52; 'Mourning and
Melancholia' 13, 15–19
future 3, 35, 54, 114–15, 116, 120, 147;
as completion 125; Heidegger on 35–6,
39; and prediction 58–9; and the
present 1, 57, 59, 66, 124, 149

Gasché, Rodolphe 65
Gedenkbuch 111–12
genius 63, 64, 65, 67
genre 24–5, 101, 102, 103
George, Stefan 130–4; *Das Wort* 130
gift, the given 27–8, 33–4, 39, 52, 61, 62,
101; of absence 117; giving again
99–100, *see also* repetition; tradition
as 27
God 41–2, 44, 47, 62, 63, 81, 98, 99;
absence of 78; in the book 146; death
of 77
Goethe, Johann Wolfgang von 82
guilt 63–4, 65, 66; and fate 63, 64–5; *see
also* fate, tragedy

Hegel, G.W.F. 1, 5, 13, 27, 43;
presentation of the Jew 105, 106, 109;
Phenomenology 85; *Philosophy of Right*
105; *Shorter Logic* 85
Heidegger, Martin 1, 4, 5, 12, 26, 32–9,
52, 54, 87, 128; and Benjamin 28, 30,
37; epochal present 33–5, 37–9, 87; on
Stefan George 130–4; on man's
homelessness 77–8, 87; sacrifice in 38,
39, 50, *see also* without (*ohne*); *Being and
Time* 34; 'Building Dwelling Thinking'
77–8; 'On the Way to Language' 36;

'Time and Being' 29, 35–9; *Introduction
to Metaphysics* 11, 78, 134; *Nietzsche* 11,
32–5, 37,
historicism 43, 87, 92, 110–11
history 47, 59, 60, 61, 66, 75, 81, 91, 94,
96–7, 104, 128, 137, 145; 'fore-' and
'after-history' 40–1, 44, 54, *see also*
after (*nach*); of philosophy 26; and time
96–7; universal 84, 96
Hitler, Adolph 93–4
home, homelessness 77–8, 95; future
being-at-home 95–6
hope x, 55, 69–70, 98, 101, 113, 114–16,
119, 120, 125, 136–7, 148–50, 152;
absence of in Celan 126–9; as caesura
57, 116; delivery of 125; and the future
9–10, 57, 114, 115; ontological
category of 69; opening of 120; an
other hope 128–9; overcoming 125,
126, 127; place of 119; and poetry's
time 120; and the present (present
hope) 2, 9, 25, 57, 61, 69, 114–15,
119; presentation of 125; propriety of
129; and time 9–10, 147; time of
128–9
Horkheimer, Max 44
humanism 34

iconoclasm 14, 106
identity 109, 118, 146, 148; concept of
149; gift of 109; *see also* Jewish being:
and Jewish identity
illusion 63–4
image 84–5; archaic 80; dialectical, *see*
dialectical image; of the past 71
incomplete, the ix–x, 2, 8, 97, 149, 152;
architecture of 115; complexity of 115;
founding incompletion 123; nature of
the present 10; ontology of xi, 1–2, 8,
129; temporality of xi, 1–2, 129, 149
infinite 43, 46, 47
interpretation 30, 36, 60, 64

Jabès, Edmond 23, 134, 146–52; and hope
120; *Dans la double dépendance du dit*
147; *Du désert au livre* 148; *Le livre des
questions* 147; *Le parcours* 147; *Le petit
livre de la subversion hors de soupçon* 148;

mimetic presentation of 74; in
mourning 20–1; recovery of 23–4
ontology 8, 26, 31, 34, 45; of becoming 8;
of the incomplete xi, 1–2, 8, 129; and
language 129; of stasis 48, 146, 149
open, opening 114, 119, 138, 146, 149,
152; anoriginal 124, 153; of the book
146; of hope 120; of the poem 121,
135; writing as 135

Padel, Ruth 77
particularity 8–9, 111; of the Jew 107; of
modernity 3, 6
particular/universal 1, 2, 5, 8
Pascal, Blaise 77, 106–7
past 70–1
philosophy xi, 1–3, 4, 13, 70, 89; history,
tradition, continuity of 2, 9, 22, 28; and
the present xi, 5, see also present:
epochal; universality 1
Plato 77, 85
plenitude 119; founding 3; impossibility
of 136
poetry xi, 1, 2, 15, 22–3, 132–3, 136;
original complexity of 127; place of
135, 136, 144; and thinking 132–3;
time and task in 137; as the work of
remembrance 131
political, the 27, 95
politics 20, 28, 91; of the caesura 91; of
the present 118; of remembrance 113;
and time 12, 26, 30, 41, 42, 44, 54, 64
power ix, xi, 107
prediction 54, 58–9, 61, 66, 68, 73, 74
present, the ix–x, 1–15 passim, 22, 25,
26–45 passim, 48–55 passim, 57, 59–60,
66–7, 78–9, 85, 91–2, 94, 98, 101–2,
103, 104, 111, 113, 114, 125, 137,
143, 149; actative dimension of 28, 34;
anoriginal complexity of 67;
chronological 5, 35; and conflict 1, 28,
31; complexity of 48, 49, 103; epochal
5, 9, 10, 11, 27–8, 34–5, 72, 77, 98,
111, 125, 134, Benjamin's 35, 51, 53,
54, 68, 94, 97, Heidegger's 33–5,
37–9, see also time: task; and the
future 1, 57, 69, 114–15; and hope
(present hope) 2, 9, 25, 57, 61, 69,

114–15, 119, 126–9, 149; as
incomplete x, 8, 97, 126; and memory
57, 67, 110; and modernity 3–4, 5, 6,
7–8, 25, 101, 123, see also Shoah; as
montage 49; ontology of 8, 10, 20, 28,
30; opening, as open 114, 129; politics
of 118; of prediction 59; repetition of
x, 55; and the Shoah 112, 118; and
tragedy 75, 76; temporality of 58; see
also remembrance
progress 89, 92
propriety 134; of hope 129; of language
130; original 38, 41; other
propriety 130

question 109–10, 112–13, 115–16,
117–8, 139–40, 148–9, 150;
architecture, building of 114, 115–16,
118; continuity of 148–9; ontology of
110; temporality of 110, 115
quotation 48–55 passim; as repetition
49–55 passim; without quotation marks
48–51, 52

Racine, Jean 101
Ranke, Leopold von 43, 92, 99
recognition 72–3
reconciliation 39
redemption 3, 58, 64, 84
relation 1; of dependancy 107, 108; of
non-relation 70
remembrance 17, 30, 54, 56, 58, 67, 68,
70, 71, 103–4, 112, 115, 116, 118,
124, 140; architecture of 103, 116;
beyond 130; and memory 68–9, 71,
110–11; politics of 113; present
remembrance 20, 23, 69–70, 74, 103,
113, 116
repetition ix–x, xi, 2, 4, 15, 20, 22, 24,
25, 27, 31–2, 38, 40, 44, 48–55 passim,
64, 73, 92, 97, 99, 101, 119, 120, 134,
135, 138, 139, 141, 143; of the present
x, 55, 120, 141; and quotation 49–55;
of the Same 1, 31, 40, 44, 50, 52, 100,
101; and memory 57; other repetition
22–3, 52, 99, 141; and rescue (Rettung)
79; see also reworking
representation 13, 18, 24, 29, 56–8, 72–4,